Bridging Early Services for Children with Special Needs and Their Families

A Practical Guide for Transition Planning

by

Sharon E. Rosenkoetter, Ph.D.
Associated Colleges of Central Kansas
McPherson, Kansas

Ann H. Hains, Ph.D.
University of Wisconsin–Milwaukee
Milwaukee, Wisconsin

and

Susan A. Fowler, Ph.D.
University of Illinois–Champaign
Champaign, Illinois

Baltimore · London · Toronto · Sydney

Paul H. Brookes Publishing Co.
P.O. Box 10624
Baltimore, Maryland 21285-0624

Typeset by Maple Composition, Binghamton, New York.
Manufactured in the United States of America by
BookCrafters, Falls Church, Virginia.

Library of Congress Cataloging-in-Publication Data

Rosenkoetter, Sharon E., 1944–
Bridging early services for children with special needs and their families : a practical guide for transition planning / Sharon E. Rosenkoetter, Ann H. Hains, Susan A. Fowler.
p. cm.
Includes bibliographical references and index.
ISBN 1-55766-160-X.
1. Handicapped children—Services for—United States. I. Hains, Ann Higgins. II. Fowler, Susan A. III. Title.
HV888.5.R67 1994
362.4'048'083–dc20

93-42078
CIP

British Library Cataloguing-in-Publication data are available from the British Library.

Contents

About the Authors

Sharon E. Rosenkoetter, Ph.D., is Associate Professor and Coordinator of Early Childhood Special Education for the Associated Colleges of Central Kansas, a consortium of private colleges. She serves as Project Director for Bridging Early Services Transition Project–Outreach and the ACCK Preservice Early Intervention Personnel Preparation Project, both funded by the U.S. Department of Education. She is a member of the Interagency Coordinating Council for Early Childhood Developmental Services in Kansas.

Ann H. Hains, Ph.D., is Associate Professor and Coordinator of the Early Childhood Exceptional Education Program for the University of Wisconsin–Milwaukee. She serves as Wisconsin Coordinator for the Bridging Early Services Transition Project–Outreach and as Consultant for the Wisconsin Personnel Development Project, Waisman Center–University Affiliated Program. Dr. Hains is Project Director of UWM's service Early Intervention Project: Respecting the Full Range of Diversity across Early Childhood Settings.

Susan A. Fowler, Ph.D., is Professor and Head of the Department of Special Education at the University of Illinois–Champaign and former President of the Division for Early Childhood, Council for Exceptional Children. She directs a federal outreach project titled Family and Child Transitions into Least Restrictive Environments and participates in numerous federal personnel preparation projects.

Foreword

The concept of transition planning recognizes that planned change meets the needs of all participants, even when that change is itself stressful. Leaving a familiar service setting or system and entering a new one is usually stressful for children with special needs and their families. Negotiating the change on their own is reported by parents to be very difficult. Without intra- and interagency planning, child needs are often not fully addressed and the child's success in the next environment is compromised. Child, parents, sending agency staff, and receiving agency staff may end up frustrated and disappointed. This volume presents a comprehensive plan for transition that, when implemented, will create a smooth road for all participants.

The need to plan for the transitions of children between infant or early intervention services and preschool services and between preschool services and kindergarten was recognized in the late 1970s. Initially, the focus was on preparing the child for the next environment and selecting the program best matched to child skills. The focus quickly expanded to include parents in program selection as they began to advocate for more naturalized, community-based settings for their children. By the mid-1980s, practitioners and researchers from around the country began collaborating to ensure successful transitions for children and families. Through this process, the needs of agencies regarding transition were identified and addressed.

The authors of this volume are leaders in family-centered transition planning from an interagency perspective. They share their years of experience in planning successful transitions for individual children and communities. They have included as comprehensive a map of strategies and practical tips as is possible in one volume. The reader will particularly appreciate their real-life case studies of children, agencies, and communities. Checklists and questionnaires for use within and between agencies are also outstanding. They include sections on common problems and possible solutions, as well as a chapter on challenges for the future in which they lay out a long-term plan for continued research to facilitate effective transitions.

Of central importance in the transition planning process are the concerns, priorities, and dreams of families for their children. The authors of this volume recognize that families, not agencies, see their children in the context of family and community. This book provides excellent suggestions for working together with families to enable children with special needs to live, play, and go to school in natural community settings.

Lisbeth J. Vincent, Ph.D.
Director
SHARE Center for Excellence in Early Intervention
California State University–Los Angeles

Preface

A bridge allows safe crossings of unknown waters. A bridge makes detours unnecessary. A bridge is sturdy and dependable. Whether simple or elaborate, a bridge allows journeys to continue without interruption. A bridge speeds people to their planned destinations.

This book is about bridges and bridgebuilding. It is a practical guide to bridging early services for children with special needs and their families. It aims to minimize the stress and increase the promise of early childhood transitions.

Chapter 1 provides a rationale for bridgebuilding. It tells why good transitions between service programs don't "just happen," but rather develop from careful planning in the community, the agency, and the individual family service team. Chapter 2 describes the federal and state laws and regulations and the current national trends that guide transition planning. Chapter 3 defines the elements of effective transitions and fits them together into a model useful for many different kinds of transitions.

Building bridges for children also involves building bridges between adults—connecting agencies with other agencies, professional disciplines with other professional disciplines, and parents with professionals. As discussed in Chapter 4, transition is inherently an interagency activity, one that accomplishes its purposes best when roles, responsibilities, and timelines are defined in writing by members of the local service system, including parents. Once the community's transition plan is in place, then each agency can determine its own transition framework, as described in Chapter 5, and share it with the families it serves.

Families, the ongoing caregivers in children's lives, are important partners in all aspects of transition planning. Chapter 6 describes ways for parents and professionals to collaborate to improve early childhood transitions. Practical strategies for incorporating the preferences and concerns of diverse families are shared in Chapter 7.

The important concepts of developmental and instructional continuity for children, along with common issues in achieving them, are discussed in Chapter 8. The following three chapters provide practical strategies to support young children during the process of transition. Chapter 9 describes actions recommended for sending programs and Chapter 10 actions for receiving programs. Chapter 11 offers guidance for interagency planning to serve young children with complex health care needs in community settings; again, careful transition planning is the key.

"How did it go?"—that's the question posed by Chapter 12, as it suggests ways for community planners and families to evaluate their local transitions in order to improve them.

Transition planning for young children with special needs and their families is happening within a much larger context of transition planning for all young children. As Chapter 13 describes this context, it encourages community networks to link to build bridges across all services for all young children, including those with special needs, and their families. Chapter 14 defines an agenda for doing just that, with suggested roles for parents, service providers, administrators, policy-makers, and researchers. Appendices subsequently provide additional resources to aid local planners.

We hope that this book will aid families and planners at both state and local levels who are attempting to improve services for children and their families. Since transition touches on nearly every aspect of early childhood intervention, transition planning is likely to enhance other services as well. We hope that readers will share with us their transition experiences and reactions to our suggestions.

This book is the culmination of a partnership initiated with colleagues nearly 10 years ago. While we have drawn on our respective experiences throughout the United States, we share much of the conceptual design with many colleagues who participated in earlier discussions, writings, and research on the topic of transition.

We acknowledge the contributions of Lynette Chandler, Tommy Johnson, Ilene Schwartz, Esther Kottwitz, and Georgia Kerns, who also staffed the first HCEEP demonstration project, titled Planning School Transitions: Parent and Professional Collaboration (#G008401758 to the University of Kansas) between 1984 and 1987; Robin Hazel, who joined the outreach project Building Effective School Transitions (#G008730177 to the University of Kansas) in 1987; and Cindy Shotts, Gay Woods, Darlene Sawatzky, Kay Streufert, and Diana Bartus, who joined the current outreach effort, Bridging Early Services Transition Project, (#H029Q00027 to the Associated Colleges of Central Kansas) first funded in 1990. We also express our appreciation to Ann Turnbull, who in 1984 helped us to envision families' roles in transitions. We thank the many families, children, and professionals who shared and continued to share their experiences and thoughts about transition, further shaping our thoughts and designs. Finally, to our families, thank you!

Bridging Early Services for Children with Special Needs and Their Families

1

The Rationale for Transition Planning

Why Do We Need a Bridge?

Each year, hundreds of thousands of young children with special needs and their families move from one service program to another (Office of Special Education Programs [OSEP], 1992). This change in programs, known as a transition, may be motivated by factors such as the child's age, health needs, readiness, eligibility, and the family's geographical location or program preference.

Joey recently moved with his mother to a large city from another state where he received no early intervention services. Joey's expressive language delay was discovered at the local prekindergarten screening. Even though it's late in the year, school personnel want to start Joey in a local special education program. Since he is 5, he is scheduled to begin kindergarten in the fall. In addition to their move to a new area, Joey and his mother could face two additional transitions: 1) starting in the local preschool or Head Start program, and 2) a few months later, starting kindergarten. How can service professionals help Joey and his mother adjust to these transitions and the many changes they involve?

* * *

One of the most cheerful and responsive children in the program, Maria shows developmental delays in several domains along with a visual impairment. Maria's parents speak only Spanish. None of the kindergarten teachers or special educators who might work with Maria speaks Spanish.

* * *

Scott has numerous sensory, physical, and mental impairments that complicate transition planning for his medical and developmental needs. Special preparations must be made to ensure that the staff in Scott's new program know how to manage the oxygen equipment and feeding tube that he requires. When Scott goes to the preschool program, he will need to ride a school bus. Scott's father is extremely worried about this because Scott has occasional seizures. What can the school district do to ensure Scott's safety, explain both seizure behavior and the special health care procedures that Scott may require to other children, and reassure Scott's father that his son will get along well on the bus?

* * *

Sylvia and her parents have been participating in the home-based early intervention program in their town since she was diagnosed with Down syndrome at birth. Soon it will be time for her to begin preschool. Sylvia's parents want her to attend the parochial preschool where their other three children have gone. Sylvia continues to need physical as well as speech therapy. Local planners have not had occasion to integrate a child with a disability into a community preschool classroom, until now.

* * *

Most 3- to 5-year-old children receiving special education services in the district are in preschool for either a morning or an afternoon session. Increasing numbers of preschoolers spend other parts of their days in child care. How can preschool teachers work with both parents and childcare providers to ease the transition between locations and continue intervention activities for children throughout the day?

* * *

Until the early 1990s, most children entered special preschool services in the fall after their third birthday. The law now says that they are eligible to receive free and appropriate services from the public school beginning on the day they turn 3. The local situation has become very confusing because children are continually qualifying for services. The local administrators need a system to monitor the number of children expected during the coming year. They also need a plan for implementing transitions at different times of the year.

* * *

Staff of the local Head Start, which serves a significant number of children with disabilities, have asked to meet with elementary school principals to discuss the transitions of their students into kindergarten. They are looking for ways to increase these students' acceptance and eventual success in elementary school. They also hope to convince the school district staff that increased family involvement and collaboration in decision-making would benefit the respective primary school programs.

* * *

Margo has been working with 5-year-old Cassandra and her parents for 2 years. It has taken a great deal of time to understand Cassandra's unusual difficulties with language meaning and use and to develop effective strategies for therapy. Margo wonders what will happen when Cassandra begins kindergarten. What can Margo do to ensure that new therapists will build upon this preexisting foundation without a lengthy period of trial and error?

* * *

Five years ago, the kindergarten teachers adopted a curriculum that set high expectations for all of their students. They even ordered workbooks to support class activities. They are generally pleased with the new curriculum, although there are always a number of children who aren't ready for the curriculum's kindergarten activities. Next fall, several children with special needs will be enrolling under the district's new inclusion policy. How can this transition work?

The two most common early childhood transitions occur at ages 3 and 5 as children move into and out of their preschool programs. Children with disabilities typically leave early intervention services by age 3 and enter preschool or other early childhood services; likewise, children typically exit preschool prior to age 6 to begin elementary school programs. Such changes may involve a transition from home-based to center-based services, from public to private programs, or from segregated to integrated classrooms. Many daily routines are thus likely to change.

Transitions between service programs are a big step for young children and their families. Transitions involve growing up and going out, confronting new challenges and learning to overcome them. They entail meeting new people, going to new places, adjusting to different schedules and new customs, and accepting altered expectations. Transitions are also a major challenge for teachers, therapists, administrators, and agencies that foster the development of young children. For professionals as well as for children and their families, transitions often bring disequilibrium. Indeed, transitions involve CHANGE!

Effective procedures for transitions reduce stress and help children, families, and professionals to bridge the differences between programs. This book is intended to guide professionals and parents as they develop effective ways to prepare for and implement transitions. It combines a philosophy with specific procedures and instruments that are useful with a diversity of agencies, families, and children. It is intended to be a hands-on manual to assist in everyday practice. Local programs may adapt the various methods for use in their individual situations. Forms may be copied or revised to serve local purposes.

Throughout these pages, reference is made to three common transitions: 1) infant/toddler programs to preschool services, 2) preschool services to kindergarten-level services, and 3) early intervention and special education services to integrated community services designed for children without disabilities (e.g., child care, preschool, or kindergarten). In addition, transitions for children with medically complex conditions are discussed in relation to general recommendations.

Investments of time and effort early in transition planning yields a significant improvement in children's adjustment to new programs. It also increases families' satisfaction with the services their children receive. Careful planning helps professionals as well as families function effectively in the climate of change.

WHAT WE KNOW ABOUT TRANSITIONS. . .

Since the early 1980s the authors of this book, together with local planners around the United States, have been studying early childhood transitions and assisting families and professionals in implementing these transitions effectively. This book is based on experience and research as well as on a review of published literature addressing early transitions for young children with disabilities and their families. Some of the basic tenets regarding transition planning may seem obvious but are nonetheless often overlooked. A brief discussion of each of these tenets follows.

Transition Is a Lifelong Process

We all face many changes throughout our lives: from hospital to home, from home to child care, from preschool to kindergarten, from residence to residence, from class to class, from school to school, from education to work, from job to job, and from employment to retirement. Families of young children with disabilities experience several additional transitional events: the initial diagnosis of disability; the beginning of intervention; and movement into or between special education programs, therapies, or community services. Life is a series of transitions, and the ways individuals and families learn to cope with early transitions will ultimately determine the course of later transitions.

Transitions Are Inevitable

Transitions cannot be avoided. All children and families who enter early childhood intervention programs must eventually move on to higher-level programs. Anticipation of this inevitable change can make it smoother for everyone involved. For instance, parents who are happy with their child's preschool program and are concerned regarding his or her readiness for kindergarten may wish to continue in preschool beyond the age of 5. But, repeated emphasis on the fact that transition is inevitable helps such families to adjust to and prepare for the coming change.

Transition Is a Continuous Process

Programs are involved in a continuous process of receiving children and their families from other programs and sending them on to future services. Soon after children and families have settled into one program, planning ideally begins for transition to the next. At any given time, a single program may have children ready to move on as well as newcomers who have just arrived. In fact, their cycles often overlap. Thus, transition policies need to incorporate procedures for both sending and receiving children, families, and staff. All personnel need to understand the transition process and their role in it.

Early Transitions Are Significant

Most young children feel comfortable in only a few environments; altering or changing one of those environments may be quite unsettling to them. Likewise, families who have successfully learned to navigate one service system must now explore others. Successful completion of early transitions can promote confidence and encourage success with later transitions. Effective skills thereby developed by children and parents are typically used again and again throughout life.

Transitions Involve Change

New programs involve knowing new adults and children, meeting new expectations, exploring new classrooms, and mastering new schedules—for both children and their families. New programs usually imply that children are growing older—and so are the parents. Transitions may entail accepting new "labels" for disabilities, new qualifying criteria to obtain services, and even new challenges to ensure that education and services are adequate and appropriate.

Transitions Are Usually Stressful

Stress frequently accompanies transitions because so many elements are changing at once. Children may worry about going to "the big school." Families may worry about the availability of services, their children's safety on the school bus, or the congruity between their children and the new program, therapist, or teacher. Alternatively, school personnel may worry about childrens' opportunities to succeed in certain classes, their own ability to meet the special needs of a given child, or the reactions of other children or their families to newcomers. This book provides some concrete ways to reduce these worries.

WHAT WE HAVE LEARNED ABOUT TRANSITIONS

Good transitions don't just happen. Rather, they result from the joint efforts of parents and professionals to make them successful. In fact, several characteristics are common to all successful transitions. Many of these are discussed in the sections that follow.

Good Transitions Require Planning

Planning helps to mitigate the changes surrounding transitions so that everyone involved has more time to adjust to them. Planning helps to prepare children, families, and related professionals for the changes to come. Written plans ensure that all relevant people contribute to the process and that their contributions are considered at appropriate times. A written transition plan for each community provides the framework for its transition process. A written transition plan for an individual child and family informs all participants of their related roles and responsibilities. In general, written transition plans help to ensure that:

- Everyone involved will have the same information about the plan.
- The plan will not be misinterpreted or its steps omitted through informal communication.
- The plan will be followed even if personnel change.
- Changes that need to be made in the plan will be shared among all participants.

Good Transitions Are Individualized

Children's abilities, disabilities, living situations, and needs for programming and environmental support differ dramatically. Likewise, parents have individual values and concerns as well as competing time commitments and varying interests in the transition process. Good transitions result from an awareness of such differences and subsequently from planning that considers these individual characteristics. The mechanisms for documenting this individualized support are the individualized family service plan (IFSP) and the individualized education program (IEP).

Good Transitions Require Shared Information, Trust, and a Great Deal of Communication

Agencies, family service coordinators, parents, teachers, and other professionals need to share information and support according to the locally established timeline. A good local transition plan enables people to work together effectively to provide less stressful transitions for children and their families.

Mutual acknowledgment of the contributions of other people and agencies as well as respect for skills in parenting, instruction, therapy, and assessment promotes effective communication and problem-solving. Indeed, shared information saves time and results in more appropriate programming. This type of collaborative approach focuses on moving children forward, rather than on issues of control.

A positive relationship such as this is tested when children no longer exhibit skills or show abilities in new settings that were regularly seen in previous environments. Instead of arguing about the presence or absence of skills and abilities, the parent–professional teams must seek ways to promote the carryover of skills between settings.

Good Transitions Empower Parents To Advocate for the Needs of Their Children

Families provide continuity across transitions. Regardless of a child's age or developmental level, decisions ultimately affect the family as well as the child. Many professionals have suggested that positive experiences with early transitions may help families and children during later transitions. Thus, by responding to families' concerns and by supporting their chosen level of involvement in early transitions, professionals can assist families in developing advocacy skills that are likely to be used again in the future.

Good Transitions Must Be Evaluated in Order To Be Improved

Local transition plans should include strategies for evaluating the local transition process over a period of several years. The opinions of parents, professionals, and agency administrators should be gathered along with measures of children's behavior in new settings. Proper data collection and thoughtful analyses can lead to a continually improving transition process that benefits children and families as well as agencies.

HOW TRANSITIONS DIFFER

Each year, parents and early childhood intervention personnel develop activities to facilitate smooth transitions. Decisions are made, children are assessed, records are transferred, and services continue uninterrupted. Whenever good transitions consistently occur, they are characterized by a sound philosophy, well-defined and written procedures, effective communication among participants, and timely decision-making. However, no single formula can govern all transitions because great diversity exists among communities and children and families served. Indeed, procedures differ based on community governance, program design, personnel, and policies established at local and state levels. In fact, routines or traditions may even dictate policies for transition.

The following factors are among many that contribute to the differences among transitions.

Age of the Child

Children may begin special services at any time from birth through age 5. Transitions occur as children move from the neonatal intensive care unit to home, home to infant/toddler programs, early intervention to preschool programs, and/or early childhood programs to primary level classrooms. Similarly, children may move into community settings such as child care, nursery or preschool programs, Head Start, or kindergarten.

Children's ages influence how they, their families, and program personnel prepare for and experience transitions. Indeed, the age of a child is a factor in determining his or her eligibility for services, and it subsequently guides which agencies participate in transition planning and which regulations those agencies must accommodate.

Child and Family Characteristics

Children's personal characteristics influence most aspects of the transition planning process, from the composition of transition teams to the various options for placement. For example, if a child has a medically complex condition, health professionals must obviously serve on the transition team.

Family resources, concerns, and preferences also influence transition planning. For example, many families require child care in addition to developmental programming for their child with special needs. The availability and location of such care, as well as families' ability to pay its rising costs, may affect choices regarding intervention services. Related issues such as the availability of transportation may also arise. Families' preference regarding their involvement in making decisions may range from primary advocacy to a desire to be informed but to have little if any involvement in the actual decision-making process.

Agency Participation

Transitions differ in the number of agencies involved and the degree of collaboration among those agencies. Transition activities are fragmented and uncoordinated in some communities, while in others they follow interagency agreements and timelines responsibly.

The local history of collaboration among agency personnel often influences interagency involvement in transition planning. For instance, in some communities, professionals may have extensive histories of working together; in others, professionals may not know one another or even the agencies that are potentially involved.

Service Delivery Options

Transition teams differ in the variety of service delivery options available in their respective localities. Some teams can consider numerous services and placements, while others are necessarily more limited in their possible choices. Appropriate services may need to be created or purchased from nearby programs. Alternatives, even if untried, may need to be considered in order to provide the most appropriate services in the least restrictive environment.

Policies

Transitions vary dramatically from place to place, even within the same region or state, due to differences in official policies. Indeed, policies often differ across agencies due to discrepancies in both sources of funding and individual agencies' missions, histories, and traditions. These differences may confuse parents as well as professionals and may subsequently hinder communication unless the respective participants understand and compensate for them.

Intra-agency policies (i.e., policies within an agency) may either assist or hinder transition planning. For example, the early childhood teachers within a given school district may want to coordinate transitions with the kindergarten teachers, but official administrative policy may not provide release time for the teachers to plan together or visit each others' programs. Such restrictive policies may limit information sharing among whole programs as well as the dissemination of information about the children enrolled in those programs.

Intra-agency policies may also be inconsistent. For example, the extent to which inclusion of children with disabilities occurs in preschool programs located in elementary schools within a single district frequently depends on the policies and beliefs of individual principals. Dramatic variations in practices often exist within a single district. The extent of such variability inevitably aids or hinders transition decisions.

Power and Control

When agencies attempt to cooperate with one another, the issues of power and control are likely to appear. Sometimes the size of the organizations involved may influence decisions regarding transitions. For example, in large urban areas, the school district may serve hundreds of preschool children with disabilities, while smaller private agencies serve fewer eligible students. Therefore, decisions may be made to accommodate existing systems (e.g., schoolbus schedules) instead of the needs and preferences of individual children and families.

Similarly, the source of funding can wield considerable influence on the degree of collaboration among agencies. For instance, school district personnel may wish to consult with early intervention providers in their communities. However, they may feel thwarted by local reimbursement policies that fund direct therapy but not transition planning time. Thus, unless early intervention providers donate their time, school district personnel may be powerless to initiate interagency collaboration.

FACILITATING TRANSITIONS

Solutions to each of these potential issues depend on the willingness and commitment of parents, service providers, and administrators to address these types of barriers in their community. Chapter 2 presents the context within which transition planning occurs for children with disabilities and their families. Chapter 3 provides a dependable plan for facilitating actual transitions. The rest of the book offers specific strategies for incorporating critical transition elements as children and their families attempt to bridge early services through transition planning.

2

Policies, Regulations, and Prevailing Philosophies for Intervention

The Context for Bridge Building

Transition planning for children with special needs and their families *must* be individualized. However, such planning is influenced tremendously by federal, state, and local laws, regulations, and priorities, as well as by prevailing philosophies for service delivery. This chapter discusses the current federal and state context for transition planning for children with disabilities and their families.

ORIGINS OF WORK REGARDING TRANSITIONS OF YOUNG CHILDREN WITH DISABILITIES

Initial work on the transitions of children with disabilities from special preschools to public school kindergartens began most notably in Kansas, Wisconsin, Utah, and Washington states, each having state and local support. Of critical importance in developing transition practices for young children with special needs was the 1980 publication of a chapter by Lisbeth Vincent and her colleagues (Vincent et al., 1980). This chapter advocates the careful analysis of kindergarten classrooms to determine functional objectives for children with disabilities who would be enrolling there. It was instrumental in guiding professionals to consider both curricular linkages and procedural collaboration in promoting continuity for children with special needs as they move from preschool to kindergarten.

Demonstration Projects

In the 1980s and early 1990s, a number of model demonstration and outreach projects on transition (Fowler, 1988) along with the Kansas Early Childhood Research Institute on Transition (Rice & O'Brien, 1990) were funded by the Office of Special Education Programs in the U.S. Department of Education. A number of manuals outlining transition procedures were developed as a result of these projects (Blair-Thomas, Wilson, Guida, & Manning, 1986; Carta et al., 1992; Conn-Powers & Ross-Allen, 1991; Fowler, Chandler, & Johnson, 1988; Gallagher, Maddox, & Edgar, 1984; Hains & Rosenkoetter, 1991; Rosenkoetter & Shotts, 1992; Rule, Fiechtl, & Innocenti, 1990; Stephens & Rous, 1992). Many of these projects continue to provide technical assistance nationwide. Appendix A of this volume lists a number of nationally funded projects relating to transition.

It is important to note that the early work on transition planning focused on the child. More recently, a family-centered approach has been adopted so that families' concerns, priorities, and resources influence the entire planning process (Fowler, Schwartz, & Atwater, 1991; Hains, Rosenkoetter, & Fowler, 1991). Moreover, much of the early work regarding transition planning for young children entering kindergarten has been broadened to include other transitions such as: 1) from hospital or institution to community, 2) from an infant/toddler program to preschool services, and 3) from self-contained and segregated programs to community-based services.

Federal Legislation and Regulations

Public Law 99-457 Even though federal agencies have been funding demonstration transition projects for young children with disabilities since the early 1980s, the first law regarding this issue was PL 99-457, the Education of the Handicapped Act Amendments of 1986.

As indicated in Table 2.1, this legislation requires individualized transition planning for every child served under the guidelines set forth in Part H. Such planning is required when 3-year-old children: 1) graduate from special services entirely, or 2) move into special preschool programs as prescribed in Part B of the law. The process outlined for an individual child and family is to be incorporated into the individualized family service plan (IFSP) and should be monitored to ensure that anticipated outcomes are achieved (McGonigel, Kaufmann, & Johnson, 1991). While this legislation specifically addressed the transition that occurs at age 3, its elements have been voluntarily included in state and local recommendations regarding other transitions as well (Rosenkoetter, 1992; cf. also *Kansas Guidelines for Implementation of Early Childhood Special Education Services,* 1992; *Michigan Inclusive Education Position Statement,* 1992).

Public Law 102-119 PL 99-457 emphasizes planning for individual children and families. The subsequent 1991 reauthorization of the Individuals with Disabilities Education Act (IDEA), PL 102-119, expanded the scope of transition planning to include a statewide system needed to support transition planning for individual children and their families. This system requires states to outline specific policies for age 3 transitions in their applications for federal funds under both the Early Intervention Program (Part H) and the Preschool Program (Part B). These policies should subsequently guide local communities in building their own transition plans.

Table 2.1. Regulations from PL 99-457 Part H (Sec. 303.344) on transition content of IFSP

(1) The IFSP must include the steps to be taken to support the transition of the child, upon reaching age three, to—
  (i) Preschool services under Part B to the extent that those services are considered appropriate; or
  (ii) Other services that may be available, if appropriate.

(2) The steps required in paragraph (h) (1) of this section include—
  (i) Discussions with, and training of, parents regarding future placement and other matters related to the child's transition;
  (ii) Procedures to prepare the child for changes in service delivery, including steps to help the child adjust to, and function in, a new setting; and
  (iii) With parental consent, the transmission of information about the child to the local educational agency to ensure continuity of services, including evaluation and assessment information required in 303.322, and copies of IFSPs that have been developed and implemented in accordance with 303.340 and 303.346.

The concept of using a timeline to coordinate transitions was introduced in the IDEA legislation in order to guide local planning (Rosenkoetter, 1992). At least 90 days prior to the child's third birthday (after obtaining the family's consent), PL 102-119 requires that the family, a representative from the child's infant/toddler program, and select personnel from the school district meet to plan transition activities. The goal of this mutual effort is to promote smoother transitions into special preschool services from early intervention programs. The IDEA legislation thus underscores the important role of families in transition planning. Table 2.2 outlines several key provisions of PL 102-119.

State Initiatives on Transition

Individual states are developing transition procedures in response to local situations as well as to accommodate federal requirements. The resulting policies may differ considerably from state to state despite the fact that they are based on the same federal legislation. Therefore, it is essential for local transition planners to acquaint themselves with their state's transition policies and procedures. Copies of these can be obtained from either the state's early intervention (Part H) coordinator or the state department of education's early childhood special education coordinator.

RELEVANT NATIONAL TRENDS IN SERVICES FOR CHILDREN WITH DISABILITIES

The 1990s have seen important changes in services for young children with disabilities (Edmunds, Martinson, & Goldberg, 1990; Meisels, 1992). These changes are having a significant impact on transition planning. Among the more salient of these changes are the following:

- Services available to more children and families
- Services utilized by a greater diversity of children and families
- Services provided in more natural settings
- Increased recognition of families as decision-makers
- Utilization of activity-based intervention that addresses the developmental and functional needs of children and their families
- Enhanced collaboration among community personnel to serve children with special needs

Each change is described in turn.

Table 2.2. Summary of provisions regarding transition from the Individuals with Disabilities Education Act (IDEA) Amendments of 1991 (PL 102-119)

State policies and procedures required

(1) Definition of how the state will ensure a smooth transition at age 3 [Part H Sec. 678(a) (8)], including a method of ensuring that when the child turns 3 an IEP (or age 3–5 IFSP) has been developed and is being implemented by the child's third birthday [Part B Sec. 613(a) (15)].

(2) Description of how families will be included in transition planning [Part H Sec. 678(a) (8)].

(3) Description of how the 0–2 lead agency will notify the local education agency and convene a conference, with the approval of the family, at least 90 days before the child is eligible for the preschool program under Part B in accordance with state law. The conference is to include representatives of the two agencies and the family and is intended to:

  (i) review the child's program options from the third birthday through the rest of the school year;

  (ii) establish a transition plan [Part H Sec. 678(a) (8)].

(4) Families are to be included in transition planning [Part H Sec. 678(a) (8)].

Individualized Family Service Plan (IFSP)

Can be used with ages 3–5 inclusive if the state, local education agency, and parents agree [Part B Sec. 614(a) (5)].

State Interagency Coordinating Council

Now must "advise and assist" the state education agency regarding the transition of toddlers with disabilities to services provided under Part B [Part H Sec. 682(e) (2) (C)].

Comprehensive System of Personnel Development

Each state's CSPD may include provisions for "training personnel to coordinate transition services for infants and toddlers with disabilities from an early intervention program . . . to a preschool program" [Part H Sec. 676(b) (8) (D)].

Flexibility in Funding

(1) States can use Part H funds to pay for children who turn 3 during the school year [Part H Sec. 679(3)].

(2) States can use not more than 20% of preschool grant funds to pay for children who are 2 but will turn 3 during the school year, regardless of whether these children have received Part H services. [Part B Sec. 619(b) (2) (B) (III)]. Part H does not apply [Part B Sec. 619(g)].

but

(3) The requirement for a free and appropriate public education applies in both cases above [Part B Sec. 619(b) (2) (B) (iii)] [Part H Sec. 679(3)].

Services to More Children and Their Families

The passage of entitlement legislation for preschool services in all 50 states means that all children with disabilities, ages 3–21, are eligible to receive free and appropriate public education. Regardless, in 1991, only 56% of all 3- to-5-year-old children with disabilities participated in preschool programs (NASBE, 1991). However, according to the *Fourteenth Annual Report to Congress* by the U.S. Office of Special Education Programs (OSEP, 1992), many new preschool services have been introduced in local communities. But, personnel may be inexperienced, which in turn inhibits the efficient implementation and subsequent development of transition planning in these new programs.

Early intervention services to infants and toddlers are also expanding rapidly. In 1990, an estimated 194,000 children and their families received intervention services, thus representing 1.77% of the total resident population of infants and toddlers between birth and age 3 (OSEP, 1992). As this growth continues, tenable transition procedures need to be established and evaluated at the local level, and time needs to be dedicated to the many children and their families who require individualized transition plans (ITPs) prior to the age of 3 when they must leave their early intervention programs. Again, because of the large numbers of new programs and the often inexperienced personnel presently involved in those programs, personnel training regarding transition is of paramount importance. (Johnson, Kilgo, Cook, Hammitte, Beauchamp, & Finn, 1992; McCollum & Bailey, 1991; Shotts, Rosenkoetter, Streufert, & Rosenkoetter, in press).

Serving a Greater Diversity of Children

Service systems are being challenged in diverse ways by increasing numbers of at-risk children: those without homes, adequate nutrition, or proper health care; those exposed to toxic substances prior to birth; those reared with violence; even those who test positive for HIV and other communicable diseases (Children's Defense Fund, 1992; Edmunds et al., 1990; NASBE, 1991).

Children like those described above present issues in transition because of the inherent complexity of child and family needs present in such situations.

Similarly, as minority populations in the U.S. expand, early intervention services must be provided to an increasing number of children from diverse cultures and ethnic groups (Lynch & Hanson, 1992; Vincent et al., 1990). Increasing instances of cultural diversity and the expanding use of languages other than English coupled with the renewed recognition of the importance of family-centered services challenges practitioners to make transition procedures and activities relevant for all involved families.

Services in More Natural Settings

Since 1975, federal law has required special education services to be provided in the least restrictive environment. Research has shown that children with disabilities, even those with multiple impairments, can be served effectively in integrated settings (Guralnick, 1981, 1990; *Mainstreaming Revisited,* 1990; Odom, McConnell, & McEvoy, 1992; Strain & Odom, 1986). The IDEA legislation, PL 102-119, requires that early intervention be delivered in natural settings "to the maximum extent possible" (Part H. Sec. 672[1] [6]).

Movement to the least restrictive or most natural environment affects transition planning in at least two ways. Primarily, it challenges local planners to change their service delivery systems to provide a variety of program options for children and their families (Allen, 1992; NASBE, 1992; Peck, Odom, & Bricker, 1993; Safford, 1989). Second, it prompts these planners to seek interventions that are effective without being intrusive (Bricker & Cripe, 1992; NASBE, 1992).

Increased Recognition of Families as Decision-Makers

Since the early 1980s, the perception of families as recipients of professional services has changed to that of families as partners in intervention—the most significant decision-makers regarding their children's services (Shelton, Jeppson, & Johnson, 1989; Turnbull & Turnbull, 1990). Family-centered intervention services begin as the priorities and concerns of family members are addressed and discussed. These services strive to meet the needs of families both now and in the future by helping them to develop effective skills for working with service systems. All family–professional interactions are thus consumer (family) driven (Dunst, Johanson, Trivette, & Hamby, 1991). Family-centered services incorporate the family's preferences concerning:

- Assessment (Gibbs & Teti, 1990; Meisels & Provence, 1989)
- Program planning (American Occupational Therapy Association, 1988, 1991; American Speech-Language-Hearing Association, 1990; Division for Early Childhood, 1993; Shelton et al., 1989)
- Service delivery (Dunst, Trivette, & Deal, 1988; McDonnell & Hardman, 1988; National Head Start Association, 1990; Turnbull & Turnbull, 1990; Wolery, Strain, & Bailey, 1992)

The passage of PL 99-457 in 1986 indicated lawmakers' intention to support family-centered early intervention, and the IDEA legislation of 1991 further underscores families' role in the development of their children's services. These statutes stress the importance of family participation in transition planning in order to ensure that families function as decision-makers throughout the entire transition process.

Family–professional collaboration in turn fosters smooth transitions throughout the lives of the children involved as it tests an agency's professed family-centeredness with regard to transition planning.

Activity-Based Intervention that Addresses the Developmental and Functional Needs of Children and Their Families

Early childhood special education and many of its related therapies once followed a highly structured, adult-directed training model with instructional targets often drawn from published checklists (Benner, 1992; Peterson, 1987). In recent years, however, intervention for young children with special needs has been developing instructional strategies that use naturally occurring activities, child-initiated interactions with people and objects, and logical consequences as reinforcers. (Bricker & Cripe, 1992; Wolery et al., 1992). Instructional targets are chosen by parents and professionals working together to determine the skills that will be useful in the everyday lives of their children.

The planning approach recommended in this book is consistent with this trend toward activity-based intervention. The examination of several potential environments (present as well as future), including the home environment if possible, is essential in order to develop appropriate goals and objectives for intervention that promotes successful transition. Published checklists of skills, though useful, frequently omit meaningful activities that can help young children enter new environments with confidence and competence. Chapter 9 provides suggestions for developing meaningful goals that can be achieved in early childhood intervention programs.

Enhanced Collaboration Among Community Agencies To Serve Children with Special Needs

Comprehensive services for young children and their families require collaboration among many agencies (Bernard, 1989; Hazel et al., 1988; Kagan, 1991b; Schorr, 1988). Limited resources and increasing need heighten the importance of eliminating the duplication of services among these agencies (Swan & Morgan, 1993). To this end, numerous policy statements advocate local interagency planning designed to meet the needs of all at-risk children and their families (Boyer, 1991; Committee for Economic Development, 1987;

Council of Chief State School Officers, 1989; NASBE, 1991; National Conference of State Legislatures, 1989; National Governors' Association, 1990).

PL 99-457 mandates interagency collaboration at both the federal and state levels. Many states have as well established local interagency councils (Morgan, Guetzloe, & Swan, 1991; NEC*TAS, 1992) to assist in implementing the Part H legislation.

The trends herein described are enhancing state and local transition planning. They encourage the collaboration of agencies and families to serve children with disabilities in natural environments with the least intrusive interventions presently available. This collaboration builds trust among agencies and promotes effective transition planning for the future (Fowler, Hains, & Rosenkoetter, 1990; Kagan, 1991b; National Policy Forum, 1991, 1992). Interagency collaboration regarding transition planning also stimulates local cooperation on other related issues (Shotts & Rosenkoetter, 1992).

IMPLICATIONS

Federal legislation provides a framework for statewide, local, and individual transition planning as children reach the age of 3, when they and their families typically change service programs. State and local agencies must therefore develop policies that comply with federal legislation. These agencies are also advised to use various principles from that legislation as a guide to improving all early childhood transitions.

Changes in population as well as in procedures for service delivery also shape policy development. Transition procedures need to reflect the increasing numbers and greater diversity of children and families receiving intervention services. Transition procedures must prepare and encourage parents and other family members to participate actively in determining the nature of their children's services. Decisions regarding program options must promote natural environments, activity-based interventions, and coordinated services.

During transition, the multiplicity of issues related to providing quality services for young children with special needs may seem overwhelming. In order to make wise decisions regarding transitions amidst the myriad of competing options, transition planners must consider theoretical data and research findings as well as proven practices. Chapter 3 provides a framework that guides that process.

3

Fitting Together the Elements of Transition

A Model for Our Bridge

Transition affects all aspects of services, from logistical issues such as service location, scheduling, and frequency of therapy, to philosophical issues regarding pedagogy and curriculum. In many cases, service eligibility is even an issue.

Several local program directors in Somerset became concerned about transition planning when two families of young children threatened litigation. The families felt that their children were automatically placed in special education programs that were neither responsive to their preferences nor in the best interests of their children. Family collaboration and partnership in building a local transition plan as well as in individual transition planning will hopefully prevent similar confrontations in the future.

* * *

A service provider for infants and toddlers in Concordia initiated transition planning when he saw that school systems were regularly ill-equipped to serve the 3-year-olds entering preschool. Through his efforts, interagency collaboration improved. The schools prepared staff and acquired the necessary equipment to serve children appropriately upon their entrance into the preschool program.

* * *

Children who had been successful in their Head Start programs quickly fell behind in kindergarten. After witnessing this pattern for several years, Elkhart's elementary school principal inquired what could be done to ease the transition into kindergarten to prevent children from falling behind. A community team worked for 2 years to answer the principal's questions and make the necessary changes.

* * *

Arborville's service providers were not concerned with transition planning, but their state agency instructed them to develop a local transition plan utilizing families' input. "We can write up something in an hour," said one local provider. However, when the parents and professionals came together, they found that there were several significant issues that required their attention. Indeed, some of the local providers were completely unacquainted with the services provided by other local agencies. Although it took 6 months to resolve several related issues, writing their local plan turned out to be a meaningful activity that benefited children and families as well as the agencies themselves.

Promoting cooperation between programs so that children and families experience smooth transitions is a complex effort that may extend over a considerable period of time. It may involve many different people and agencies who may have dissimilar ideas and policies regarding how best to serve young children with special needs. Indeed, in most cases, disparate regulations must be reconciled. For families, an upcoming transition often elicits heightened and mixed emotional responses while providing greater possibilities for their children's development and programming.

Although the dynamics of each transition are different, several basic elements are common to all transitions. The way that these elements relate to each other is shown in Figure 3.1. This transition model is based on both research and practice in numerous demonstration projects that deal with early childhood transitions.

As indicated by the rectangular perimeter of the model, several forces shape the context within which local transition practices are developed:

- Federal and state policies and national trends
- Family leadership and advocacy
- Local issues and practices

Each is discussed in turn.

Chapter 2 describes the federal and state laws and regulations regarding service availability for young children with disabilities and their families. Indeed, legislative initiatives, such as PL 99-457, should give direction to local planning. Similarly, national trends (i.e., efforts promoting community-based services and making programs more responsive to families' preferences) also affect local planners' priorities.

Likewise, at the national, state, and local levels, families have effectively expressed their desire to participate actively in planning for their children's transitions. Various parents have articulated their individual needs and preferences regarding transition and have suggested ways that service systems may respond. For instance, the strong feelings of two Somerset families who disapproved of the local process for placing children in special education programs helped to reshape transition planning in their community. The families' advocacy pushed transition to the fore of the local agenda and subsequently forced local planners to provide a variety of options for preschool services.

Indeed, communities often differ with regard to their values and traditions, and these differences also affect transition planning. For instance, in Arborville, parents regularly accompany their children on the first day of kindergarten. In Elkhart, however, children ride the school bus independently on the first day of school. Transition planning for children with special needs in Arborville and Elkhart was influenced by the existing customs in each community, respectively. Indeed, issues that may be inflammatory in one area may not even be discussed in another (busing is one such issue). Similarly, local practices, union contracts, administrative patterns, and a community's history of interagency collaboration each may greatly affect transition planning on a local level.

TRANSITION BUILDING

Regardless of children's age or the respective characteristics of the programs involved, all transitions share certain elements in common. Children with disabilities and their families are likely to experience at least four types of transitions requiring service intervention before they reach the age of 6. These may include:

- The transition from hospital to home
- Entry into early intervention services
- Entry into preschool services
- Entry into kindergarten

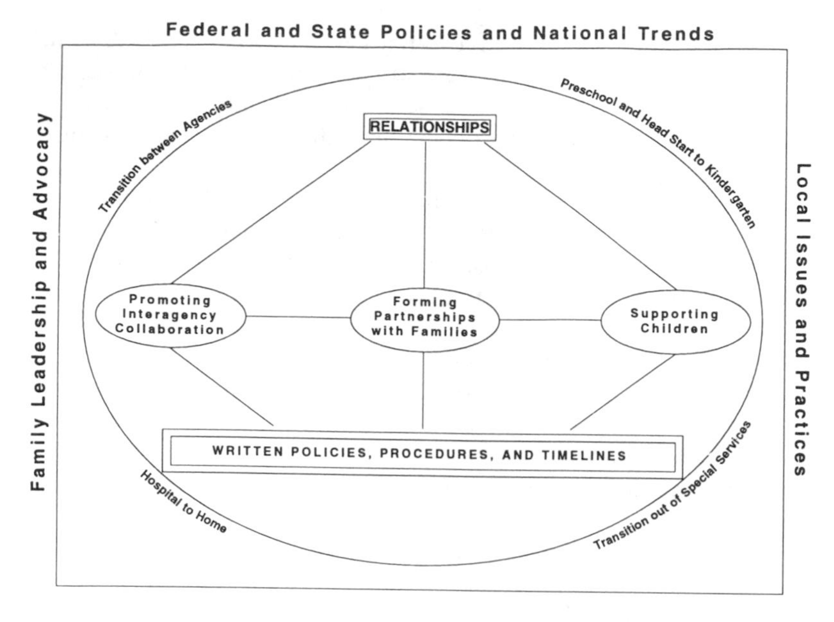

Figure 3.1. The Bridging Early Services transition model.

Additional changes may involve movement into and between childcare services, residential relocations, the birth of a sibling, or the sudden unemployment of a parent, each potentially leading to changes in the service delivery model (e.g., from home-based to center-based).

Families may enter the service system at any point. Some families choose to begin receiving services prior to discharge from the hospital, while others will identify their need for services and obtain them during their children's infant, toddler, or preschool years. Some families subsequently exit the early childhood intervention service system entirely when their child no longer exhibits a need for specialized assistance. Regardless of the time at which services are initiated or discontinued, each change in the service system and every subsequent change in service providers constitutes a transition. For most transitions, however, careful planning with families and professionals is required to ensure that services are not interrupted and thus continue to be available in a timely and appropriate manner.

Selma Schumann and her family experienced many transitions during her early childhood years. Selma was born after 28 weeks

gestation and subsequently received intensive services in a level III nursery at the medical center 3 hours from her home in Somerset. When the baby's condition stabilized, she was transferred to a level II nursery closer to home. Selma was brought home 2½ months after her birth. Although the family continued to receive Home Health Care medical services, those services were judged to be unnecessary after 8 months. Thus, the Schumanns enrolled in Somerset's local early intervention program when Selma was 9 months old; a home visitor began to come to their home twice each week. Her assistance was greatly appreciated. However, when Mrs. Schumann resumed her factory job after Selma's first birthday, the home visits were discontinued and center-based intervention was initiated at Happy Children Care, where Selma's sister was enrolled.

When Selma was 28 months old, both parents lost their jobs. The family consequently moved to another state where Mrs. Schumann had lived as a child. Despite the fact that the early intervention system was less developed there, the social services agency arranged for Selma to receive physical therapy at the local hospital. When Selma was 32 months old, Mr. Schumann was called back to work. Therefore, the family moved back to Somerset and reinitiated home visits through Somerset's early intervention program. Planning for Selma's transition into preschool began when she was 33 months old.

In accordance with the regulations of their state, the Schumanns worked with personnel from the early intervention program in developing an IEP for Selma. Home visits continued for several months until the fall semester began in the local schools. Selma was then enrolled in the neighborhood Head Start Program and there began receiving special education services.

Upon Selma's fourth birthday, an evaluation indicated that she no longer required special education services or related therapies. A transition plan was thus drawn up by her planning team (including her parents). Selma meanwhile continued to attend Head Start and participate in developmental activities, until her transition was at hand. In sum, during her first 4 years, Selma and her family experienced and successfully traversed eight major transitions.

TWO CRITICAL TASKS TO FACILITATE SUCCESSFUL TRANSITIONS

The foundation for successful transition planning is local coordination. Each of the transitions described above will depend on:

1. The relationships that develop among professionals, families, and children

2. The written policies, procedures, and timelines that guide agencies and families in supporting transitions

Each of these components is discussed in turn.

Positive Relationships

Successful transition planning requires collaboration among professionals representing various agencies and disciplines, among parents and professionals, and among support systems for children as well as families. The effective initiation of transitions depends on establishing open, honest relationships among these various participants to make decisions and solve problems. Such relationships must then be carefully nurtured over time. In fact, transition planning is often aided by seemingly unrelated activities that help participants to understand and appreciate one another. For example, in one community, families and agency directors ate lunch together while working to pass a local bond referendum regarding children's issues. Later, when a transition issue came to the fore, they were able to work effectively with one another, thus avoiding many potential problems.

Indeed, time is well spent nurturing positive relationships among parents and professionals from varied agencies and disciplines. People typically need a history of communication and shared interests in order to create a sense of trust and respect among one another. Initially, local planning teams often find it easier to discuss important but nonthreatening issues (e.g., how we can coordinate screening activities) rather than issues that entail immediate costs (e.g., how shall we allocate the funding base necessary for transition services).

Much literature that is directly relevant in this field has dealt with the second critical task of transition planning—the production and subsequent implementation of effective local transition procedures. Problems may arise in implementing exemplary written transition plans, however, if the community lacks positive relationships among its transition participants.

Policies, Procedures, and Timelines

The remainder of this book provides specific suggestions for developing a local framework for early childhood transitions and strategies to apply or adapt that framework in promoting effective transitions for infants, toddlers, and young children with special needs and their families.

ELEMENTS OF TRANSITION PLANNING

There are three areas in which transition planning must focus:

1. Promoting interagency collaboration
2. Forming partnerships with families
3. Supporting individual children

A local team may work concurrently in all three of these areas or may instead target one area at a time.

Regardless, each is closely related to the others, and all depend on both positive relationships and defined transition procedures to promote successful transitions on a regular basis.

Somerset, Concordia, Elkhart, and Arborville are communities of varying sizes located throughout the United States. Each has different resources to contribute to its intervention efforts, and each was motivated to initiate transition planning for different reasons. Nevertheless, all four communities were successful in building the positive, honest relationships required for effective transitions to occur. All have developed written policies, procedures, and timelines to guide their transition efforts, and data from planned evaluations will guide future changes in their individual transition processes.

IMPLICATIONS

This chapter provides a framework that families as well as agencies can use in planning healthy transitions. Though transition planning will generally occur locally, outside forces will significantly affect the directions taken by local planners.

4

Local Interagency Collaboration

Building the Bridge

Most early childhood transitions necessarily involve personnel from two or more service agencies. Transferring children and families into and between these agencies is thus an interagency effort. However, this effort is oftentimes informal, with each agency fulfilling its responsibilities but leaving the parents to serve as intermediaries between agencies. Nevertheless, collaboration among individual agencies is the key to orchestrating the most effective transitions possible.

Agencies in Arborville confronted state directives to develop a plan for children and their families moving between early intervention and special preschool services. They also needed to plan for children moving out of early intervention services who were ineligible for special education services after age 3. Agency heads realized that they needed to work together on this project to enable children and their families to move smoothly between programs.

Through collaboration, agencies can develop timelines that define responsibilities and outline systematic procedures for gathering and sharing information, making decisions, supporting children and families, and evaluating transition activities (Bennett, Raab, & Nelson, 1991; Hains, Fowler, & Chandler, 1988). Ultimately, local interagency collaboration results in a *system* for transitions that:

- Eliminates gaps and promotes continuity in services for children and families

- Avoids duplication
- Assures that needed information is available for wise decision-making
- Provides peer support for parents and professionals
- Defines financial responsibility in advance
- Ensures that transitions are evaluated and improved as needed
- Promotes understanding regarding the guidelines and constraints under which various agencies work
- Eases the process for everyone involved

Initially, building an interagency transition system can be demanding, but such a system will ultimately save both time and effort as families and professionals are able to work together in accomplishing smooth transitions.

THREE LEVELS OF TRANSITION PLANNING

As illustrated in Figure 4.1, teams of people are involved in interagency transition planning at different levels (Shotts & Rosenkoetter, 1992). The first level of planning addresses the development of policy at the community level that will guide agencies in outlining specific transition procedures. The second level addresses those specific procedures necessary for the successful implementation of all transitions within that community. The final level of planning focuses on individual situations—adapting the general policies and procedures identified in the first two levels of planning to fit the specific priorities, resources, and needs of individual children and their families. Although the primary purpose of interagency collaboration is to provide appropriate services to individuals, services may be compromised if insufficient time is spent in first developing adequate policies and procedures.

It is beyond the scope of this book to speak to each of the issues regarding the formation and successful continuation of local interagency councils. For such assistance, the reader is directed to excellent publications on the topic (Elder & Magrab, 1980; Hazel et al., 1988; Magrab, Elder, Kazak, Pelosi, & Wiegerink, 1981; Morgan et al., 1991; Morgan & Swan, 1988; Swan & Morgan, 1993) as well as to resources compiled by individual states for local use (California Infant Preschool/Special Education Resource Network, nd; Commonwealth of Virginia Early Intervention, 1988; Indiana First Steps, 1991; Moore & Toews [Oregon], 1985; Ohio Department of Health, 1989a, 1989b; Pennsylvania Office of Mental Retardation, 1991).

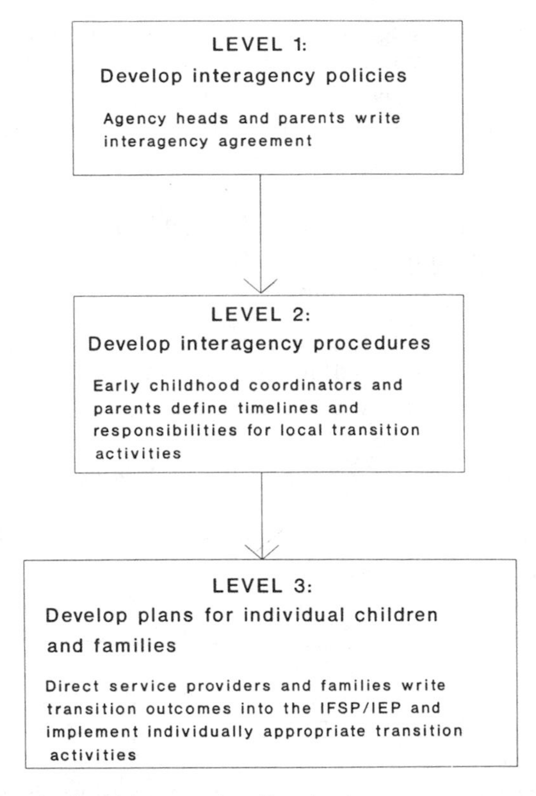

Figure 4.1. Three levels of interagency transition planning.

These resources provide specific strategies for advancing interagency collaboration as they validate the interagency approach to improving early childhood services.

Level 1: Developing Interagency Policies for Transition

A team may be formed explicitly for the purpose of planning transition policy, or it may emerge as part of a pre-existing body that deals with broader issues regarding early childhood or disability. This team should include people who have the authority to act on the behalf of their respective organizations in making decisions and committing resources. These individuals are typically agency directors. For example, a team of local policy-makers may include the director of the health department, the superintendent of schools, the president of the local childcare association, the coordinator of special education services, the director of the mental health center, the Head Start director, the chairperson of the parent group, the director of the human services agency, and the head of the recreation commission. Public representatives such as school board members and business leaders may even wish to participate. Parent members also contribute essential viewpoints as they share their experiences before and after participating in the transition process and help to critique proposed policies.

This team establishes the broad, flexible policies under which more specific transition procedures will later be developed. Some typical policy issues will include:

- When, how, and by whom transition will be initiated
- How service eligibility will be determined
- Guidelines that will govern funding for various aspects of transition
- Who will facilitate personnel coordination among different agencies
- How services that are not the responsibility of the local lead agency will be arranged and provided
- Timelines to be established for initiating transition activities
- How transitions will subsequently be evaluated and how that evaluation will be conducted
- If various agencies employ service coordinators or case managers, how these individuals will collaborate to assist individual children and their families
- How information will be shared among the three levels of interagency teams working to improve transitions for children and families

The results of these policy decisions are typically incorporated into an interagency transition agreement like the one shown in Figure 4.2. Additional sample agreements appear in Appendix B. Although some interagency agreements resemble legal documents, others are much less formal. Some are parts of more lengthy agreements that describe collaboration in multiple areas of service. Conversely, some are merely one-page documents that deal with a single transition or one limited area of transition services.

Written interagency transition agreements are intended to serve a number of purposes (Kagan, 1992; McNulty, 1989; Swan & Morgan, 1993). Among the more salient of these are the following:

- To expand service options
- To commit program administrators to joint efforts
- To specify procedures

Participants in this agreement include representatives from the Republic County Special Education Cooperative (representing five school districts), the Republic County Head Start, the Daisy Center for Infants, the Arborville Memorial Hospital, Parents as Teachers, Parents as Partners, the Arborville/Republic County Association for Young Children, the Republic County Health Department, the Midstate Mental Health Center, the Republic County Family Life Center, and the Future Horizons Developmental Center. Each agency will designate a transition coordinator. These people will work together to refine the plan outlined below.

Purpose

The purpose of this interagency transition agreement is as follows:

To define a mutually agreeable system for the transition of toddlers with special needs from early intervention services to special preschool services or to other appropriate placements if they are no longer eligible for special services

To involve the parents of these children in planning the transitions and to provide assistance as necessary

To ensure that young children with disabilities receive appropriate services without interruption due to program changes

To encourage that those services, to the maximum extent possible, be provided in environments where children without disabilities are served

The plan outlined below will be shared with parents as well as with relevant personnel in the participating agencies. Each November, the plan will be reviewed by the local interagency council for continuation or modification. The plan has eight parts: notification, planning, assessment, eligibility, placement, information sharing, funding, and evaluation.

Notification

Nine months prior to the child's third birthday (12 months prior if the birthday occurs during the summer months), the early intervention family service coordinator will share specific information about the transition process with families, ask whether they want a specific person to participate with them in the planning, determine their informational needs, and work with them to develop outcomes for the individualized family service plan.

No later than 90 days prior to the child's third birthday, the family service coordinator for the early intervention program will, with parents' permission, arrange a meeting with representatives from the early intervention program, the Republic County Special Education Cooperative, and the family. This meeting will be convened at a mutually agreeable time and place. In the event that the child's birthday occurs during the summer months, this meeting will take place at least 90 days before the end of the school year.

Planning Meeting

At the planning meeting, participants will discuss procedures to be followed in determining eligibility, options for assessment and placement, the interagency timeline, parent rights and due process, and any remaining issues of concern to the participants. This meeting also signifies a referral to special education, which begins the 40-school-day timeline for completion of evaluation.

Assessment

Recent evaluation results from the early intervention program will, with parents' permission, be shared with the Special Education Cooperative. Procedures that provide

(*continued*)

Figure 4.2. Republic County interagency agreement for the age 3 transition.

Figure 4.2. (*continued*)

current information will not be repeated. Information will then be gathered, again with parental permission, from all the programs serving the child. The schools will coordinate the planning of additional assessment in consultation with parents and staff from the Daisy Center and the Future Horizons Developmental Center. Cooperation in assessment will help ensure that results obtained are valid indicators of the child's present level of performance.

Family input at this point is highly desirable. Representatives from the Family Life Center and Parents as Partners will work with the early intervention programs as well as the Special Education Cooperative to develop procedures to assess family priorities and concerns at the time of transition.

Once it is determined that the child is eligible for special education services at age 3, the family will be invited to visit possible placements to screen their appropriateness for the child's needs.

Eligibility

Eligibility for special education services will be determined according to the state's special education guidelines. For each eligible child, an individualized education program will be developed.

Placement

When a child who has been served by early intervention but is now found to be ineligible for special education services, the family service coordinator will work with the family, Head Start, the executive board of the Arborville/Republic County Association for Young Children, and other agencies, as appropriate, to locate suitable preschool or childcare arrangements.

The Special Education Cooperative will convene a meeting with the parents, in conformity with legal precedent, to develop an individualized education program for each child found to be eligible to receive special education services. The child's present level of development and his or her special needs will guide decisions regarding placement and service. To the maximum extent possible, preschool-age children with special needs will receive services in environments where children without special needs are served.

It is likely that some services provided through early intervention will not become the school's responsibility after the child's third birthday. Consequently, the signers of this agreement pledge to work together through the local interagency council as well as in individualized planning in attempting to continue meeting those needs when the child is receiving preschool services.

An IEP will be in force by the third birthday or at the time of enrollment in preschool, whichever occurs first. The signers of this agreement acknowledge that multiple transitions are difficult for the child as well as the family. Accordingly, the participating agencies agree that, if the child turns 3 after April 1, he or she will continue to be served in the early intervention program until the following school year. If the child's birthday is after the beginning of school but before November 1, he or she may start preschool at the beginning of the school year. In both cases, services will be free of charge to the family.

With regard to birthdays occurring at other times of the year, local agency heads will work with the family to determine appropriate start dates. The needs of the child are paramount. Free and appropriate public education is guaranteed either when a child turns 3 or when he or she enters services sponsored by the Republic County Special Education Cooperative.

Information Sharing

Procedures, including common intake forms, are being developed by the participating agencies. With the permission of parents, information will be shared among the

(*continued*)

Figure 4.2. *(continued)*

agencies that jointly serve the child, and records will be forwarded in a timely manner to the new service provider that works most closely with the child. Specific procedures for this exchange are under development at this time and will be added to this agreement later.

Funding

With parental permission, the early intervention programs and other involved community programs will share current assessment information without charge to the Special Education Cooperative. The Cooperative will assume responsibility for further assessment, although some additional testing may be conducted by Head Start or other early childhood programs in the community.

As discussed above, there will be no charge to parents for special education services either after the child's third birthday or after the child begins special preschool services. The early intervention programs will absorb the costs for late spring and summer services contained in the IEPs of children with birthdays after April 1. The Special Education Cooperative will assume the costs for 2-year-olds who begin school prior to their birthdays in August, September, or October. In the case of individual decisions regarding start dates, participating agencies will negotiate funding.

The Family Life Center and Parents as Partners agree to work together, in consultation with other agencies, in developing a parent mentoring and information program to assist families approaching the age 3 transition.

Evaluation

The plan presented in this agreement will be implemented immediately. It will subsequently be evaluated for benefits and costs to children, families, individual staff members, and agencies. The transition coordinators will plan and conduct the evaluation and present its results to the Republic County Interagency Transition Taskforce next November with the aim of prompting improvement in the transition plan for Republic County.

Signatures

- To specify the financial responsibilities and time commitments required of each agency
- To guide transition procedures if and when personnel change
- To ensure the delivery of appropriate services on an uninterrupted basis

In some areas, a written interagency transition agreement is required by the state as part of the local plan to deliver early intervention services to eligible infants and toddlers and their families.

The local written plans must comply with federal and state regulations as well as with existing state interagency agreements. Indeed, many states recognize agreements between Head Start and the public school system and/or the developmental disabilities system and the schools.

After a viable interagency transition agreement is developed, the interagency policy team shares it with the staff members most likely to be responsible for its implementation. This team will probably meet once or twice a year to resolve problems that arise as this policy goes into effect, to review evaluation data, and, if needed, to refine the interagency transition agreement.

Level 2: Developing Interagency Procedures for Transition

Once the general policies are in place, a second team is formed that consists of a transition coordinator from each agency as well as parent representatives and others who can help in developing specific procedures for transition planning. Members of this team are aware of the day-to-day problems that confront children and their families during periods of transition, and consequently work together to prevent them. The interagency transition procedures team is also familiar with personnel in different agencies who have relevant past experience and may thus be helpful in planning future transitions. The functions of this team may include:

- Developing common forms for use across agencies
- Developing a timeline for transition activities that specifies responsible personnel in various agencies
- Delineating specific evaluation questions and the procedures for answering these questions in order to minimize time and money spent while increasing the amount of information gained for decision-making
- Defining the expected patterns of communication among agency personnel
- Developing collaborative parent activities and peer support networks for families experiencing transition
- Helping to educate new members of the interagency policy team regarding how the local transition system functions

The interagency transition procedures team meets quite frequently, especially early in the process of developing a local transition plan. Its members should maintain regular contact to discuss issues that arise among agencies or to resolve dilemmas related to individual transitions that have implications for interagency functioning as a whole.

Level 3: Developing Transition Plans for Individual Children and Their Families

A transition team is created for each child who becomes eligible for new programs. This team includes the child's parents, teachers and therapists who presently serve the child, and other people whom the parents specifically designate (e.g., the child's primary care provider, a grandparent, an advocate, or a parent mentor). It may include the same members as the IFSP/IEP team. The names of current service providers are included in the transition plan of the child's IFSP or IEP, whereas the names of receiving or future service providers become obvious as transition planning proceeds. Once identified, the new service providers also join in transition planning.

Members of this team consult one another both before and after the transition actually occurs in order to maximize service continuity (Hains et al., 1988). Professionals and parents serving on such teams need to communicate regularly with their agency's representative on the interagency transition procedures team in order to shape interagency activities that really work for communities, children, and families. In addition, they must ensure that the practices being followed conform to established policies and procedures or else that they deviate for a valid reason.

THE INTERAGENCY TRANSITION PLANNING PROCESS

A community's transition planning process necessarily involves all the participants in each of the three levels discussed above. Its primary steps are outlined in Figure 4.3. The critical first two steps involve defining the particular transition(s) for which to plan and specifying the relevant agencies to involve in the planning. Transition planners often forget to include important participants (i.e., Head Start, Chapter 1 or state-sponsored early childhood programs, family life education programs, home or public health agencies, or community preschools and childcare services) on the interagency policy teams. These agencies (and potentially others) may be key contributors in the planning process, as their participation facilitates the development of individually appropriate intervention services in natural environments. Initial invitations to all agencies that serve young children and families will thus promote an inclusive approach to service provision.

It is essential that policy-makers view the transition as a shared challenge, rather than as a discrete problem of a single agency. With regard to any given transition, one agency may have greater responsibility than others; but, only by working together can the relevant agencies adequately support children and their families throughout the transition process. Conflicts can be resolved more easily or averted completely if the focus remains on solving jointly owned transition dilemmas (Hazel et al., 1988; Kagan, Rivera, & Parker, 1990). This

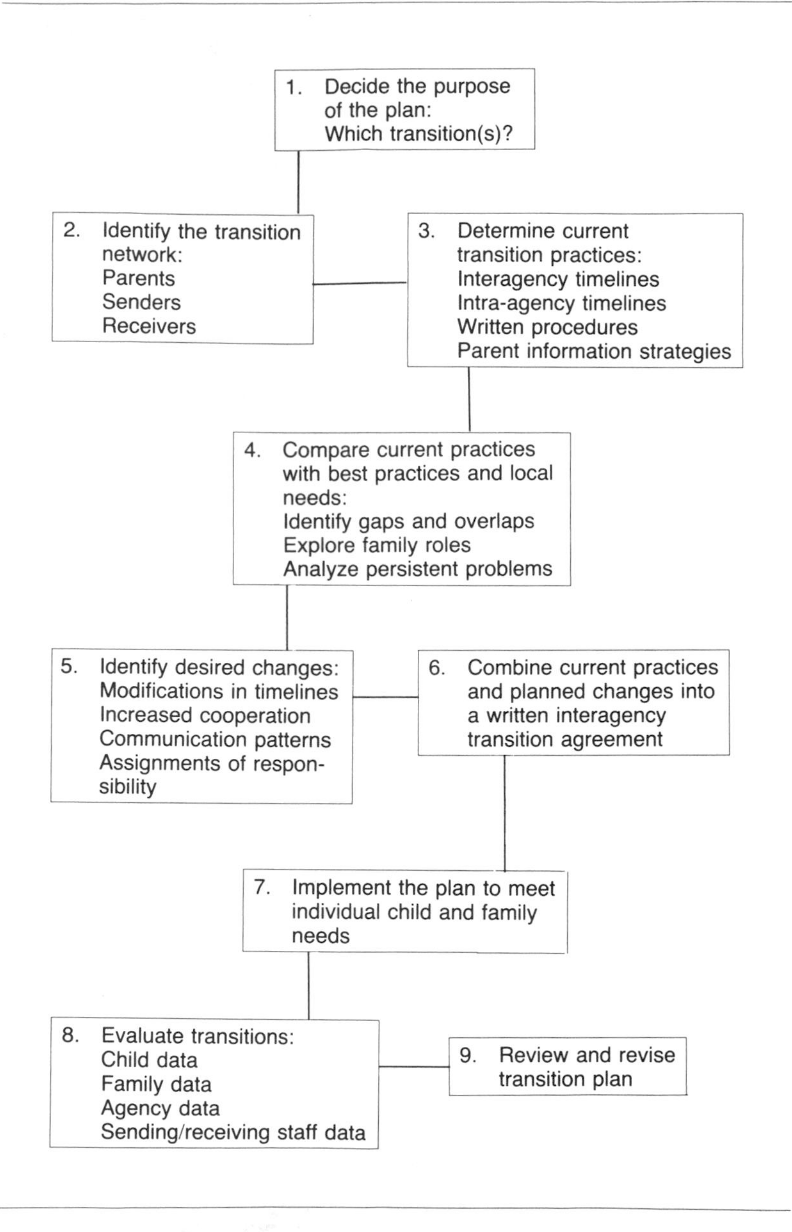

Figure 4.3. The interagency transition planning process.

shared responsibility may best be achieved if receiving agencies acknowledge the historical and emotional commitments of personnel from the sending agency to the children and families they have been serving. Despite the fact that the direct responsibilities of the sending staff will soon cease, their knowledge of the child and family and their ongoing concern for them should entitle sending agency personnel to a major role in the transition. The sending staff should participate in the assessment process and goal setting, but they must recognize that legal and financial responsibilities will soon rest with the receiving agency. Finally, both agencies must acknowledge that families are the primary decision-makers regarding the futures of their young children. Therefore, both sending and receiving professionals need to respect the pivotal role of families in transition planning. The smoothest transitions occur when the three major planners—senders, receivers, and families—share in the transition planning process and realize the importance of the decisions being made. This concept is diagrammed in Figure 4.4.

The third step in the interagency planning process is to determine current transition practices within and across agencies. This step helps team members appreciate the constraints under which

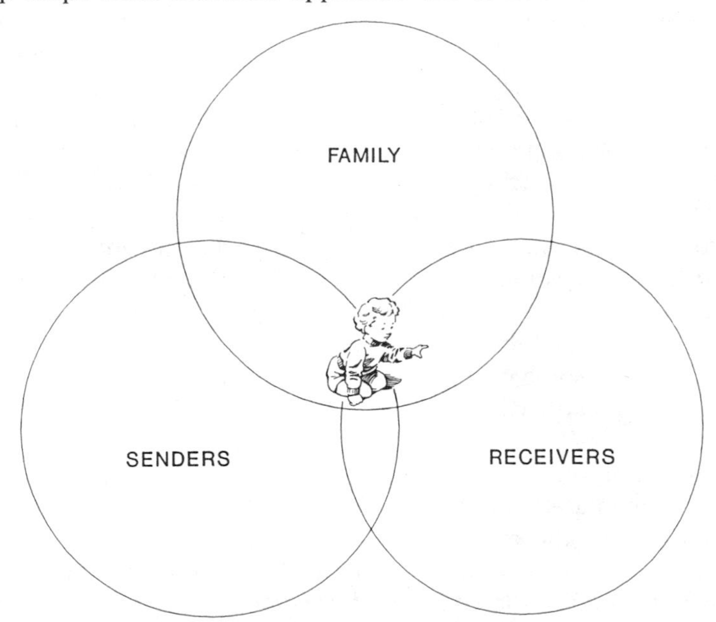

Figure 4.4. Participants in transition planning.

other agencies work (i.e., the real world of transition planning and application). Some elements of the local transition plan have most likely been established. Delineating pre-existing elements helps determine what works well, and these strengths can subsequently be incorporated into the new plan. Thus, the task of transition planning becomes less formidable as members realize that many necessary elements are already in place, albeit informally.

Fourth, policy-makers can note gaps and overlaps in transition services, establish a partnership with families in decision-making, and analyze persistent problems plaguing children, families, or professionals in achieving the particular transition presently under study. A good resource for comparing present practice with best practice is the transition planning self-assessment checklist shown in Figure 4.5. This checklist helps all team members to focus on the entire transition process for which they share responsibility.

Discussions regarding desired changes in transition practices will lead to the creation of a list of possibilities for future action. These might include revisions in the present timeline, pooling of resources for assessment, additional communication, form sharing, preparation of a transition manual for parents, formation of a parent mentoring group, and strategies for the development of new evaluation. Some suggestions will be jointly implemented, whereas others will be managed by a single agency or individual. The suggestions should be discussed (by the policies team) in terms of desirability and feasibility and subsequently prioritized for action (by the procedures team or by individual agencies).

The sixth step in the interagency transition planning process is to combine current practices and planned changes into a written interagency transition agreement. Development of this agreement requires cooperation within the interagency transition procedures team. It is essential that the director of each agency sign the written agreement. In some cases, attorneys for the agencies bearing financial responsibility will peruse the document before signatures are obtained.

Actual implementation of the plan follows. Evaluation of both the implementation and its outcomes should precede periodic interagency review and revision. These practices ensure that the interagency transition agreement continues to promote smooth and effective transitions for children, their families, and the involved agencies.

Indicators	Occurs?			Target for Change?		Priority for Change					Comments
	No	Somewhat	Yes			Low		Medium		High	
1. Leaders and/or staff of sending and receiving programs are acquainted with one another.	N	S	Y	N	Y	1	2	3	4	5	
2. Sending and receiving programs have a designated interagency group to work on transition planning.	N	S	Y	N	Y	1	2	3	4	5	
3. Sending and receiving programs have an action plan to improve transition in the future.	N	S	Y	N	Y	1	2	3	4	5	
4. Staff members use written transition procedures to plan activities both to receive new children and families and to send children and families to their next placement.	N	S	Y	N	Y	1	2	3	4	5	
5. Sending and receiving programs have developed a timeline of transition activities that is adapted to meet individual child and family needs.	N	S	Y	N	Y	1	2	3	4	5	
6. Sending and receiving programs have developed and periodically revise an interagency agreement.	N	S	Y	N	Y	1	2	3	4	5	
7. Families have access (in their native language) to information, support, and opportunities for participation in transition planning.	N	S	Y	N	Y	1	2	3	4	5	
8. Parents receive an information manual to help them become involved in the transition process.	N	S	Y	N	Y	1	2	3	4	5	
9. Sending and receiving programs have identified staff who will coordinate the transition or will assist families in coordinating the transition process themselves.	N	S	Y	N	Y	1	2	3	4	5	
10. Sending and receiving programs have a system for exchanging information and are familiar with the services of each (e.g., exchange visits, share curriculum materials).	N	S	Y	N	Y	1	2	3	4	5	

Figure 4.5. Transition planning self-assessment checklist.

(continued)

Figure 4.5 (*continued*)

Indicators	Occurs? No / Somewhat / Yes			Target for Change		Priority for Change Low / Medium / High					Comments
11. The family and the sending service coordinator discuss the transition process, review the steps, and determine the family's desired level of involvement.	N	S	Y	N	Y	1	2	3	4	5	
12. Transition issues are considered, and appropriate outcomes/goals and objectives are included in the child's IFSP/IEP.	N	S	Y	N	Y	1	2	3	4	5	
13. Sending program notifies receiving program(s) well in advance about the number and birth dates of children who are likely to enter the receiving program(s).	N	S	Y	N	Y	1	2	3	4	5	
14. Sending program prepares a transition progress report, including information on the child's experiences and accomplishments in that program.	N	S	Y	N	Y	1	2	3	4	5	
15. The sending program obtains written permission from the parents to share information about the child with the receiving program(s).	N	S	Y	N	Y	1	2	3	4	5	
16. The sending program, the receiving program, and the family meet at least 90 days prior to the child's third birthday to discuss the child's progress as summarized in the transition report, consider possible program options for the future, and explore differences in educational services, eligibility, and paperwork between the current program and potential receiving programs. They review the transition timeline, plan for the family's desired level of participation in the transition process, and outline any additional evaluations needed to determine eligibility and program placement.	N	S	Y	N	Y	1	2	3	4	5	
17. Parents and the transition coordinator or sending teacher visit potential placements for the child.	N	S	Y	N	Y	1	2	3	4	5	

Item					
18. The family and the sending and receiving program staff participate in the placement conference. They make decisions regarding placement, starting date, special services, and new IFSP/IEP plans based on the current IFSP/IEP and the transition progress report.	N S Y	N Y	1 2 3 4 5	
19. Sending program transfers records in a timely manner.	N S Y	N Y	1 2 3 4 5	
20. Receiving program visits the child in present placement to begin planning for the child's special needs, to identify similarities and differences between the two programs, and to plan strategies to ease the child's transition.	N S Y	N Y	1 2 3 4 5	
21. Sending program and/or parents implement strategies to ease the child's transition into the receiving program.	N S Y	N Y	1 2 3 4 5	
22. Child and family visit the new program.	N S Y	N Y	1 2 3 4 5	
23. The family exchanges information with the receiving program on their child (e.g., his or her likes and dislikes, effective motivators and approaches to discipline, or current medical information related to the child's special needs), their goals and dreams for their child's scholastic experiences, and strategies for effective communication between school and home.	N S Y	N Y	1 2 3 4 5	
24. Prior to the child's entry, the new program obtains necessary resources, including staff, instructional materials, and equipment and completes necessary building changes and staff training.	N S Y	N Y	1 2 3 4 5	
25. Receiving teacher implements strategies to ease the child's transition into the program.	N S Y	N Y	1 2 3 4 5	
26. Family and sending and receiving programs communicate regarding appropriateness and satisfaction with the placement and strategies to overcome difficulties.	N S Y	N Y	1 2 3 4 5	
27. Interagency transition group conducts evaluations of the transition process and considers changes to improve the process for the next year.	N S Y	N Y	1 2 3 4 5	

THE INTERAGENCY TRANSITION TIMELINE

Transition planning for both agencies and individual children must occur within a specific timeframe. This is necessary in order to comply with legal mandates as well as to provide continuity in services for children and families. It is thus important to have a written interagency timeline that indicates when particular activities will occur. This timeline, which is developed by local transition planning teams, should consider the following factors:

- Necessary legal requirements
- Different birthdates, screening schedules, and family moves that may shift children out of and into service programs at various times of the year
- Personal and unrelated professional responsibilities of program personnel that may absorb time from transition activities
- Normalization: families of children with disabilities should know about their children's future placements at the same time of year as families of children without disabilities
- The time required to gather information, conduct assessment, transfer relevant records, visit potential programs, and meet with individual child transition teams for discussion and decision-making
- The extraordinary amount of time required to locate funding, prepare materials, obtain necessary equipment, or train staff in unfamiliar procedures essential for some children with complex needs

The transition planning self-assessment checklist (Figure 4.5) may serve as a starting point for developing a local interagency timeline. It may indeed be helpful to dissect the elements of transition and arrange them independently (as in Table 4.1), deleting unnecessary elements and adding steps according to local need. The right timeline must be responsive to the local situation and that of its families and agency personnel, as well as to federal and state regulations and requirements.

Timelines may employ a variety of formats. Perhaps the most common is the linear type—a collection of boxes organizing activities into a proper sequence, as illustrated in Figure 4.6. Other timelines may use a matrix that lists dates (either actual dates like "July" or relative dates like "6 months before the child's birthday") horizontally and individual participants vertically, as shown in Figure 4.7. With this format, a reader can easily determine what each party

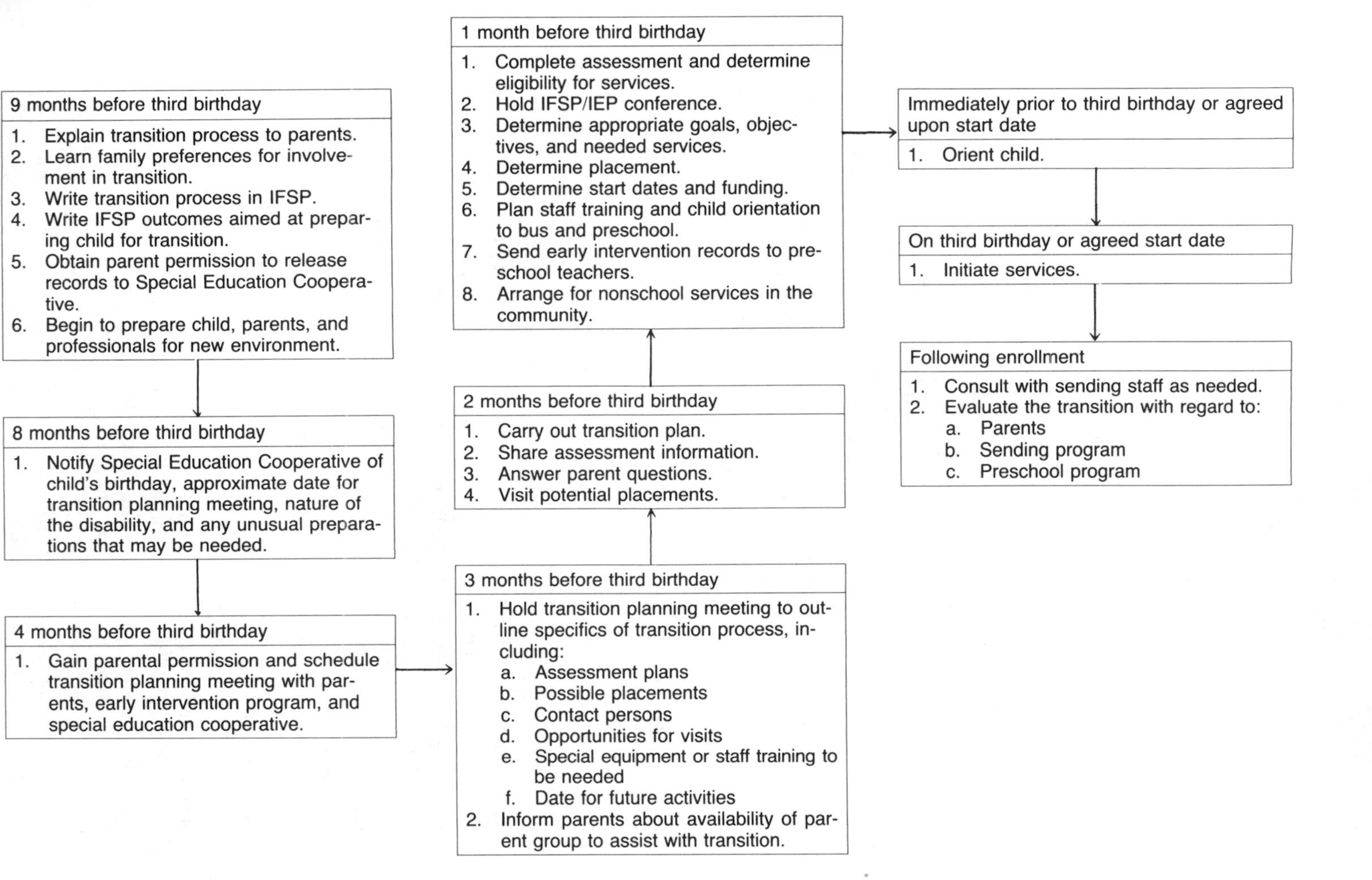

9 months before third birthday
1. Explain transition process to parents.
2. Learn family preferences for involvement in transition.
3. Write transition process in IFSP.
4. Write IFSP outcomes aimed at preparing child for transition.
5. Obtain parent permission to release records to Special Education Cooperative.
6. Begin to prepare child, parents, and professionals for new environment.
8 months before third birthday
1. Notify Special Education Cooperative of child's birthday, approximate date for transition planning meeting, nature of the disability, and any unusual preparations that may be needed.
4 months before third birthday
1. Gain parental permission and schedule transition planning meeting with parents, early intervention program, and special education cooperative.
3 months before third birthday
1. Hold transition planning meeting to outline specifics of transition process, including:
a. Assessment plans
b. Possible placements
c. Contact persons
d. Opportunities for visits
e. Special equipment or staff training to be needed
f. Date for future activities
2. Inform parents about availability of parent group to assist with transition.
2 months before third birthday
1. Carry out transition plan.
2. Share assessment information.
3. Answer parent questions.
4. Visit potential placements.
1 month before third birthday
1. Complete assessment and determine eligibility for services.
2. Hold IFSP/IEP conference.
3. Determine appropriate goals, objectives, and needed services.
4. Determine placement.
5. Determine start dates and funding.
6. Plan staff training and child orientation to bus and preschool.
7. Send early intervention records to preschool teachers.
8. Arrange for nonschool services in the community.
Immediately prior to third birthday or agreed upon start date
1. Orient child.
On third birthday or agreed start date
1. Initiate services.
Following enrollment
1. Consult with sending staff as needed.
2. Evaluate the transition with regard to:
a. Parents
b. Sending program
c. Preschool program

Figure 4.6. Arborville timeline for the transition at age 3.

	9 months before			3 months before		2 months before					1 month before						(portions omitted)	Follow-up	
	Explain transition process	Define family preferences for involvement	(portions omitted)	Attend transition planning meeting	(portions omitted)	Share assessment data	Complete assessment	Visit potential placements	Answer parent questions		Determine eligibility	Write IFSP/IEP	Determine placement	Plan staff training	Share records	Assist in arranging for nonschool services		Consult with early intervention as needed	Evaluate the transition process
Family	X	X		X				X				X	X			X		X	X
Early Intervention Program	X	X		X		X	X	X	X			X			X	X			X
Special Education Cooperative				X			X		X		X	X	X	X		X		X	X
Local Interagency Council																X			X

Figure 4.7. Portion of an alternative timeline for Arborville

should be doing at any point in time. Conversely, some communities prefer a single list delineating activities for each participant. This type of timeline is illustrated in Table 4.1. Further examples of interagency timelines may be found in Bennett et al., (1991); Conn-Powers & Ross-Allen, (1991); Lazzari, (1991); and Stephens & Rous, (1992). Additional sample timeline formats may be found in Appendix C.

Some communities include their completed interagency timelines in the written interagency transition agreement, whereas others list only key activities there and subsequently expound upon them in the interagency procedures delineated by the interagency procedures team. Regardless, the interagency timeline should be used by individual agencies to project activities for all involved parties. All relevant personnel should receive a copy of the timeline, and it should be posted in a place where responsible parties may glance at it frequently. Individual professionals should consult it regularly as they develop personal time management plans for working with families in transition planning. The interagency timeline should then be adapted for individual children and their families and subsequently incorporated into their IFSPs and IEPs. Indeed, specification of the transition schedule helps everyone involved both to anticipate

Table 4.1. Sample format for timelines

(portions omitted)

1 month prior to the child's third birthday:

- ____ Complete assessment (SE).
- ____ Determine eligibility for services (SE).
- ____ Convene and attend IFSP/IEP conference (F, EI, SE).
- ____ Determine appropriate goals, objectives, and services needed (F, EI, SE).
- ____ Determine placement (F, SE).
- ____ Determine start dates and funding (F, EI, SE).
- ____ Plan staff training (SE).
- ____ Plan child orientation (F, EI, SE).
- ____ Share records among agencies (EI, SE).
- ____ Assist in arranging for necessary nonschool services (EI, SE, ICC).

F = Family; EI = Early Intervention Program; SE = Special Education Cooperative; ICC = Local Interagency Council.

forthcoming activities and to meet individual responsibilities (Fowler et al., 1991; Hains et al., 1991).

INTERAGENCY SUPPORT FOR PLACEMENT OPTIONS

In many communities, early intervention centers and special education programs have developed strong relationships that promote placements that are nearly automatic. Two important trends in early childhood services, however, encourage services that are more community-based and family-centered (see Chapter 2) (Peck et al., 1993). Therefore, as part of their planning processes, local interagency teams must analyze the broad array of settings for service delivery available in their community. Table 4.2 lists many of these settings. Strategies to ensure the consideration of these multiple placement options should be included in the interagency transition process.

Table 4.2. Possible placement options for children (birth through age five)

Family childcare home	Pre-kindergarten
Childcare center	Early childhood education center
Public health home visitor program	Head Start
Early intervention center	Respite care
Early intervention home visitor program	Early childhood family education center
Preschool	Kindergarten
Nursery school	Before and after school care programs
Community play group	Nongraded primary program
Neighborhood community center	Employer-sponsored child care
Cooperative child care	Residential-sponsored care (e.g., shelters)
Library children's hour	Community recreation program
Parochial school	

When Arborville received the state directive to develop a transition plan, several agency directors, prompted by their early childhood coordinators, convened a meeting to discuss the situation. The following persons attended: three parents who had recently experienced the age 3 transition with their children; one parent of a 15-year-old child who had experienced many transitions within the school system; administrators of the two regional agencies providing family service coordination for early intervention programs within the community; the director of special education for the county special education cooperative that encompasses five school districts; the director of the local Head Start; the president of the local early childhood association; and various administrators from the county health department, the local hospital that provides most of the therapy for early intervention services in the community, the county human services program, the local YMCA that sponsors a widely used recreational program for preschool children, the local council of churches, and the local library that sponsors a weekly storytime for preschool-age children.

The members decided to call themselves collectively the Arborville Interagency Transition Taskforce. Initially, they planned to define their mission and outcomes using the flowchart shown in Figure 4.3. The members decided to meet from 4 to 5 P.M. on Mondays when all were able to attend. Child care funded jointly by the early intervention and special education agencies was provided for parents. The Taskforce set a timetable of 2 months to complete an interagency agreement, realizing that it would be reviewed and revised based on future evaluation data.

The Interagency Taskforce developed the interagency agreement contained in Figure 4.2. Few options were available for children graduating from early intervention programs if they no longer qualified for special education services. Therefore, more options were to be explored by this Arborville team in conjunction with local preschool and childcare providers.

Members then turned the interagency agreement over to early childhood administrators in various agencies to develop more specific procedures and a detailed timeline. Those administrators coupled with the parents from the Taskforce constituted the interagency procedures team. This group then composed the detailed timeline shown in Figure 4.7 as well as several written descriptions of tasks that may potentially be confusing. For instance, the assessment process was streamlined by including data released from the early intervention programs, thereby reducing the amount of required testing and the subsequent duplication of information. The interagency transition procedures team also defined specific strategies for evaluating local age 3 transitions. They plan to work on developing common intake forms to reduce the strain of transition on families. Additionally, they decided to create a menu of potential family support activities. One of the parents suggested that a transition mentoring program be established that pairs par-

ents facing the age 3 transition with parents who have already experienced it. The team eventually plans to develop a common transition planning manual for parents.

Thereafter, the agency administrators presented the timeline and newly developed procedures to their respective agencies to guide them in developing both intra-agency transition procedures and individual child/family transition plans.

Arborville's transition planning process built upon existing practices. It clarified agency, individual, and shared responsibilities, and provided a framework for future decision-making. The activities described above took less than a year to complete. However, the processes of evaluation and revision as well as the enactment of planned supporting activities will undoubtedly continue into the next year and beyond.

IMPLICATIONS

This chapter outlines a procedure for convening community personnel from various agencies and levels to work together with parents in building a coherent transition system. This process begins with the interagency policy team, which develops a general interagency agreement regarding transition. The interagency transition procedures team then delineates everyday operations necessary to promote smooth transitions between agencies. This planning is then applied by an IFSP or IEP team in moving an individual child and his or her family successfully from one program to another. Parents play key roles on all three levels of interagency planning. Individual communities develop a transition timeline that specifies the schedule of forthcoming transition activities. Interagency efforts are subsequently evaluated under the direction of the interagency policy team, and the information thus gained is used to refine and improve the local transition process.

Intra-agency Coordination

Smoothing the Roadbed

The success of an individual transition depends on relevant professionals performing their assigned jobs in a timely manner. But what are their assigned jobs, and when is the right time?

The Daisy Center provides service coordination for 250 families of children with disabilities, birth through age 3, who live in an urban area. The Center receives referrals from four public health departments, hospitals, physicians, and individual citizens. Upon reaching the age of 3, children and their families may transfer into a variety of programs: five school districts, one special education cooperative, three Head Start agencies, four private schools for children with disabilities, and numerous community preschools and childcare centers. Obviously, transitions are complex matters for the Daisy Center personnel and the families with whom they work.

This chapter aids local agency personnel in translating a community's timeline into a mutually acceptable schedule delineating specific tasks to be carried out by designated people. The resulting agency plan for transition should both support the pre-existing interagency plan and help individual professionals manage their time effectively. Most importantly, however, when such a plan is incorporated into IFSPs and IEPs, it helps families learn what the future holds regarding their child's transition, from whom future action will come, by what date, and when and how they may participate in that action if they choose to do so.

IS MY AGENCY A SENDER OR A RECEIVER?

The answer is "both." All agencies receive new children and their families into their service programs while they either send children and families to new special education programs or arrange for them to graduate from special services entirely. Each role—receiving and sending—necessarily entails its own set of responsibilities.

Receiving Programs

Effective receiving programs efficiently perform many functions throughout the transition process. Some of these pertain to placement:

- Participate positively in the decision-making process regarding placement.
- Oversee the child's multidisciplinary evaluation that includes securing appropriate parental permissions and coordinating with present service providers to avoid unnecessary duplication of evaluation activities.
- Learn about the incoming child and his or her family's resources, priorities, and concerns.
- Provide information about their program to both the sending program and the family.

Other functions of the receiving program include making preparations to serve the child and family effectively:

- Learn about the philosophy and service history that the entering child and family experienced in their previous program(s) and/or home.
- Welcome the child and family for a pre-transition visit.
- Plan carefully to make initial interactions between the child and family and new program personnel pleasant and encouraging.
- Receive and review records; make copies available to staff members who will be working with the child and family.
- Ensure that necessary equipment, menu modifications, transportation, and other special adaptations are in place prior to the transition.
- Ensure that staff members have appropriate training and support to manage the special needs of the child.

Staff members from the receiving program act to help the incoming child and his or her family in adjusting to the new setting:

- Modify existing program practices to ensure success for the entering child and family.
- Emphasize similarities and minimize differences between instructional programs to ease the child's transition.
- Communicate frequently with the family, especially during the first days after the transition.
- Consult with staff members from the sending program after the initial transition to solicit their expertise in resolving problems.

Finally, staff members from the receiving program participate in the local interagency effort to help ease transitions for young children and their families:

- Assist in locating needed services that are not presently available.
- Help in evaluating the transition.
- Contribute suggestions for improving the local interagency transition plan.

It is of course true that the respective importance of these functions will vary with regard to both the characteristics of individual children and their families as well as the resources and priorities of agency personnel. Nevertheless, each function deserves careful attention as each agency evaluates its effectiveness in bridging services for children and their families.

All three Head Starts in Republic County have been working to develop procedures for welcoming incoming children and their families. Each of these Head Starts is using a list like the one printed in this book to facilitate comprehensive transition planning. The activities of each Head Start differ, however, from those of the other two because each operates under unique circumstances.

San Juan's Head Start serves many families that recently migrated from regions near the Mexican border to work in Republic County's meat packing plants. Two new Spanish-speaking staff members have been hired to improve communication with families during their children's transitions into Head Start.

Paulson's Head Start is training its staff regarding the home visits that occur prior to children's enrollment in Head Start. Similarly, Merrimac's Head Start is putting special effort into developing procedures for records transfers. Its staff are also attempting to improve relationships with the local public health department in order to decrease referral time for eligible children.

Sending Programs

Programs also carry responsibilities as senders. These functions mesh with those of receiving programs to ensure smooth transitions for children and their families. Some activities of the sending program are initiated long in advance of an anticipated transition:

- Positively share information regarding the forthcoming transition process with the family.
- Help the family prepare for the transition.
- Affirm the level of involvement chosen by the family.
- Research potential receiving programs.

The sending program initiates the transition, with parental permission, and subsequently participates in the decision-making process:

- Provide current and appropriate information to initiate the comprehensive evaluation process as stipulated in the interagency transition plan.
- Visit potential receiving programs with the family, if so requested.
- Recommend goals and objectives appropriate for the child and family that focus on desired outcomes rather than on the service delivery model necessary to achieve those outcomes.
- Participate in the actual placement process by making recommendations regarding various options.

Once a decision regarding placement has been reached, the sending program acts to ensure its success:

- Serve as a liaison between the family and the receiving program.
- Help to prepare the child for transition into the new program.
- Emphasize instructional similarities between the programs to ease the child's transition.
- Write a transition report for the receiving agency.
- Transfer records according to the interagency transition plan.
- Consult with the receiving program both before and after the actual move.

Finally, the sending program, like the receiving program, participates in the interagency effort to help ease transitions for young children and their families:

- Assist in locating needed services that are not provided by the receiving agency.
- Help in evaluating the transition.
- Contribute suggestions for improving the local interagency transition plan.

Agencies generally tend to be more comfortable with receiving children than sending them. Indeed, sending agencies are often concerned about how "their" children and families will be served in new program(s). This paradoxical situation tends to be true for all transitions, regardless of when they occur.

The three Republic County Head Starts are working with their local school districts in developing effective procedures that facilitate transitions into kindergarten. In this situation, Head Start acts as the sending agency. Head Start both shares information regarding transition with all of its families and sponsors an annual "homecoming" when families formerly involved in Head Start return to describe their transition experiences for other parents.

Because transition is incorporated into each family's IFSP, families know in advance what to expect throughout the transition process. Children and their parents are invited to visit their neighborhood kindergarten, and children are told stories about kindergarten.

The Head Start teachers are also working with the local kindergarten teachers to promote curriculum continuity across the two programs. In the past, some Head Start teachers were apprehensive about sending their students forward into "the big school," but transition planning is helping to ease their concerns. By working closely with their counterparts at the kindergarten level, these Head Start teachers believe that appropriate services will continue to be provided for their students with special needs after their transitions into kindergarten.

WORKING TOGETHER

This situation suggests the need for an increase in the amount of time allocated in each agency's transition plan for increased consultation, frequent visits to other programs, and joint staff training and curriculum development. This recommendation is consistent with the recommendations of the U.S. Department of Education as well as those of various other national organizations. Indeed, as understanding, trust, joint planning, and cooperative inservice training develop, the relationships among direct service personnel in various agencies will certainly improve. Additionally, families will benefit from contact with professionals who are able to communicate effectively and positively regarding other service agencies.

Intra-agency transition planning should ideally address each of the functions listed above. Many agencies, however, presently have only informal, individually determined procedures to handle most of these functions. Oftentimes, when agency personnel are asked who is responsible for what function, the ensuing response is "the team." Although, teamwork is vital to providing quality early childhood services, individual people must assume discrete responsibilities within the team's framework to ensure that each transition function is properly addressed. Of course, different people may assume these responsibilities at various stages of transition. But, knowing in advance who those people are is vital to ensure efficiency and continued success.

HOW DO WE PROCEED?

The goal is to specify in writing who is responsible for each discrete task, in consultation with whom, and by what date. Who may refer to a specific person, or, better yet, to a professional role (like the child's speech-language pathologist, for instance).

The Intra-agency Transition Planning Process

The processes of interagency and intra-agency planning are quite similar. Intra-agency planning is profiled in Figure 5.1. The goal of this process is to develop a written statement of an agency's transition procedures (Stephens & Rous, 1992). This statement should be given to each employee, explained to every involved family, and incorporated into each IFSP or IEP. It should be shared with new employees during their agency orientation, incorporated into job descriptions, and referenced in personnel evaluations. Because evaluation, review, and revision are parts of the transition process, this agency transition plan will change over time and will subsequently become more and more helpful to agency personnel in their effort to bridge early services. Portions of sample agency transition plans appear in Figures 5.2 and 5.3, and a sample transition monitoring form (i.e., an individual child approach to an intra-agency plan) is shown in Figure 5.4.

Variations in Transition Coordination

Some transitions, especially those in smaller communities, are relatively simple to coordinate (e.g., when a child moves from a single

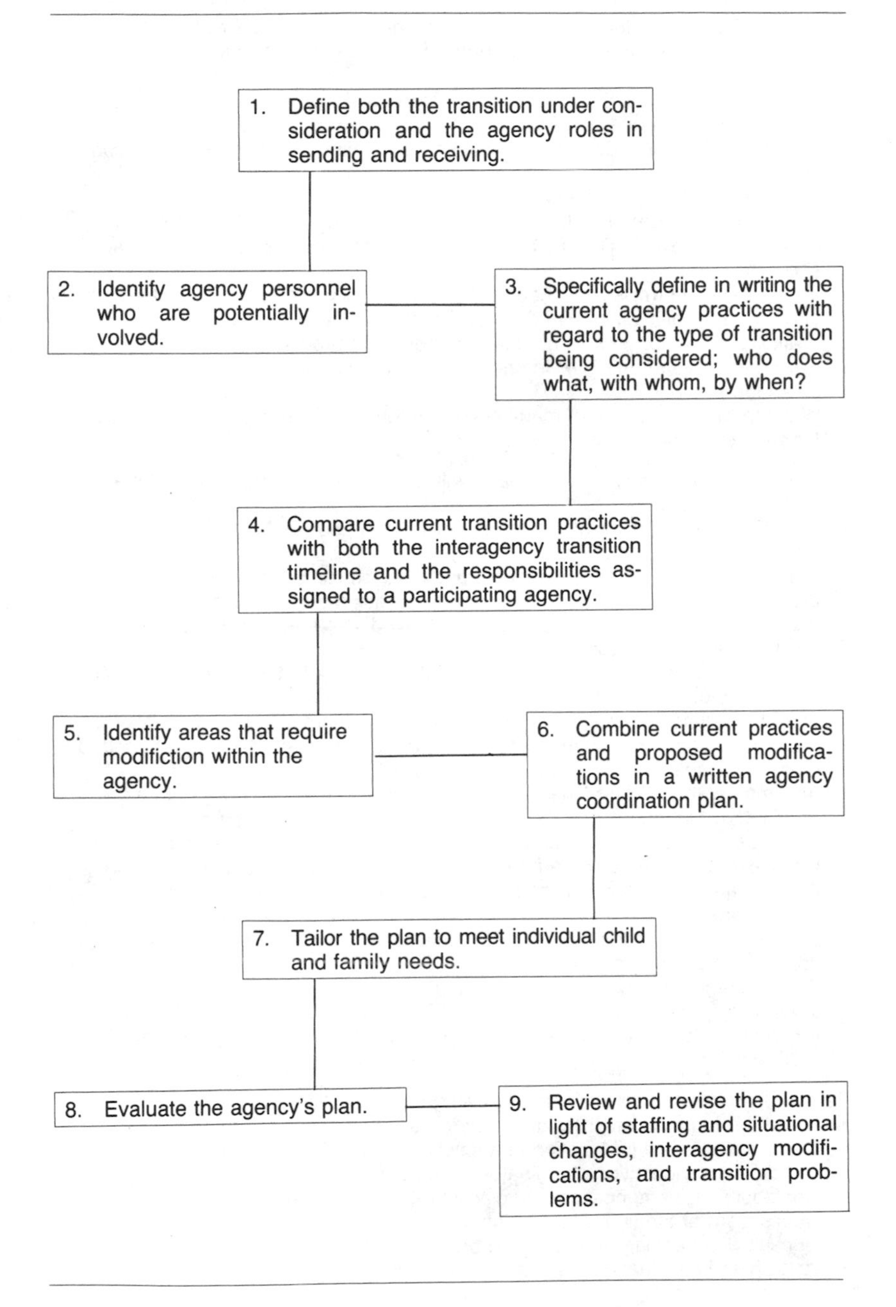

Figure 5.1. The intra-agency transition planning process.

The Daisy Center employs a transition coordinator to coordinate all transitions into or out of the Center's service program. Responsibilities of the coordinator include:

- Lead the agency in complying with provisions of the Arborville interagency agreement for the age 3 transition.
- Represent the Daisy Center in developing and refining interagency transition procedures.
- Summarize monthly intake data.
- Summarize projected numbers of children graduating from the Center and coordinate the sharing of information with relevant schools, Head Starts, and childcare centers.
- With parental permission, schedule transition planning meetings at least 90 days prior to each child's third birthday.
- Train Daisy Center personnel regarding transition procedures.
- Seek information from IFSP teams to evaluate and improve transition procedures.
- With the help of other staff members, keep the transition monitoring form current for each child (see Figure 5.4).

Each family's family service coordinator will assist with the transition, undertaking the following responsibilities:

- Orient the family (including pre-enrollment visits) prior to their participation in the Daisy Center program.
- Nine months prior to the child's third birthday, explain the transition process to the family, learn how actively they wish to participate in transition planning, determine whom they want to become involved with them, and assist them in drafting transition outcomes for the IFSP.
- Obtain the family's permission to share information with the appropriate school district and/or Head Start.
- Provide relevant information to the transition coordinator 8 months and 4 months prior to the third birthday respectively, using the forms specifically designed for those purposes.
- Accompany the family to the transition planning meeting 90 days before the child's third birthday.
- Share assessment data as agreed in the transition planning meeting.
- If requested, accompany the family to visit potential placement sites.
- Answer family questions or refer parents to the transition coordinator from another agency.
- If requested, attend the IFSP or IEP conference and aid in formulating appropriate goals and objectives.
- Write a summary report (incorporating information from teachers and therapists) to be sent to the receiving program prior to the child's entry.
- If requested, consult with the receiving program to aid in the adjustment of the child and family.

Teachers and therapists share the following responsibilities:

- Assist the family in attaining appropriate transition outcomes for the child.
- Share assessment information in a timely manner with the family service coordinator or transition coordinator, as requested.
- Contribute recommendations for placement and suggestions for goals to the child's team at the time of transition.
- Consult with sending and receiving professionals to aid in the child's adjustment.
- Participate in evaluating the transition process.

Figure 5.2. The Daisy Center transition plan.

	Family	Transition coordinator	Family service coordinator	Teacher or therapist
9 months prior to the child's third birthday:				
• Explain the transition process to the family.			X	
• Decide who will participate in developing transition outcomes.	X			
• Determine transition-related IFSP outcomes.	X		X	X
• Seek and give parental permission to release information about the child to the appropriate school district.	X		X	
• Report the above information to the transition coordinator.			X	
• Share demographic information with the school district.		X		
• Begin implementing transition-related IFSP activities.	X		X	X
8 months prior to the child's third birthday:				

(Form continues)

Figure 5.3. A portion of an alternate transition plan for the Daisy Center.

Transition monitoring form for: ____________ (Child's Name) ____________
Date of third birthday ____________

Note: Responsible staff should date and initial when tasks are completed

9 months before Date: ________	8 months before Date: ________	4 months before Date: ________	3 months before Date: ________	
____ Explain process to parents ____ Determine people parents want to participate ____ Include transition plan and outcomes in IFSP ____ Share additional information as requested by the family ____ Obtain parental permission to release demographic information to the school district	____ Inform school of child's birthdate and demographic information	____ Obtain parental permission to schedule transition planning meeting ____ Schedule transition planning meeting with family and school	____ Convene transition planning meeting ____ Define possible placements ____ Determine how parents can visit potential placements if they choose ____ Set transition timeline ____ Determine how evaluation will occur	(Form continues)

Figure 5.4. A portion of the transition monitoring form.

home-based early intervention program run by the local school system to a community-based preschool program with special education services, and subsequently into a kindergarten offering supportive special education services). Indeed, in a very small community, this may be the typical progression for all but a few children.

Other communities employ much more complex service systems, with multiple early intervention programs feeding into numerous public school systems, Head Starts, and private preschool and childcare programs, which then send children to kindergartens and special education classrooms that are sponsored by several school districts as well as to various parochial and private elementary schools. Thus, an agency's individual transition plan must reflect its place within a larger interagency milieu, be it simple or complex. Each agency should employ a transition coordinator who monitors the overall transition process within his or her agency while at the same time maintaining contact with other agencies. This person is typically the agency's representative on the interagency transition procedures team. In order to function effectively, this individual must be knowledgeable about the people and practices both in that agency as well as in other agencies. He or she need not be an agency director or early services coordinator, but must nonetheless be capable of individual problem-solving while maintaining a positive attitude.

In the type of small community described above, a single individual might serve as transition coordinator for all children presently involved in the local service system. Transition procedures thus remain relatively simple. Indeed, in this situation, the transition process serves comparatively few children per year. Therefore, many relevant personnel may already be familiar with one another, thereby simplifying the establishment of clear lines of communication. Some personnel may in fact serve in all three programs, thus further facilitating the transition process (e.g., in some small communities a school psychologist, a social worker, or a family life specialist may serve as transition coordinator for all local early childhood transitions).

Conversely, in a complex system, large numbers of children are moving among numerous agencies employing personnel who are unfamiliar with one another. In this case, each agency needs a transition coordinator who spends considerable time fostering positive relationships with other agencies. Additionally, he or she must communicate the diverse practices and expectations of other agencies to personnel within the home agency who are serving on individual transition teams. Thus, in these large and complex systems, an efficient means of communication must be established and subsequently shared with all relevant personnel. Indeed, regarding the Daisy Center's situation (see Figure 5.2), the transition coordinator reports to each of the five school districts to which it sends children about the numbers of children who may soon be eligible to receive special education services, their birthdays, the types of disabilities as well as the amount of support they may need, and any special needs that may require additional planning and attention. In the event that parental permission cannot be obtained, children's names may be omitted from these reports.

It is obviously more efficient for a single transition coordinator to circulate information than for all involved early interventionists and family service coordinators to report individually to each of the five school districts. Therefore, agency transition plans must ensure that the transition coordinator is provided with the appropriate information in a timely manner.

Getting Started

The process outlined above may at first glance seem formidable. However, the actual implementation will be less time-consuming than it seems here, and significant amounts of time and confusion will be averted over the long term. Agencies are well-advised to choose a "test" transition for initial work because the procedures developed may be modified to aid further transition planning. Family collaboration and partnership throughout the planning process is critical for developing smooth and effective intra-agency plans.

After transition policies and procedures were developed for the community, the Daisy Center's director appointed Charlene Meyers to draft an intra-agency transition plan. She consulted with parents and experienced staff members and produced the plan shown in Figure 5.2. It will of course be modified in the future based on feedback from its users. Regardless, staff members have already expressed appreciation regarding the organization it brings to their transition planning efforts. Ms. Meyers and her staff have also recently produced an alternate form for the intra-agency transition plan, shown in Figure 5.3.

IMPLICATIONS

Chapter 5 outlines a procedure for delineating intra-agency responsibilities that will operationalize the interagency transition agreement described previously. It also suggests the appointment of a transition coordinator within each agency to develop and monitor intra-agency transition efforts and to coordinate transition activities that involve other agencies. With this framework soundly in place, transition planning for individual children and families can move forward.

6

Family–Professional Collaboration

Drawing the Map Together

Transition is experienced many times by all families (Barber, Turnbull, Behr, & Kerns, 1988; Brotherson, Backus, Summers, & Turnbull, 1986). Families with young children often experience stress during early transitions, regardless of whether their child has special needs (Brotherson et al., 1986; Gwost, 1992; Ziegler, 1985). A planned approach encouraging parent–professional collaboration can help families to prepare for and cope successfully with early transition, thus alleviating at least some of this accompanying stress (Hanline, 1993).

A definition of transition is a change accompanied by loss and/or gain. Preparing for transition is very important, and very difficult. As the word implies, it is an ongoing process. For some parents who have children with disabilities, change seems to be the norm and at the same time things seem to happen very slowly and laboriously.

I am still in the midst of my son's transition, or should I say, my own. I now realize that my son has adjusted well to his new school. It is I who have not. I am still grieving the loss of my son's early intervention teacher and therapist—my friends.

I have not been able to replace that loss with his new teachers and therapists for different reasons. One of those reasons is

Portions of this chapter appeared in Hains, A.H., Rosenkoetter, S.E., & Fowler, S.A. (1991). Transition planning with families in early intervention programs. *Infants and Young Children, 3,* 38–47. Adapted with permission.

the change in location. My friends used to come into my home and we would talk while we worked. Now a note is sometimes sent home telling me what has been done in school that day.

Any change in personnel is hard. My friends valued my opinion, saw how I lived, and respected me for who I was as well as for being my son's mother. Now I am just "his mother" and I am consulted only when things are not going as planned. Not only have new people entered our lives, but so has an institution (school) with rules of its own.

JoEllen Kilkenny, parent
Wisconsin

* * *

I am really excited about the transition. It will be so wonderful for Casey to make new friends and encounter new challenges in kindergarten. This is an important time for us. I just hope I'm doing everything I can to help Casey like school.

Anonymous parent,
Kansas

* * *

I'm not celebrating this transition at all! My daughter can't talk to me and tell me what's going on. I don't know what they're doing to her up there in kindergarten—it's just not like preschool. And I'm mad! Don't take it personal, but I just want this to work, and I don't know if it is, cause she can't tell me. That's why I'm mad at everybody.

Anonymous parent,
Kansas

* * *

I hope Marci will have friends, be invited to birthday parties, be invited over to play—but I just don't know whether that will happen.

Anonymous parent,
Kansas

THE BENEFITS OF COLLABORATION

Collaboration between professionals and families results in obvious benefits to the family as well as the child (Bennett et al., 1991; Hains et al., 1988). Because the family is the child's primary caregiver providing continuity throughout the child's life, a positive experience with early transitions may indeed facilitate later transitions (Barber et al., 1988; Hains et al., 1991; Lazzari & Kilgo, 1989; Ziegler, 1985). The strategies that families develop to cope with early transitions will likely be utilized in the future as they continue to advocate for their children, both during the early childhood years and beyond.

Families as well as children are affected by transition decisions. Transitions into new service programs may entail such changes as the termination of home visits, a decrease in parent–teacher contact, and a shift from family-focused to child-centered intervention. Other adjustments may require parents to alter routines, coordinate child care, arrange transportation, develop trust in new educational services and personnel, and adapt to a number of program differences. Parent–professional collaboration ensures that families' concerns and priorities are recognized and that planning thus responds to the unique situations identified. Children consequently profit from: 1) anticipatory guidance that is consistent in both home and school, 2) personnel equipped to serve their special needs, and 3) increased understanding of the home culture and school practices by professionals and parents, respectively (Love, Logue, Trudeau, & Thayer, 1992).

Community agencies also benefit as a result of family–professional communication and planning. Indeed, when families and professionals devise appropriate transition timelines and activities, parents, teachers, therapists, and administrators are aware of not only who is responsible for providing services, but also when and where those services will be provided. As a result, service continuity is maintained, service quality improves, and litigation diminishes (Swan & Morgan, 1993). Overall, interagency coordination of community resources assists professionals in discussing program options with families and subsequently helps families in making informed decisions regarding future programs.

The benefits of collaboration have even been recognized in legislation that identifies families as key decision-makers for their children during transition planning. PL 99-457 dictates that the IFSP must include steps that lend support to the family during the age 3 transition. Required activities thus include "discussions with, and training of, parents regarding future placements and other matters related to the child's transition" (*Federal Register,* 1989, June 22). The school-age regulations (including those for preschool) allow "parent counseling and training" to be listed as a related service in the IEP (Strickland & Turnbull, 1990). These activities are intended to assist "parents in understanding the special needs of their child and provide parents with information about child development" (Individuals with Disabilities Education Act, 1990).

FAMILY CONCERNS REGARDING EARLY TRANSITIONS

In order to support families during transitions, early intervention professionals should be aware of concerns that arise for many families throughout the transition process (Fowler, Chandler, Johnson, & Stella, 1988; Hanline, Suchman, & Demmerle, 1989). Whereas some concerns are readily verbalized, others may never be shared with professionals, and still others may go unrecognized altogether, even by family members. A number of issues raised by families regarding early transitions are discussed below.

Transfer of Friendship

Many families develop strong relationships with program staff members during their initial encounters with the service delivery system (Summers et al., 1990). Indeed, family service coordinators, nurses, teachers, therapists, social workers, and other professionals are often dependable sources of emotional support for families enrolled in early intervention programs. After building high levels of trust and communication with professionals over several months or years, however, transitions ultimately force parents to take leave of their current intervention team and form new relationships with different service professionals. Even in center-based programs where the infant/toddler and preschool programs are located in the same building, many families find the transition to be traumatic (Hanline & Knowlton, 1988; Summers et al., 1990). "It can feel like abandonment by the professionals, even though the parent knows the relationship is different from an ordinary friendship" (A. Spooner, personal communication, January, 1993).

Changes in Service Delivery

Families may express concern regarding the many changes in service delivery that can occur during early transitions (Fowler, Chandler, Johnson, & Stella, 1988b; Hanline, 1988; Johnson, Chandler, Kerns, & Fowler, 1986). Indeed, many variables differentiate various service delivery agencies (Peterson, 1987). Several of these are discussed below.

Differences in Focus of Services The IFSP identifies both the child and his or her family as targets for early intervention services, whereas the primary target for preschool and primary-level services is usually the child (Lazzari & Kilgo, 1989). Families of infants and toddlers enter the system by participating in identifying their own resources, priorities, and concerns as part of the IFSP process. Thus, the determination of outcomes is largely a function of individual family preferences. However, these issues are seldom addressed in the written IEPs of preschool-age children. Consequently, few services remain family-centered (Harbin, 1988).

As the emphasis on family participation diminishes, families may face difficulties in remaining actively involved in the decision-making and monitoring processes of early childhood intervention. Families may consequently experience confusion and frustration as a result of these changes. Some of the differences in the IFSP and IEP approaches to planning are summarized in Table 6.1.

As a result of the challenges described above, the reauthorization of the Individuals with Disabilities Education Act (1991) allows continued use of an IFSP until the child reaches the age of 6, provided that the state, school district, and family agree unanimously to do so. Similarly, the Head Start Act (1990) encourages use of a Head Start IFSP through the primary grades. Although these practices may ultimately be adopted by most communities, they are presently used in only a few regions of the United States. Nonetheless, regardless of the age at which intervention shifts from being family-centered to child-focused, the family will be required to make numerous adjustments during transition between the two.

Differences in Types of Services and Their Coordination The types of services provided and their coordination are likely to differ among service programs. Families generally have a greater variety of service options in early intervention programs than in preschool programs (Fowler et al., 1990). For instance, suppose the family identifies respite care as a necessity during the IFSP process. Although preschool programs may refer families to agencies that are equipped to provide respite care, the provision of such support is usually not addressed during the IEP process because respite care is not an "educationally-related service." This need might well be addressed, however, during interagency discussions as part of the transition planning process.

The administrative structure, underlying philosophy, developmental curriculum, and intervention activities of two service programs may differ. Changes such as these may be especially difficult for families if services shift from being home-based to center-based (Hanline & Knowlton, 1988) or from being play-oriented to structured programming (Barbour & Seefeldt, 1993). Consequently, families may worry about or even question the philosophy or practices of a new program. They may ask questions like, "If there are differ-

Table 6.1. Differences between the preschool/school-age (Part B) and infant/toddler (Part H) approaches to services based on the Individuals with Disabilities Education Act (IDEA) and the 1991 Amendments (PL 102-119)

Issue	Infant/toddler (Part H)	Preschool (Part B)
Individualized plans	Individualized family service plan (IFSP): • A statement of the child's present level of development • With the concurrence of the family, a family-directed assessment of their resources, priorities, and concerns • A statement of the major outcomes expected to be achieved for the child and family, and the criteria, procedures, and timelines used to determine: 1) The degree to which progress toward achieving outcomes is being made 2) Whether modifications or revisions of outcomes and services are necessary • A statement of the specific early intervention services necessary to meet the unique needs of the child and family in achieving the outcomes identified, including: 1) Frequency, intensity, location, and method of delivering services 2) Arrangements regarding payment, if any 3) Other services not required by this act but that are needed by the child, and steps to secure those services from other sources • The projected date for initiation of services and the anticipated duration of those services	Individualized education program (IEP): • A statement of the child's present levels of educational development • A statement of annual goals, including those regarding short-term instructional performance • A statement of the specific special education and related services to be provided for the child, and the extent to which the child will be able to participate in regular education programs • The projected date for initiation of services and the anticipated duration of those services • Appropriate objective criteria and evaluation procedures and schedules for determining, at least annually, whether short-term instructional objectives are being achieved • Transition services • At local or state discretion and with the concurrence of the family, 3- to 5-year-olds may have an IFSP instead of an IEP, so long as the IEP requirements are met

	• The name of the service coordinator (who is qualified to carry out the responsibilities of the position as designated under Part H) to be responsible for the IFSP as well as coordination with other agencies and persons • Steps to be taken to support the transition of the child at age 3 • A statement of the natural environments in which early intervention services shall be provided appropriately • Requires informed, written consent from parents before services in the IFSP are provided (if parents do not provide consent for all services, services for which consent is not given must not be provided)	
Eligible children	Birth- through 2-year-olds: • Showing developmental delays (as defined by state) • Having a diagnosed physical or mental condition which has a high probability of resulting in developmental delays in one or more of the following areas: 1) Cognitive 2) Physical 3) Communication 4) Social or emotional 5) Adaptive • At-risk for developmental delay at state's discretion • Who are in need of early intervention	3- through 5-year-olds: • With disabilities: mental retardation, hearing impairment, speech or language impairment, visual impairment, serious emotional disturbance, orthopedic impairments, autism, traumatic brain injury, other health impairments, specific learning disabilities; or at state discretion, eligibility may include children experiencing developmental delays, as defined by state in one or more of the following areas: 1) Physical 2) Cognitive 3) Communication 4) Social or emotional 5) Adaptive • Who need special education and related services.

(*continued*)

Table 6.1. *(continued)*

Issue	Infant/toddler (Part H)	Preschool (Part B)
Services	Early intervention services documented on individualized family service plan (IFSP) include but are not limited to: • Audiology • Service coordination • Family training and counseling as well as home visits • Health services • Medical services (for diagnostic purposes) • Nursing services • Nutrition services • Occupational therapy • Physical therapy • Psychological services • Social work services • Special instruction • Speech-language pathology • Early identification, screening, and assessment • Vision services • Assistive technology devices and services • Transportation and related costs	Special education and related services documented in individualized education program (IEP) include but are not limited to: • Audiology • Counseling services (provided by qualified social workers, or other[s]) • Early intervention • Medical services (for diagnostic purposes) • Occupational therapy • Parent counseling and training • Physical therapy • Psychological services • Recreation • School health services (provided by a school nurse or other qualified person) • Speech pathology • Social work services in the schools (social or developmental history; group and individual counseling with the child and family; working with problems in a child's home, school, and community that affect the child's adjustment in school; mobilizing school and community resources to enable the child to receive maximum benefit from his or her educational program) • Transportation

Costs to parents	State must establish a sliding fee scale if state law permits; however, families may not be denied services because of inability to pay • Certain services must be provided at no cost: 1) Child Find 2) Evaluation and assessment 3) Service coordination 4) Development and review of IFSP 5) Procedural safeguards • If a state provides "a free appropriate public education" (FAPE) from birth, all services are at no charge	All special education and related services must be at no cost to parents
Integration	"To the maximum extent appropriate, [services] are provided in natural environments, including the home and community settings . . . in which children without disabilities participate."	"Least restrictive environment": • "to the maximum extent appropriate, children with disabilities, . . . are educated with children who are not disabled, and that special classes, separate schooling, or other removal of children with disabilities from the regular educational environment occurs only when the nature or severity of the disability is such that education in regular classes with the use of supplementary aids and services cannot be achieved satisfactorily."

Adapted from Smith, Rose, Ballard, & Walsh (1991).

ences, which one represents the best approach?" or "Will my child be able to cope successfully with the demands of the new program?" (Rosenkoetter & Rosenkoetter, 1993). Regardless, the primary issue is likely to be whether the new program will be as successful as the old in facilitating their child's development.

The manner in which these services are coordinated is also subject to change. Early intervention services typically involve numerous agencies that have coordinated the administration of their services through interagency agreements. In these cases, the family service coordinator assists the family in consolidating, organizing, and interpreting pertinent information from all participants involved with early intervention services (Bailey, 1989). When families and children transfer into preschool programs, however, the public school system assumes the role of coordinating many of these services. This situation may challenge families in several ways during transition. First, the family is no longer able to rely on a single designated person to assist with service coordination. While teachers and therapists can be supportive of the family's involvement, they may not possess the skills or authority necessary to evaluate and monitor other services. Second, the family alone must now advocate for the delivery of appropriate services for the child. Indeed, when the service coordinator is also the service provider (i.e., the public school), a conflict of interest may arise regarding advocacy (Bailey, 1989). As of now, for instance, few school districts offer a full continuum of preschool services (Smith & Strain, 1988). Thus, families who prefer a preschool service option not presently available in their community may fear that their wishes will be ignored (Safford, 1989). Consequently, many parents are concerned regarding the best way to advocate for their child's needs—how to accomplish their own goals (for their child) without either alienating professionals or resorting to due process legal procedures.

Alternatively, when families move out of early intervention/special education services to a child care or typical preschool/kindergarten program, the careful planning of goals and objectives through the IFSP/IEP process is no longer available. This situation may be of concern to parents because their child's individual needs will no longer be considered formally in daily lesson planning. Moreover, only informal means of influence are available to parents under the auspices of these new programs.

Differences in Location of Services The location of services necessarily influences the types of services that are available. For example, in a home-based infant/toddler program, the early interventionist or teacher may, using familiar objects, focus on supporting interactions between the child and parent during the family's domestic routines. By contrast, a center-based preschool program may have a teacher or therapist initiating group activities by using commercially prepared materials with minimal parent contact. As the locality of services moves from home to center and subsequently from preschool to kindergarten, opportunities for parents to communicate with the professional staff are less frequent. This is especially true if children rely on public transportation instead of the family in commuting from place to place (Fowler, Chandler, & Johnson, 1988). Parents may not recognize these changes as problems; rather, they may fault the new program's personnel for having less interest in their child.

Indeed, many family anxieties emerge regarding the issue of transportation. Some parents are apprehensive about being separated from their children (Hanline, 1988) or, conversely, feel confusion about their delight in the newfound personal time that the school bus represents (Hanline et al., 1989). Parents may have legitimate fears for their child's safety during lengthy bus rides to preschool or kindergarten. Some families who are uncomfortable about the label of "special education" may dislike having neighbors see a conspicuous vehicle pull up to their homes. Siblings of children with disabilities may need to explain the reasons for the bus's presence and feel embarrassment in doing so (Lobato, 1990). The use of public transportation may even entail massive schedule changes for the family, new roles in dressing and feeding, changes in sleeping and meal times, and alterations in childcare arrangements (Hains et al., 1988).

In order to ease concern regarding the use of public transportation, many school districts schedule bus rides for new children and their parents so they can become familiar with the new routine. In areas where insurance regulations prohibit parents from riding the bus, the familiar early interventionist or the new preschool teacher may accompany the child on his or her first trip.

Differences in Service Personnel The introduction of new service personnel may cause anxiety for both the child and his or her family. For example, the early interventionist or consulting teacher for community programs may function as a member of a transdisciplinary team. Here, a single team member represents the others regarding service delivery and subsequently conducts activities with the child and family based on information gained through consultation with professionals of other disciplines (Peterson, 1987). In this situation, the family works with one professional. By contrast, at the preschool and kindergarten levels, the teacher and therapists may comprise an interdisciplinary team and subsequently deliver either cooperative or individual services to the child. Families may find it difficult to communicate with multiple professionals, especially if these professionals are itinerant. Indeed, families may even receive contradictory recommendations for teaching their children if the professionals do not work cooperatively.

Discrepancies in Eligibility

While in early intervention or special preschool programs, some children will overcome their developmental delays and will no longer require special services. Other children, who have been served under the at-risk provision of PL 99-457 (Part H) are not eligible for special preschool services unless they qualify because of a specific disability or developmental delay. Parents may thus be delighted that their children are not disabled, but concurrently sad to acknowledge the termination of high-quality, perhaps free, developmental services. The regulations of PL 99-457 do, however, require the IFSP to include specific guidelines for transition planning for those children who are ineligible to receive special education services. Regardless, planning is not likely to eliminate parental concern if options for continued early childhood education are limited, inappropriate, unaffordable, or unavailable (Smith & Strain, 1988).

Variations in Labeling

PL 99-457 authorizes young children to receive early intervention and special education services from birth through age 5 either categorically (e.g., "visually impaired," "mentally retarded," "severely emotionally disturbed") or under the label of "developmental delay." Each state must determine the ages at which it will recognize the use of "developmental delay" as well as the term's definition (states do *not,* however, determine definitions of *categorical* labels). A large number of states require categorical labeling at age 3 (Mallory & Kerns, 1988; Smith & Strain, 1988), others at age 5 or 6 (NEC*TAS, 1992a). However, this system of labeling and diagnosis may cause great concern for families (Wolery, 1989). First of all, a categorical label implies that a child *is* disabled, not merely developmentally behind. Second, the use of the label itself may become a painful issue. If parents have never heard professionals use the term *mental retardation* with regard to their child's level of functioning, then its introduction at a time of transition may trigger strong emotional reactions regarding the child's as well as family's future (Smith & Schakel, 1986).

Social Acceptance

Any time a child enters an unfamiliar environment, the family is likely to wonder whether he or she will be accepted. In fact, many parents verbalize to professionals their hopes and concerns regarding social acceptance (Fewell, 1986; Fowler, Chandler, Johnson, & Stella, 1988; Hanline & Knowlton, 1988; Rosenkoetter & Rosenkoetter, 1993). This issue is especially prominent as the child moves from: 1) home-based to center-based services, 2) a segregated to an inclusive program, 3) a community-based to a public school program, or 4) a small center to a larger, multi-classroom building.

Gaps in Children's Skills

Some parents worry about deficits in their children's experience or skill level that may potentially hinder adjustment in new programs (Noonan, 1989; Rosenkoetter & Rosenkoetter, 1993). By the age of 3, a considerable number of children have never been separated from their parents. They may regress in toileting, begin to cry, or act out when their families leave them for even a brief period. At age 5, some children enter academically focused kindergartens that have high expectations (Hains, Fowler, Schwartz, Kottwitz, & Rosenkoetter, 1989; Shepard & Smith, 1988). Consequently, many parents wonder what they can do at home to help their children prepare for preschool, child care, or kindergarten, respectively (Murphy & Vincent, 1989).

In a 1993 study, the concerns of parents of children with disabilities were compared with those of parents of normally developing children experiencing transition (Rosenkoetter & Rosenkoetter, 1993). The results showed that parents of children with disabilities were twice as likely as parents of children without disabilities to express anxiety about their children's transitions into kindergarten. In fact, the more severe the disability, the greater their concern. However, regardless of whether their children appeared to have disabilities, parents of girls were more likely to express a generalized worry, whereas parents of boys voiced more concerns about issues of readiness.

Other Concerns

Parents may have many other practical concerns such as:

- What the child should wear in the new setting
- What school supplies are needed
- What menu items are available
- What safety precautions are employed
- What programs are available other than regular programming (e.g., after-school care, swimming, recreation)
- What procedural safeguards are in effect
- What support programs are available to families
- Who are the people in the new setting
- Who is the contact person(s) with whom to discuss a question or problem

These issues and many others must be addressed during transition planning.

Joey and his mother are adjusting after their move from another community. Joey's mom is a single parent who works as a nurse in a local hospital. She was delighted to enroll Joey in the on-site childcare facility. He loves his new friends and teachers. However, the results of the recent prekindergarten screening confirm his mother's suspicions about Joey's language delays. The ensuing discussion regarding the possibility of moving Joey into a half-day Head Start or preschool program to receive services concerns her. Joey just recently started at the childcare facility, and he will be eligible to move into kindergarten in a few months. His mother thinks that the additional move to a half-day program for special services would be simply overwhelming. Local planners need to work with Joey's mother in minimizing change while Joey receives the help he needs. This will require a style of service delivery different from any utilized previously in this community.

* * *

Since Maria's parents speak only Spanish, the early childhood teacher arranged to meet with them at their neighborhood's community center where a friend could interpret for them. Maria's parents expressed concern about both her limited skills in speaking English and, considering her visual impairment, the upcoming transition into kindergarten. What about Maria's linguistic and visual needs? How can her parents help her in preparing for kindergarten? None of the kindergarten teachers or consultant staff speaks Spanish. Maria's parents are additionally concerned about her ability to adjust to the big school building, given her visual impairment. They say that Maria loves preschool and wonder if it is possible for her just to stay there. Her parents also wonder if any of Maria's playmates will be in the same kindergarten class next fall. If not, could she meet some of her potential classmates during the summer?

* * *

Scott's father is concerned about Scott's age 3 transition because preparations need to be made for his special health care needs. Specifically, the new staff must learn to manage Scott's oxygen and feeding apparatus. Scott's dad also wonders if it would be possible for his son to go to the neighborhood school, thus shortening the bus trip considerably. That placement would allow Scott's dad to be closer in case problems should arise. In the past, all children with complex medical needs have been sent to the early childhood special education classroom located in a school on the other side of town. Scott's father is eager for Scott to experience new independence and is thus looking forward to planning this transition.

* * *

Sylvia and her family have received most early intervention services through a home-based program. Sylvia's parents want their daughter to start preschool at age 3 in the local parochial school where her older brothers and sister are enrolled. The school has never served a child with Down syndrome, but it is willing to accept placement on a conditional basis. The public school system resists her parents' suggestion that physical and speech therapy be provided at the parochial school because of its legal interpretation of the separation of church and state. Sylvia's parents want to know what "conditional" placement entails, how her therapy will be provided, and what they can do to prepare their daughter for preschool.

IMPLICATIONS

Family involvement in developing early childhood transition procedures benefits children, families, professionals, and agencies. This is true both in developing overall transition policies and procedures as well as in making plans for individual children. The concerns and priorities of families should always guide collaborative planning. Together, parents and professionals can indeed develop comprehensive, coordinated transition plans.

7

Family Concerns and Preferences in Transition Plans

Partnership for the Journey

Effective transition planning is flexible and responsive to the individual concerns of each family (Hains et al., 1988; Kilgo, Richard, & Noonan, 1989). Additionally, it also remains sensitive to individual differences regarding the family's ability and desire to participate in the transition process. Every family has a right to participate in transition planning to a degree that is comfortable for each of its members (Fowler, Chandler, & Johnson, 1988). Some families prefer extensive involvement, whereas others desire minimal involvement. Families may thus assume a variety of roles in transition planning: as teachers (educating professionals about their child and teaching their child transition skills), as sources of information (communicating with other parents and with professionals), as coordinators (linking agencies with one another), as decision-makers (identifying transition goals), or as advocates (pursuing available services and/or specific placements for their child). However, families' interests and resources may change over time (Barber et al., 1988). Consequently, the nature and degree of their involvement may also change. Certainly, not all families want or are able to be involved in transition planning to the same degree or in the same capacity.

A Parent's Perspective

A child. My child. A child with special needs. A challenge . . .

The daily existence of a child with special needs may depend greatly on early assertive intervention. This can be quite overwhelming for most parents; my husband and I know this from personal experience!

When our young son first began seeing a number of specialists and therapists, my husband and I felt that we were losing control of what we wanted for our son. We did not understand many of the medical terms or procedures, nor did we feel comfortable asking a lot of questions. We were unsure of our "proper place." We soon learned that as responsible, loving parents, it was our responsibility to make decisions concerning our child's life. There is an old proverb that advises, "Action is the proper fruit of knowledge." It was at this time that we had to make a very determined effort to become more knowledgeable. My husband and I had spent much time in the local library and sought advice from other parents who have experienced similar challenges. It was necessary for us to ask the professionals involved in our son's care many questions and even to ask for further explanation in words we could understand! We shared our feelings and concerns at every opportunity and made decisions for our child's medical care and therapy visits that fit the needs of our entire family.

We chose to assume that medical professionals, service providers, and educators had our child's best interest in mind, but that they just did not understand life with a child with special needs. We can see that these people are now becoming more aware that the parents' role is of major importance. Indeed, attitudes are being changed and programs are being adapted to meet the needs of families. As parents, though, we must remember that it is essential that we be prepared and remain positive. To become more knowledgeable is to gain power. Our child's future depends on us!

Jeannie Wanless, parent
Wisconsin

* * *

A Sending Professional's Perspective

It is hard to say good-bye to children after you have worked with them. You develop a real bond with them and with the family as well. Sometimes you regret not doing enough to assist them. To smooth the transition, you can arrange a meeting with personnel from the new program to share what ideas work with the child, to introduce the family, and then to offer support and just be available if any trouble crops up. The parting gift you can give is your confidence in the family's strength to successfully negotiate this stress-filled time.

Pamela Phillips Olson, social worker
Wisconsin

* * *

A Receiving Professional's Perspective

So many children and families enter at once! I want to know about each family—its makeup, culture, and members' goals for their children. I want to learn how to keep each family excited about their child's development and involved in school activities. These things are important to help children learn, and they help me know how to teach. But there are so many families and very little time to get to know them all.

Anonymous teacher
Missouri

* * *

A Family's Perspective on Involvement in Transitions

Linda's family was eager to plan her age 3 transition from the early intervention program into preschool. The agency staff learned that Linda's mother was concerned about the changes Linda would be experiencing and thus wanted to prepare her daughter for the new school.

Linda's mother planned to visit several public school and community early childhood programs before meeting with Linda's transition team to discuss possible placements. Her mother's plans changed, however, with the early arrival of her third child. Thus, the family was coping with both a premature baby and an 18-month-old toddler when it came time for Linda's transition. Although the family's level of involvement was not to the degree initially envisioned, other family concerns necessarily took priority. Professionals on the transition team did, however, consult with the family regarding Linda's transition. Consequently, the family's participation in transition planning met its members' needs despite the other pressing events in their lives.

Anonymous parent
Missouri

Professionals need to be sensitive not only to a family's need for information and support, but also to their degree of readiness for transition planning. Kilgo and colleagues (1989) found that the child's age and the severity of his or her disability are inversely related to the parents' readiness for considering future educational programs. That is, the more severe the disability, the less interested parents are in planning for transition. Thus, although transition planning must accommodate individual timeframes, researchers and practitioners recommend that information be shared months in advance in order to provide the family with an adequate amount of time to learn about and prepare for the actual program change (Fowler, Chandler, Johnson, & Stella, 1988; Kilgo et al., 1989; McDonald, Kysela, Siebert, McDonald, & Chambers, 1989).

If the process delineates short-term as well as long-term planning, then families have the opportunity to formulate and share their ideas for both the present and future. Therefore, future planning should begin as early as possible: "Parents must constantly look ahead to the skills, choices, and responsibilities that their disabled child will need, make, or acquire next year, in the next five years, in the next 10 years, and so forth" (Brotherson et al., 1986, p. 22).

One strategy for identifying families' preferences in planning for the future is to use the McGill Action Planning System (MAPS) (with adaptations for early childhood settings) shown in Table 7.1. The MAPS process is used to facilitate full inclusion of all students—including those students with severe or multiple disabilities—in typical classrooms (Forest & Lusthaus, 1990; Vandercook, York, & Forest, 1989). When adapted for use in early childhood settings, the MAPS process helps both families and professionals in creating a plan for providing supportive and effective services that are consistent with families' values. This planning process may begin with initial evaluation and assessment and can be continued throughout childhood into adult life. MAPS may even be incorporated into IFSPs or IEPs to help accomplish desired outcomes.

Table 7.1. Integrated family-centered birth to age 3 services: MAPS (rewritten) to get you there

1. *What is the history of your family and child?*

   A short time should be spent talking about the family. Discussions about family members, activities, and milestones could be recorded.

2. *What is your dream for your child and family?*

   An important goal of pre-assessment planning is to develop a vision for the family and child. It is important to look beyond current reality and help families to identify a viable direction. This direction will help families identify planning options and work toward growth for the family and their child as well as the community.

3. *What is your greatest fear regarding your family and child?*

   This difficult but important question helps team members to prevent future problems.

4. *Who are you as a family?*

   Again, a short time should be spent describing the family and its individual members. All descriptions are acceptable.

5. *What are your family's and child's strengths and abilities?*

   Building on strengths and abilities is the prime task of family-centered services. A list can be made that outlines the strengths and abilities of the family as well

(*continued*)

Table 7.1. (*continued*)

as the individual child. It is important to talk about what each can do, likes to do, and subsequently does well.

6. *What are the needs of your family and child?*

   This question provides an opportunity for family members to identify *their* needs from *their* unique perspective. This is the beginning of program design.

7. *What would an ideal day consist of for your family and child?*

   All planning should be responsive to the family's routines. The family service coordinator, the family, and possibly other team members can devise ways of integrating individuals' needs into a balanced daily routine that is agreeable to all involved.

Source: Schauls (1991), adapted from R. Paisley, *Interagency Transition Guide*. Cumberland, WI: Northern Pines Area Early Intervention Project.

SUPPORTING FAMILY INVOLVEMENT IN TRANSITION PLANNING

The key to family-centered transition planning is that the planning process remains flexible and responsive to the family's concerns, priorities, and resources. Thus, the professional staff should provide information and a menu of involvement options open to the family.

Consider These Options. . .

I am the parent of a 7-year-old child with cerebral palsy. Because of her disability, she is in a wheelchair.

As a parent, I needed to know all the options available for my child when she left birth to 3 services. Some questions I had were:

- **Would she benefit most from day care, early childhood special education, or a Head Start program?**
- **What if we like a couple of different programs? Will they work together and complement one another?**
- **Does she have to attend all day every day?**
- **How do I tailor a program to meet my child's and family's needs?**

The more choices that are considered, the more likely the program developed will fit the needs of your child. Taking a close look at programs as well as working with and getting to know the people involved will make the best options available for your child.

Barb Featherly, parent
Wisconsin

Initial Planning

Most sending programs recommend that initial conferences with families regarding transition planning should occur 6 months to a year prior to the scheduled program change (Fowler, Chandler, Johnson, & Stella, 1988; Hanline, 1988; Kilgo et al., 1989; McDonald et al., 1989). Although the transition itself is a discrete series of events, preparation should occur throughout the time spent in the previous service program. Therefore, in order to help families in planning ahead, the transition coordinator should ensure that the following issues are discussed with them in a timely manner:

A review of the transition timeline as it pertains to both the current program (e.g., child assessments) and to future programs (e.g., record transfers)

The determination of precisely who will be involved with the child's transition (including family, friends, or advocates as well as current and future staff). The name and phone number of the transition coordinator should be provided, and families should be urged to contact this individual whenever questions arise.

A discussion regarding the family's role in the transition and their subsequent need for information. When professionals discuss transitions with families, they should be prepared to "repeat information in several formats, if necessary, as families' changing emotional states allow them to attend to the information" (Summers et al., 1990, p. 91). Information should therefore be provided in writing to enable parents to review it at their leisure. Indeed, families of young children often want many types of information regarding various aspects of transition (Hanline, 1988; Johnson et al., 1986; Spiegel-McGill, Reed, Konig, & McGowan, 1990). Professionals need to remember, however, that "families may not always be 'ready' to hear, understand, or accept some information, but that it should be available for later use" (Summers et al., 1990, p. 91). Many programs have developed transition notebooks or handbooks so that families have materials (viz., timelines, program observation checklists, assessment information) that they can refer to at any time before, during, or after the child's move between programs (Pensacola ARC, 1992; Vincent, Madrid, & Martinez, 1992).

A review of the IFSP or IEP to ensure that all relevant transition goals and outcomes have been included. Table 7.2 outlines a few sample goals and outcomes.

During their initial interactions with families, professionals can help families prepare for transition by:

- Providing parents with opportunities to meet with parents who have already been through the transition at hand (see Table 7.3 for suggested procedures for establishing a parent-to-parent net-

Table 7.2. Sample outcomes and goals for transition planning

- We want Shandell to begin walking so that he can become more independent and explore more.
- Maria will babble with more sounds so that she will start using words.
- Bob will schedule a health screening at the community center sometime next month in order to meet Head Start requirements when Tyrone turns 3.
- Twanda would like to meet another parent of a child with spina bifida so she can share ideas, successes, and challenges while receiving support.
- Cia will reach for toys so she can play alone.
- Mary, the public health nurse, will visit the neighborhood kindergarten with Carmen and Jose—Conchita's parents—to see how Conchita's medical needs can best be met at school.

work; see Brown and Irwin [1992] for a booklet describing that process).

- Providing opportunities for families to question or otherwise receive information from potential programs.
- Talking positively with both the child and the family about transitions (e.g., mention how exciting it was to observe growth and development in the child since he or she entered the present program; discuss the strengths the child brings to the new situ-

Table 7.3. Parent-to-parent program: transitions from early intervention programs to the ECSE Program at Algonquin School

Goals

- To assist parents of children with disabilities who are initially entering the public school program
- To provide an informal network of support for parents
- To assist parents in making connections (outside of the public school system) in order to facilitate the easy access of services for their children
- To promote the speedy adjustment of children to new programs

Procedures

1. Identify parents of present or former students who have made transitions from various agencies
2. Call parents individually to explain the parent-to-parent program and ask if they would like to participate
3. Invite parents to meet with the program coordinator to discuss issues relating to transition
4. Identify issues that are important to parents as they experience the transition process
5. Identify and answer questions parents may have regarding either the ECSE program or any transition issue
6. Group parents on the basis of disabling condition and/or other appropriate characteristics
7. The ECSE coordinator continues to serve as a facilitator for the group: matching parents, organizing training sessions as needed, monitoring program efficiency, and establishing and maintaining program continuity

ation; praise the new program, teacher, principal, or whatever is honestly praiseworthy).
- Encouraging parents to express concerns (e.g., informally asking if parents have questions regarding either the transition materials they have received thus far or the event itself).
- Referring parents, as needed, to appropriate resources outside the receiving program or agency to answer questions.
- If they wish, providing families with activities to help their children prepare for the new program (see Table 7.4)

Planning for Future Placement

Professionals can help families to prepare for future IFSP/IEP activities as they encourage them to participate in the process of choosing new services for their children. Conversations between families and their service coordinators that span several months may help to ensure that upcoming transitions are anticipated and planned. Interventionists and families alike are advised to consider transitions when developing IFSPs or IEPs, perhaps as much as 12 months in advance of actual program changes. At the IFSP or IEP development meetings, discussions cover transition timelines, procedures, information and training desired by parents, and relevant goals for children. These elements are then written into planning documents for the transition year.

Before any formal transition meetings regarding future placement occur, however, the differences between IFSPs and IEPs must be specifically clarified for families as well as professionals. Such clarification may preclude unrealistic expectations and thus help in preparing informed advocates to develop the most effective combination of services for children and families. Published manuals, worksheets, and meetings as well as parent-to-parent training may help to explain local processes to families who are confronting their first IFSP/IEP meetings.

Conversations regarding the specific elements of transition for an individual child and his or her family should begin prior to the meeting to be convened (with parents' permission) 90 days before the age 3 transition, as required by PL 102-119 (Hanline & Knowlton, 1988). The family's representatives and their service coordinator should:

- Review the transition timeline and discuss upcoming events (e.g., the 90-day meeting, possible assessment procedures).

Table 7.4. Getting ready for new programs: tips for parents

- Help your child to be excited about going to the new school. Talk often about how much fun it will be at the "big school" and about the activities he or she will do there. This will help him or her to anticipate making the transition.
- Tell your child often how proud you are that he or she is growing up, how pleased you are that the child is doing so many things by himself or herself, and how sure you are that the child will do well in the new school. This will help your child feel confident about handling new experiences.
- Place your child in situations where he or she must follow directions—one step at first, then two at a time, then three. Teach your child to rehearse directions in order to remember them.
- Help your child to learn self-care skills that are age appropriate (e.g., putting away toys, handwashing, independent toileting, buttoning, zipping, and shoe tying). Teach your child to recognize his or her name and the basic colors. Busy teachers often value these skills.
- Challenge your child with situations where he or she may not be able to do the expected task and must therefore ask for help. If he or she doesn't know how to ask for help, demonstrate the procedure and wait for the child to imitate you before assisting.
- Read books with your child each day. Discuss the pictures and the story. If your child doesn't like to sit still, read for a brief time; even if the book time is only 2 minutes per day, make it a happy time. You will see your child's attention span increase.
- Watch television with your child, especially shows like *Reading Rainbow, Mr. Rogers,* and *Sesame Street.* Discuss what you are seeing. If you allow your child to watch cartoons, watch them with him or her. Ask your child to tell you what happened in the cartoon story or help him or her to reconstruct the sequence of events.
- Let your child help sort laundry, set the table, cook, bake, put away groceries, and organize his or her books and toys. All of these tasks involve classification, which is a foundation for skills learned in school.
- Teach the child to do simple tasks at home. Most young children can learn to hang up their coats, pick up their toys, and put things away. Preschoolers can even keep a school box at home where they are expected to keep crayons, scissors, pencils, and an eraser. Let your child help you vacuum, sweep, dust, and clean. These very practical jobs develop discipline and physical coordination.
- Be sure that your child has many opportunities to run, jump, climb, and play outside. These activities can be done in a city neighborhood, a rural area, or a park; they cannot, however, be done inside a house. Children who have learned to control their bodies in space are usually more confident in new situations and more capable of managing complex motor tasks like walking in a straight line.
- Anytime you teach your child to perform a task, break it into parts and teach each part discretely in sequence. Reward (with praise) each part of the task the child does successfully. Very few people praise a child too much; in fact, most of us praise too little.
- When you go places with your child, talk about what you are seeing. Point out characteristics (e.g., color, size, shape) and names of objects you view. Try to be conversational (as you would be with an adult) rather than constantly quizzing the child (e.g., "Oh, look at the red house" rather than "What color is this house?"; "I like the big pumpkin best; which one do you like?" rather than "Show me the big one").
- When you get home from a trip to the store, church, or party, ask your child to tell another family member what you did. If the child has difficulty retelling the

(*continued*)

Table 7.4. *(continued)*

event, help and support so that the story can be told. This skill is called *recasting*. It is closely related to reading comprehension.
- Point out letters, words, and numbers in the world around your child (e.g., McDonald's, house numbers, names of family members on letters, the numbers of hymns in a songbook at church). This will provide a foundation for learning symbols in reading.
- Frequently count objects, touching each as you go along. This will help your child to realize that numbers represent sets of real things.
- Talk often about interesting jobs your child might have when he or she grows up. Be sure that your child knows that most jobs require hard work and doing well in school.
- Teach your child to appreciate that every person is unique and special, that human differences are a wonderful part of our world and are not a threat, and that all people need to help others as well as be helped by others in order to live happily.
- Enjoy the time you spend with your child. Positive, trusting attitudes about people and the world that your child learns now will remain with him or her throughout life.

- Seek parents' permission to convene the 90-day meeting for children graduating from early intervention services at age 3.
- Review the IFSP/IEP process (including procedural safeguards, parents' legal rights, and, if appropriate, the implications of moving from an IFSP to an IEP for both the family and the child).
- Discuss eligibility and categorical labeling, if appropriate.
- Identify the family's preferences regarding their desired levels of involvement in transition planning.
- Assist the family in clarifying their goals regarding the new placement (see Table 7.5).

Representatives from the sending program(s), the receiving program(s), and the family subsequently participate in a meeting to discuss the transition activities timeline and potential placement options. By law, this meeting must occur at least 90 days prior to the age 3 transition. Although this meeting is not legally required for transitions other than the one at age 3, such a conference is generally beneficial for both families and agencies during other transitions as well.

When options regarding placement are discussed, it is useful to have available a locally developed directory listing all the early childhood services available in the community (see Appendix D for a sample format). Parents should be encouraged (by the transition coordinator) to visit possible placements prior to the meeting at which decisions regarding placement will be made. The transition coordinator should also ensure that family members have adequate op-

Table 7.5. Placement: Questions parents can ask themselves (compiled by Jo Gwost, parent, Topeka, Kansas)

- What placement do I prefer as the first step toward attaining the vision I have for my child's future?
- What are the possible programs from which my child could receive services locally? As placements are considered, what will be the reasons for eliminating some of them? What features will make a setting appropriate for my child? Am I satisfied that all placement options have been explored?
- Who will ultimately decide on placement for my child? If one placement has been proposed, what others were discussed? What type of brainstorming was done in selecting the proposed placement? Why were other placements dismissed?
- What does "meaningful progress" mean to me?
- List and prioritize the child's needs. How can each need be met in each possible placement?
- Does it matter to either my child or myself whether he or she is at the top of the class?
- How much time will my child spend with children with disabilities? Is this necessary? Will this time help my child to become more typical?
- Does the proposed placement "feel" good to me?
- If a particular setting is not ideal, what can be done to make it work better for my child and family?

portunity to develop criteria for choosing a new program before decision-making actually begins. The questions listed in Table 7.5 were developed by a parent to aid in defining her goals for her children's future placements, thereby enabling her to refine those goals as the IFSP/IEP was written and the placement process initiated.

Ideally, decisions regarding eligibility and placement are made at different times. Oftentimes, however, these decisions are made during a single conference. Without adequate time to evaluate assessment information, generate IFSP/IEP goals, and explore alternative placement options, the planning team may rely on historical precedents in making its decisions. This situation creates serious problems for family–professional partnerships in transition planning. For instance, for a child with a developmental delay in only one domain, the transition coordinator and the child's parents may initially be uncertain regarding the child's eligibility for special education services. Thus, discussions of potential placements may be inadvertently misleading because they are either too broad or too narrow in scope. The resulting dissatisfaction on the part of the family may in turn hinder future collaborative planning efforts.

In order for families to be active participants in the planning process, they need time both to clarify their priorities and to visit potential program placements before a placement decision is made. Several approaches in this regard are possible:

1. Eligibility determination and placement decisions may be made on different occasions, as dictated by a community's standard operating procedure.
2. An IFSP/IEP meeting may be reconvened if the family and their service providers need more time to generate and explore potential placement options.
3. If eligibility and placement must be determined simultaneously, then the team (including the parents) may generate a variety of service options in advance, covering both eligibility and ineligibility for special education services (as appropriate). This should occur early in the planning process to allow families time to investigate possible placements and therefore participate actively in transition decision-making.

One parent recommends that the initial IFSP/IEP meeting (to establish a partnership between the family and professionals in the new service system) be held in the family's home ("around the kitchen table" if the family desires) (Gwost, 1992).

Everybody had done their best to help us understand and participate. The placement choice was a good one that fit our family's values. I felt like I was taking my child from the loving arms of the preschool teacher and placing her in the welcoming hands of the kindergarten teacher. It felt very natural.

Anonymous parent
Kansas

Conversations with Families Entering New Programs

When a child is enrolled in a new program, the family and the new teacher as well as other staff members must establish working relationships. The family's relationship with their child's new teachers will likely be different from that shared with previous professionals. The new teacher may have different expectations for the child and family as well as different ways of sharing information. Because initial introductions and subsequent conversations may be awkward for families as well as teachers, the *Guide for Sharing Information with the New Program* shown in Figure 7.1 was developed to help families provide pertinent information. It in turn encourages parents to collaborate with the new teacher in establishing open lines of communication as it helps both parties to prepare for the final stages of transition.

Prior to or shortly after the child's entrance into the new program, the receiving teacher and the family discuss the following issues. In some cases, this information may be collected by the sending teacher and subsequently sent to the receiving teacher.

A. *Child Information*

1. What are some of the activities your child most enjoys doing at home?
2. What are some things that are most difficult for your child to learn?
3. What activities would you like to see continued in the new program?
4. What types of rewards work best with your child?
5. What types of discipline work best with your child?
6. What other things would you like the new teacher to know about your child?

B. *Family Involvement Information* There are many ways that families can become involved in their child's programs. Please indicate the ways that your family would like to be involved.

—— Observe my child in the new program
—— Volunteer in the new program
—— Work with my child at home
—— Participate in parent–teacher meetings
—— Help select learning goals for my child
—— Participate in parent organizations such as PTA/PTO
—— Be informed regarding my child's successes and problems in the classroom
—— Other ____________________

C. *Communication with the New Program* Teachers and families are busy and may have difficulty in finding the time to communicate with one another, yet, both want to share information. What would be your preferred way of communicating with the new teacher?

	How Often?	Best Times?
1. Notes	______	______
2. Informal meetings	______	______
3. Parent–teacher meetings	______	______
4. Telephone calls	______	______

Figure 7.1 Guide for sharing information with new programs. (See also Fowler, Chandler, Johnson, & Stella [1988] and Hains, Rosenkoetter, & Fowler [1991].)

Ideally, both the family and the transition coordinator complete the guide prior to the child's entrance into the new program. This may be important for the sending staff as well as the family in that it provides a positive forum for discussing the future. If the family and child visit the new classroom after placement has been finalized but before the child is officially enrolled, the guide may be discussed with the new teacher during that visit. For example, if the parents and teacher arrange to meet after school, the child may explore the new classroom with a paraprofessional while the teacher and parents exchange information. Subsequent visits and conferences may also be scheduled to accommodate the preferences of both the parent and the teacher(s).

In some cases, the only opportunity to discuss the guide comes after the child begins the new program. The family is, however, advised to request a meeting with the new teacher(s) no later than 2 weeks after the child's entry. Although teachers are generally busy at the start of the school year, the timely exchange of information is of the utmost importance to both teachers and parents.

Home Visits

Another strategy designed to welcome families entering a new program is the home visit. Either the new teacher alone or the sending teacher along with the receiving teacher may coordinate a home visit. In Polk County, Florida, for instance, both the receiving teacher and the the school principal visit the homes of incoming families to welcome them into the new program and to assure them of the school's concern for their child. Although this strategy takes a great deal of time to plan and implement it pays benefits by:

- Helping school staff to meet parents and subsequently begin to understand their culture, lifestyle, and values
- Making initial contact in the family's home where they are likely to feel most comfortable
- Building a positive relationship prior to the onset of crises or problems
- Assuring the family of their child's safety in the new school
- Allowing the child to see parents and professionals working together, thus creating a visual bridge between home and school
- Supporting the family's involvement with their child and the school system and encouraging continued interaction with both
- Allowing the staff to meet other family members, including siblings and pets, who are important to the child and are thus likely to be topics for discussion

Home visits are indeed rewarding for all involved parties. Programs that have instituted them (at the families' discretion, of course), include Head Start as well as many special education programs and a few kindergartens. Home visits upon entry into kindergarten are indeed a recommended strategy for *all* children (Love et al., 1992), not only for those with disabilities.

Because it was already April—just 2 months prior to Joey's transition into kindergarten—the evaluation team (including Joey's

mother) hesitated to recommend placing him in a public school or Head Start program. In addition, the team thought that Joey would continue to require child care after either half-day program. The team respected the mother's decision to keep Joey enrolled in the employer-supported childcare program at the local hospital.

The team was charged with deciding how speech therapy could best be provided for Joey. After discussion, the team suggested two solutions: the school district could provide a consultant teacher and a speech therapist for Joey through the hospital's childcare program, or the school district could collaborate with the early intervention program (also located at the hospital) in providing services for Joey. Joey's mother preferred the second option, as did the program administrators who had additional incentives for fostering collaboration. The IEP team left the writing of the interagency agreement (including the financial arrangements) to the program administrators.

* * *

Maria's parents discussed their concerns regarding Maria's limited English-speaking skills with the early childhood special education teacher. The teacher reassured them that Maria's pleasant disposition and excellent social skills would help her to overcome her language barriers in kindergarten. Services of the school's *English as a Second Language (ESL)* program would also be available for Maria as well as her family. The special educator suggested that Maria and her parents visit the new classroom (with an interpreter) to meet both Maria's new kindergarten teacher and the school's consultant for children with visual impairments.

The special education teacher assured the family that, because Maria was nearly 6, she would surely move into kindergarten. Several of Maria's preschool friends—including one who speaks Spanish—will also be enrolled in the same kindergarten. The teacher asked if Maria's parents would like to meet the other enrolling families, and she later arranged a family picnic at the preschool. With parental permission, she compiled a list containing the names of all families who had children graduating from the preschool program and where those children planned to attend kindergarten. The teacher also outlined a number of summer programs available in the community and suggested activities for parents to do at home or in their neighborhoods. As a result, several families decided to start an informal play group. Maria's parents were delighted that their daughter could participate in a play group such as this that encouraged her development as an English speaker.

Meanwhile, the school's consultant for children with visual impairments will interview Maria's ophthalmologist, meet with Maria and her family prior to the start of school, and plan a way to orient Maria to the physical environment of the classroom in ways that are appropriate to her special needs.

* * *

Scott's father has expressed concern regarding Scott's complex medical needs as they pertain to his safety while riding a bus to school. Nevertheless, he wanted to place Scott in a typical classroom, if possible. Prior to his placement, Scott's transition team (including Scott's father) invited the local special education director and the director, health coordinator, disabilities coordinator, and preschool teacher from the local Head Start program to a meeting. The preschool teacher invited the rest of the team to visit the classroom and talk with her about Scott. While there, Scott's father found that the elementary school in which Head Start was located employed a full-time nurse. Both the teacher and the nurse were willing to learn how to care for Scott and supervise his oxygen and feeding programs. The school district was willing to provide a paraprofessional to work in the classroom with Scott and one of his classmates who has spina bifida as well as with their typically developing peers.

Scott's father told the Head Start disabilities coordinator that he was still concerned about the issue of transportation. Therefore, they called the special education director who explained that the bus driver as well as the bus aide were certified in both first aid and pediatric cardiopulmonary resuscitation. Both of those adults, the classroom staff, and any involved substitute teachers would receive special training (from the local hospital) in emergency procedures that are useful for children with complex health conditions. Each bus was equipped with child safety car seats; Scott's father additionally requested that a cellular telephone be installed to ensure easy access to medical services in the event of an emergency or accident. Because Scott's seizures are unpredictable, his father felt that this was critical to his safety on the bus. The special education director subsequently referred them to the special education social worker who was familiar with the funding system for family support of children with complex health needs. The social worker helped the family to apply for the cellular phone through the medical assistance program.

The school district and the local Head Start developed a written agreement that delineated the services to be provided by each agency. Final decisions regarding all matters of health management were made when Scott's health plan was finalized. Scott is scheduled to begin Head Start (with other 3-year-olds) in September.

* * *

Sylvia's parents want Sylvia to attend the local parochial school with her older brothers and sister. The school's early childhood program agreed to accept Sylvia on a "conditional" basis. Evaluation results showed that Sylvia continues to require speech and physical therapy. The parents invited the parochial school principal to attend the placement meeting to discuss how therapy could be delivered and what a conditional placement might entail. In addition, they wanted the school's preschool teacher to prepare her class to welcome Sylvia and to educate the children's families about Down syndrome.

At the placement meeting, the team agreed that Sylvia's parents will be responsible for taking their daughter to a nearby public elementary school once a week for speech therapy and once a month for physical therapy. The therapists at the school agreed to show the parents how to incorporate therapy into Sylvia's daily routines. They will also prepare instruction sheets for the parents to share with any of Sylvia's caregivers—including her preschool teacher.

IMPLICATIONS

By responding to families' priorities and concerns and subsequently building their strengths and resources, service providers can support families experiencing early transitions and help them to prepare for the future. The tools discussed in this chapter may assist families in becoming involved in transition planning as they help agencies to consider families' perspectives in early childhood intervention. The resultant family–professional interaction improves transitions as a whole and subsequently enriches the early childhood programs that they bridge.

8

Creating Continuity for Children

Planning a Smooth Route

Transitions are milestones—times when families and service systems re-evaluate the child and current intervention efforts on his or her behalf. These efforts are then redefined and redirected as needed. The stakes often seem very high when adults are making decisions regarding transition for vulnerable young children (Kilgo et al., 1989).

There are some things I would like to tell the kindergarten teachers in our town.

Preschool teacher,
Missouri

* * *

There are several comments I would like to make to the preschool teachers in our community.

Kindergarten teacher,
Missouri

* * *

Will you be talking to the kindergarten teacher?

Parent to
preschool teacher,
Missouri

* * *

At a PTA meeting a couple of years ago, an irate father asked just what we were doing to his son. When his son was at the preschool program next door, he could choose his activities . . . he loved reading books, telling stories, and writing messages. Kindergarten the following year wasn't too bad, it seems. The child could occasionally paint and make some choices after he had completed his alphabet pages. The father's real anger came after his son entered first grade. He began losing all interest and delight in a school where he had no choice and was being made to feel he couldn't read. The father questioned whether first grade had to be so rigid. He was seeing his son go from loving books to developing a dislike of reading . . . There were many different reactions and lots of dialogue. Eventually, we began to realize that children really ought not to have to adjust to major changes as they move from home to childcare experiences to kindergarten and primary grades. It was then that we started to reach out to the teachers in the preschool in our neighborhood. We are really trying to make smoother transitions for the kids as they move from preschool to the public schools. We are also reorganizing parts of our instruction within and across classrooms to provide continuity of curriculum for children from preschool through the primary grades. We are including the childcare director and some of the teachers in the planning.

Kindergarten teacher, quoted
in Barbour and Seefeldt (1993)

* * *

The preschool teachers saw Rilla as more capable than I did. They encouraged me to stop carrying her, and let her walk. They wanted us to have her talk, rather than letting her twin brother say all the words for her. At first, I was angry about what they said, but then I realized that they were right. It is time for us to treat Rilla like a little girl, rather than a baby.

Parent,
Nebraska

THE VALUE OF CONTINUITY

Will (1984) describes transition as a bridge between the security offered by the current service program and the opportunities and risks of future programs: "Any bridge requires both a solid span and a secure foundation at either end" (p. 1). This chapter discusses planned, system-wide efforts designed to connect the solid foundations of early childhood transitions in promoting service continuity for children with special needs. Special services—and the transitions between them—are most beneficial when specialized to meet the individual needs of children and families. As discussed in Chapter

9, the IFSP and the IEP are vehicles that provide continuity and thus help to span the differences among foundational service programs.

Professionals necessarily see individual children and families from the perspective of the agency that employs them and as part of the group of children and families currently served by that agency. They are likely to have little if any knowledge regarding the past or future experiences of a particular child and family (Carta, Atwater, Schwartz, & Miller, 1990; Carta, Sainato, & Greenwood, 1988; Love et al., 1992). Although the purpose of all service systems is to aid children and their families, each may approach this task differently. The resultant programs and services are therefore likely to seem very different to children and families in transition.

These differences may consequently affect a child's satisfaction with, and behavior and learning in a new program. Transitions may serve as springboards for increased learning and social interaction (Ziegler, 1985). But, they could also cause children to regress and subsequently display behaviors associated with vulnerability and uncertainty (i.e., increased or reduced levels of activity, crying, exaggerated or limited talking, apathy, separation anxiety, tantrums, nausea, toileting problems, or even fear of school) (Fowler, 1982; Johnson et al., 1986). These behaviors may discourage friendships (Ladd, 1990; Odom, McConnell, & McEvoy, 1992), hinder learning (Barbour & Seefeldt, 1993), and negatively influence professional perceptions of children's ability and potential levels of functioning. Problems in adjusting to new settings may even result in a child's being transferred into a segregated classroom (Carden-Smith & Fowler, 1983).

Careful community planning for curricular continuity and ongoing family involvement both supports children in transition and prevents problems in adjustment that may have long-term consequences (Caldwell, 1991; Futrell, 1987; NASBE, 1988). Continuity (in people, curriculum, and routines) helps children to feel comfortable and confident in new settings and encourages the anticipation of continued success during future transitions (Diamond, Spiegel-McGill, & Hanrahan, 1988; NAESP, 1990).

The numerous strategies that promote service continuity may be divided into two subgroups: system-wide strategies and individually appropriate strategies. Chapter 9 deals with strategies to be used with individual children to reduce the risks and subsequently increase the benefits of moving into new environments. The remainder of this chapter thus deals with system-wide strategies for facilitating early childhood transitions.

THE CHALLENGES OF TRANSITION FOR CHILDREN—AND SOME SOLUTIONS

The challenges for *families* inherent in the transition process are discussed in Chapter 6, and some strategies for agency–family collaboration are outlined in Chapter 7. Alternatively, this chapter describes some of the common differences to which *children* must adjust during transition between programs, as well as some innovative ways that local service systems have attempted to mitigate these differences and consequently increase continuity for young children.

Home-Based Versus Center-Based Services

The Challenges Although the transition from home-based to center-based services may be developmentally appropriate for both children and families, it may nevertheless present challenges for children that must be addressed in transition planning. In home-based services, all intervention activities are personalized for an individual child and family and their home setting. Thus, siblings, pets, and familiar toys may be easily included in intervention activities. Conversely, center-based services are provided in unfamiliar settings with unfamiliar toys and equipment. This situation is further aggravated when the child is served in a group, away from parents or siblings.

Some Solutions To minimize discontinuity in transitions, some early intervention programs sponsor toddler groups—groups of parents and their children that meet for short weekly sessions (Early Education Center, 1992; Noonan & Ratokolau, 1991; Ratajczak, 1992). With this arrangement, home visits continue; the toddler group simply provides both children and their parents with additional opportunities to become acclimated to the new surroundings, meet the preschool staff, and develop a positive feeling about center-based services. Forms for the establishment of such a group are contained in Appendix D of this text.

A joint home visit by early intervention and preschool teachers may also provide continuity for the child. It allows him or her to interact with the new teacher as he or she is prompted by the well-known home visitor. In addition, the familiar surroundings free both children and adults to initiate communication with personnel from the new service program (Gwost, 1992).

Alternatively, the home visitor and the toddler may attend the preschool or childcare program together for 1 day per week for several weeks prior to the actual program change (Rosenkoetter, 1990a).

Although this replaces the home visit, it introduces the child to his or her new surroundings in the presence of a familiar adult who can interpret unfamiliar events. The preschool staff in turn meet the child and observe his or her particular needs, preferences, and communication patterns as the early interventionist provides explanations regarding the child's level of functioning as well as information about his or her previous service program. Possibly most importantly, the visit allows for brief trial separations of the child from his or her parents—perhaps even including a bus ride—with the trusted home visitor.

Regardless of other methods of promoting continuity, most programs encourage parents to visit the center with their children several times prior to initiating center-based services. This, in turn, allows the child to meet staff, locate physical landmarks, and choose special toys for future enjoyment (Hains et al., 1988; Logue & Love, 1992).

Differences in the Inclusiveness of Various Placements

The Challenges New placements may be more or less restrictive than previous placements. If they are more restrictive, professionals and parents may worry about social stigma when the child attends a special education class. They may also worry about the absence of higher functioning children to model appropriate behavior for their child. If the new placement is less restrictive, families and professionals may have concerns about safety, the appropriateness of the intervention to be provided, or the impact of the incoming child on other children in the classroom.

Some Solutions The National Association of State Boards of Education (NASBE, 1992) has recommended that all children attend their neighborhood schools. If such a plan were adopted in every community, all children with disabilities would begin out-of-home intervention programs in their neighborhood Head Start, preschool, or childcare center and continue in their neighborhood schools through kindergarten and the elementary grades. Of course, appropriate support would be provided to ensure the continuing development of each child.

Obviously, such community-based placements promote continuity in unrestrictive environments from the time of initial enrollment. With this approach to service delivery, typically developing peers, children with disabilities, parents, and educators alike become accustomed to diversity in the classroom on a daily basis (Peck et al., 1993; Safford, 1989). Aided by the Americans with Disabilities

Act (1989) and the reauthorization of the Individuals with Disabilities Education Act (1991), parents and professionals together are seeking to promote service continuity for children with special needs in natural environments where children without disabilities are served. Progress is made when a community becomes *philosophically* committed to inclusive services. However, many *practical* matters may need to be resolved before appropriate education is provided for every eligible child (Peck et al., 1993).

Regardless, many communities are not even philosophically committed to providing services in inclusive schools. Indeed, in many areas, young children with special needs still receive some or all of their education in classrooms serving only children with disabilities or that include only a few typical peer models. Achieving effective community-based placements across the age span may require months or even years of advocacy, problem-solving, and careful preparation, both before as well as after transition decisions are formulated.

How can parents and professionals promote continuity for children moving from a segregated facility into an integrated classroom? Planned transition activities can support children as well as their families during such a move:

- Introduce the incoming child to the new staff without drawing attention to his or her disability. Videotapes showing the child interacting with others and enjoying everyday routines as well as classroom visits will help to reduce the staff's fear and win acceptance for inclusion.
- Ensure ongoing support and adequate resources from the local special education program.
- Precisely define the learning and social goals for each child and establish the means for monitoring and achieving them.
- Ensure adequate staff preparation, including orientation and training of nonprofessional personnel such as bus drivers and cafeteria workers.
- Transfer written records to the appropriate teachers and therapists, and allow time for ongoing consultations with the sending teacher.
- Ensure that each child's health and safety needs are met.
- Provide training for all staff members in team collaboration (McCollum & Hughes, 1988) and define their respective classroom roles (Heron & Harris, 1993).
- Explain, in a developmentally appropriate way, any unusual equipment needed by, or behaviors and routines of, the child

with special needs to his or her classmates and their parents (see Table 8.1).

- Explain the family's expectations to parents of typically developing children when the child's disability is obvious or puzzling (parental permission in this regard is required—the letter to parents in Figure 8.1 is one solution).

These activities should also be incorporated into the interagency and intra-agency transition timelines. Additional suggested materials for facilitating inclusion may be found in the resource list shown in Table 8.2.

For a variety of reasons, young children are sometimes placed in settings that are more restrictive than past placements. Although the goal is to provide intervention services in natural environments (according to the IDEA Amendments of 1991), educators recognize several issues that may affect placement, including parental preferences in identifying placement options (Peck et al., 1993) and the quality of available services (Strain, 1990). Although current data delineate clear advantages to serving children in integrated settings,

Table 8.1. Resources for educating young children about disability

New Friends: Mainstreaming Activities To Help Young Children Understand and Accept Individual Differences (S. Heekin & P. Mengel [Eds.], Copyright © 1993) is a training program designed for teachers who want to create a more supportive classroom environment. It consists of a teacher's manual, a trainer's supplement, and classroom materials. Notebook, including doll patterns—$20. Teacher's manual—$15. Available from the Chapel Hill Training and Outreach Project, 800 E. Town Drive, Suite 105, Chapel Hill, NC 27514. 919-490-5577.

The Kids on the Block is a set of puppets and accompanying curricula. The program includes puppets, props, scripts, audio cassettes, a training guide, follow-up materials, resource suggestions, and continued manufacturer support. Thirty-four programs are available covering a range of physical conditions, illnesses, and disabilities. Available (for varying prices) from The Kids on the Block, Inc., 9385-C Gerwig Lane, Columbia, MD 21046. 301-290-9095 or 800-368-KIDS.

Dolly Downs (a doll with Down syndrome) includes a 15″ cloth doll, a 5-minute cassette tape introducing Dolly Downs, and a small primer-type booklet contained in Dolly's backpack. Available for $29.95 from Camp Venture, 100 Convent Road, Nanuet, NY 10954.

Numerous books and videotapes are available that depict children with disabilities performing various tasks. Current books specifically addressing the issue of disability can be located in *Bookfinder* and *The Best of Bookfinder,* both published by American Guidance Service, 4201 Woodland Road, P.O. Box 99, Circle Pines, MN 55104-1796. 800-328-2560. These volumes are also available in most public libraries.

Dear Parents,

Our daughter Elizabeth is in the kindergarten class at Swanson. Your child may talk about the girl who doesn't talk or do the same things they do. That's Elizabeth.

The reason I am writing this is so you can know a little about her for your own information and so you can answer some of your child's questions.

Elizabeth was born with a genetic disorder that left her with multiple disabilities. She is generally very healthy, but the disorder resulted in delays in development.

Elizabeth has been getting educational services from District 66 since she was about 6 months old. When she was 20 months old, she started classes at Sunset. She has since been to Westbrook, Oakdale, and back to Sunset. These have all been "special" classes where there have been mostly other children with disabilities. During this time, we have used regular child care and preschool as well.

We wanted to stop bouncing around schools and have both of our children go to school in our own neighborhood with all the other kids. I want to stress that we did not want to just show up at Swanson (the local kindergarten) on the first day of school to drop Elizabeth off. All during the spring and summer, I have spent countless hours on the phone and in meetings with everyone involved to plan how Elizabeth would be able to participate in the Swanson kindergarten program.

You know how scary it is to have your child encounter challenging new environments. However, I have seen Elizabeth rise to challenges before and surprise us all. She has learned so much! In addition, District 66 staff have spent a lot of time in making sure that there is enough support in the classroom when Elizabeth is there so the program is not affected adversely.

I also want to stress that we don't expect the kindergarten staff to "fix" Elizabeth and teach her all the things the other kids are learning (I wish we could pull off such a miracle). Rather, Elizabeth is in the class to get to know other children, to learn how they behave and play, and to learn how to communicate more easily with them. Otherwise, she has her own education plan. The other children will, in turn, learn so many things from her. Kids her age are much more perceptive than we give them credit for. They have few preconceived notions and they ask good questions.

I tell 5-year-olds her brain doesn't always work very well so she has trouble talking, walking, and learning how to use toys. Even though she doesn't always answer when you talk to her, she does understand a lot of what is said to her. And she will make choices about what she wants to do. In fact, she can be very determined.

Please don't tell your child that Elizabeth is "retarded." That term only labels her in a negative way by describing one characteristic. She is a bright, happy child who is very determined to explore her world. She swims and swings and plays in sandboxes. She hates television, but loves books. She has many friends and is learning a simple sign language that the other kids enjoy using.

Obviously, I have a lot to tell people about Elizabeth. If you have read this far, I hope you have found it interesting. Please call me any time if you have any questions or just want to visit.

Yours truly,
Susan Christensen,
Nebraska

Figure 8.1 Letter to parents.

Table 8.2. Materials to facilitate inclusion of young children with disabilities

Allen, K. E. (1992). *The exceptional child: Mainstreaming in early childhood education* (2nd ed.). Albany, NY: Delmar Publishers Inc.

Bricker, D., & Cripe, J. J. W. (1992). *An activity-based approach to early intervention.* Baltimore: Paul H. Brookes Publishing Co.

Circle of Inclusion Project. (1993). *The process of communication* [videotape and manual]. Lawrence, KS: Author. (University of Kansas, Learner Managed Designs, Inc., 2201 K West 25th Street, Lawrence, KS 66047).

Circle of Inclusion Project. (1993). *The process of instruction* [videotape and manual]. Lawrence, KS: Author. (University of Kansas, Learner Managed Designs, Inc., 2201 K West 25th Street, Lawrence, KS 66047).

Cook, R. E., Tessier, A., & Klein, M. D. (1992). *Adapting early childhood curricula for children with special needs* (3rd ed.). New York: Macmillan Publishing Company.

Derman-Sparks, L., & the A.B.C. Task Force. (1989). *Anti-bias curriculum: Tools for empowering young children.* Washington, DC: National Association for the Education of Young Children.

The Family Child Learning Center. (1991). *The preschool integration handbook: A daycare provider's reference for inclusion of children with disabilities.* Tallmadge, OH: Author (Children's Hospital Medical Center of Akron, 90 West Overdale Drive, Tallmadge, OH 44278).

Foyle, H. C., Lyman, L., & Thies, S. A. (1991). *Cooperative learning in the early childhood classroom.* West Haven, CT: National Education Association.

Hanline, M. F., & Graham, M. A. (1991). *Mainstreaming works! A manual for training child caregivers and integrating children with disabilities in child care settings* (rev. ed.). Tallahassee, FL: Center for Prevention & Early Intervention Policy, Florida State University.

Mulligan, S. A., Morris, S. L., & McMurray, D. (1992). *Integrated child care: Meeting the challenge.* Tucson, AZ: Communication Skill Builders.

Musselwhite, C. R. (1986). *Adaptive play for special needs children: Strategies to enhance communication and learning.* Austin, TX: PRO-ED.

Odom, S. L., Bender, M. K., Stein, M. L., Doran, L. P., Houdin, P. M., McInnes, M., Gibert, M. M., Deklyen, M., Speltz, M. L., & Jenkins, J. R. (1988). *The integrated curriculum: Procedures for socially integrating young handicapped and normally developing children.* Seattle: University of Washington Press.

Odom, S. L., McConnell, S. R., & McEvoy, M. A. (Eds.). (1992). *Social competence of young children with disabilities: Issues and strategies for intervention.* Baltimore: Paul H. Brookes Publishing Co.

Peck, C. B., Odom, S. A., & Bricker, D. D. (Eds.). (1993). *Integrating young children with disabilities into community programs: Ecological perspectives on research and implementation.* Baltimore: Paul H. Brookes Publishing Co.

Safford, P. L. (1989). *Integrated teaching in early childhood: Starting in the mainstream.* New York: Pitman Publishing Inc.

Trostle, S., & Yawkey, T. (1990). *Integrated learning activities for young children.* Boston: Allyn & Bacon.

Wolery, M., Strain, P. S., & Bailey, D. B. (1992). Reaching potentials of children with special needs. In S. Bredekamp & T. Rosegrant (Eds.), *Reaching potentials: Appropriate curriculum and assessment for young children.* Washington, DC: National Association for the Education of Young Children.

research studies have been conducted largely in state-of-the-art programs (Strain, 1990). The characteristics and subsequent quality of the care provided in integrated community programs that are not federally funded demonstration projects or that do not have access to additional financial support varies greatly across settings (Carta, Schwartz, Atwater, & McConnell, 1991). This may in turn cause some parents to choose segregated programs for their children. Some questions to consider when children and families participate in segregated programs are:

- Does the program provide opportunities for children to participate in activities with normally developing peers?
- Are IFSP/IEP goals appropriate to make community-based or integrated placement more likely in the future?
- Does the program provide staff training to ensure that special educators teach with emphasis on student independence, problem-solving, and social initiation and responding, thus laying the groundwork for less restrictive future placements (Carta et al., 1992; Rosenkoetter & Fowler, 1986; Rule et al., 1990; Sainato, Strain, Lefebre, & Rapp, 1990; Striefel, Killoran, & Quintero, 1991)?
- Do program personnel respond to parents' concerns about potential stigma by determining whether administrative changes or facility modifications would reduce the separatism caused by special class placement?

There are so many pros and cons about presenting disability to the class. For example, before my son returned to school after chemotherapy—with no hair—his class watched a Charlie Brown video about cancer that helped children to know what to expect. But some of the understanding just happened. At one point he just pulled up his shirt to show his Hickman catheter. Sometimes it's a fine line to know whether to explain differences or ignore them.

Ann Spooner, parent
Wisconsin

* * *

We were prepared to talk to the children in the kindergarten class about Down syndrome if questions arose. There were none. In kindergarten, children are pretty accepting of each other. Nicholas does have some speech difficulties, but some other children in kindergarten also have speech difficulties. Thus, he didn't stick

out from other children in the class. We may have done something different if Nicholas had a more obvious handicapping condition.

There were some concerns from the parents of a few other children. These were assuaged by the principal. Their fears were laid to rest when he assured them that this was the right placement for our son and that the teacher certainly was not slighting their children.

In first grade, we visited the class to tell the children what Down syndrome was and to answer their questions honestly. We told them that you can't "catch" Down syndrome. We also said that Nicholas has one mother at home and doesn't need a lot of little mothers in the classroom. The children pretty much accepted him as he was.

Barbara Balistreri, parent
Wisconsin

* * *

I think people need to use a certain amount of creativity about this—not to be too heavy-handed about *disability,* but rather to include people with disabilities in books, dolls, and dramatic play and then be ready to answer children's questions honestly.

Barbara Lawrence, Region VI
Head Start Resource Access Project

Differences in Program Guidelines

The Challenges As discussed in Chapter 6, many children and their families move from having an IFSP to having an IEP at age 3. Others make this change at age 5 or 6. The significant difference between the two approaches is that the IFSP serves the child with a family-centered approach to providing services that relate to and support his or her development (McGonigel et al., 1991), whereas the IEP outlines a process that is exclusively child-centered. Thus, although the IEP is developed with regard to the family's desired level of participation and is ideally responsive to the family's needs and preferences (Brinkerhoff & Vincent, 1986), its focus is on providing services to the child rather than to the family as a whole.

Additionally, the law requires schools to provide only special education and educationally related services after the child's third birthday, whereas early intervention and Head Start coordinate more comprehensive services. This means that some child services that were previously available under the auspices of an IFSP may not be provided by the schools (once an IEP is enacted) unless they are "educationally related."

As families change planning documents, some procedures, such as those related to due process, are also likely to change across service programs (e.g., early intervention, Head Start, preschool, kindergarten). Most states are, however, trying to align these due process procedures across programs, but the match remains imperfect (Mental Health Law Project, 1990; NEC*TAS, 1992b).

Another significant difference between early intervention and special preschool provisions is that the 1991 reauthorization of the IDEA legislation allows families to reject any discrete service offered through early intervention. Once the child enters preschool services, however, the IEP as developed by the child's planning team (including his or her parents) is treated as a package to be either accepted or rejected in its entirety.

Considering these program differences, it is rather easy to see how confusion or misconceptions can occur. Indeed, professionals frequently see only *their* agency's procedural approach and consequently fail to appreciate that families are forced to comply with the procedures of multiple service agencies.

Some Solutions Chapter 6 discusses ways that professionals and parent mentors can educate families regarding the differences between IFSPs and IEPs and the varying ways that these plans may be implemented. We urge system planners to inform professionals about perceived as well as real differences between the two approaches in order that accurate information can be shared with families. Similarly, parental rights and due process procedures must be fully explained so that parents understand their rights and responsibilities within new programs.

Actions must also be taken to ensure that the continuing needs of children and their families are met. Service gaps between early intervention and preschool or Head Start and kindergarten should be identified and addressed as part of the interagency planning process discussed in Chapter 4. Indeed, more than one agency must often be involved in order to meet the special needs of children and their families (NASBE, 1991; National Commission on Children, 1991). Thus, when additional services are needed for families moving between programs with different eligibilities and regulations, but are beyond the auspices of local schools, local interagency policy teams should promptly address the problem and determine how these services can best be obtained (NASBE, 1991; Peterson, 1991).

The IFSP/IEP transition issue serves as a precursor to the lifelong process of transition planning. For instance, school districts and families often begin to plan for the transition into adulthood for students with disabilities by the early high school years (Halpern, 1985; Leach, 1992; Rusch & Phelps, 1987). Indeed, many of the issues faced during the IFSP/IEP transition are again experienced in the move to middle school (York, Doyle, & Kronberg, 1992) and in subsequent transitions to adulthood. Each of these transitions requires both support from families and collaboration among agencies that provide education as well as health and social services. With similar initiatives to conduct interagency planning for the transitions of young adults from school to work (Johnson, Bruininks, & Thurlow, 1987), school district and community agencies can begin to develop a uniform plan for orchestrating transitions throughout a person's lifespan, rather than dealing with each transition discretely. Of course, parental participation in this development process is essential.

Changes in Service Delivery Models for Therapies

The Challenges One of the most volatile issues regarding transition is the question of whether a given therapy will be available through a new service program. Assuming that a specific therapy will be available, who will provide that therapy and for how long after the transition are questions that frequently arise. For example, a child may have been receiving physical therapy from a registered physical therapist for 1 hour per week in her early intervention program. After the child's transition into special preschool services, however, the local school system may intend to provide occupational therapy in attempts to accomplish the same goals. The system may even choose to have the occupational therapist train a paraprofessional to administer the therapy on a daily basis, rather than weekly, with the therapist's supervision only once a month. Can the OT obtain the same or better results as the PT? Is daily service from an OT paraprofessional likely to be superior, inferior, or equal in effectiveness to weekly service from a PT? Will this method of providing therapy work for this child? These questions and many others must be addressed primarily at the agency level; the answers may have significant implications for this child's development.

Some Solutions The most useful strategy here is the sharing of information, including research data, about the efficacy of various service delivery models. When parents and professionals are aware that a proposed service delivery model has been highly effective with other children, they are generally more apt to consider it for use in their own situation. Another strategy that promotes service continuity across agencies is to arrange a meeting between the therapy teams from the sending and receiving programs to discuss their respective philosophies and intervention strategies, both with each other and with involved parents. Collaborative planning will thus promote continuity in therapy, even if personnel and models for service delivery change.

Differences in Philosophy, Curriculum, Schedules, Activities, and Routines

The Challenges Bettye Caldwell wrote, "The transition between early childhood and elementary education programs should be as normal and routine as continuity between second and third grades" (quoted in Futrell, 1987, p. 252). Unfortunately, movement between early childhood programs is often not very smooth, regardless of the child's age. Immense differences concerning philosophies, curricula, schedules, activities, and routines may exist between sending and receiving programs. Many of these differences can be attributed to differing levels of awareness as well as varying interpretations of developmental appropriateness, as summarized briefly in Table 8.3 (Bredekamp, 1987; Bricker, 1989; NAEYC, 1990).

One major issue concerns the characteristics of children's learning. Varying interpretations foster different ways of teaching young children, specifically: 1) activities, 2) allocation and use of time, 3) learning materials, 4) patterns of communication, 5) adult roles, and 6) classroom structures (Bredekamp & Rosegrant, 1992; Mahoney, Robinson, & Powell, 1992). Indeed, teachers and schools vary considerably regarding this dimension (Carta et al., 1990; Love et al., 1992).

A second issue concerns the question of whether the program accommodates individual differences, or simply uses a single stan-

Table 8.3. Developmentally appropriate practice in early childhood programs serving children from birth through age 8

The concept of *developmental appropriateness* has two dimensions: age appropriateness and individual appropriateness.

Age appropriateness

- Predictable sequences in growth
- Learning environment reflective of the child's developmental stage

Individual appropriateness

- Uniqueness of each child
- Curriculum responsive to individual differences
- Learning experiences that are experiential, interactive, and challenging

Bredekamp, S. (1987). *Developmentally appropriate practice in early childhood programs serving children from birth through age 8.* Washington, DC: National Association for the Education of Young Children. Reprinted with permission.

dard for teaching and evaluating all children. Although this issue is especially important for children with disabilities, it is truly relevant for all children. A national survey (Boyer, 1991) found that 35% of all American children entering kindergarten were performing below levels expected by teachers. However, an equal percentage performed markedly above these levels. Even those children deemed to be average had discernible areas of strength and weakness. Classrooms differ markedly in how they accommodate this natural variation in performance (Love et al., 1992).

As a result of this diversity, highly teacher-directed academic preschools and kindergartens exist alongside programs that feature child-directed, play-based, or experiential learning. Similarly, programs that encourage children to explore materials and solve problems cooperatively are often proximate to classrooms featuring independent problem-solving with worksheets.

Moving from one *type* of program to another entails tremendous change for young children (Barbour & Seefeldt, 1993). In many parts of the country, it has been expected that children simply adapt to new programs (O'Brien, 1991), without the collaborative support of sending programs, receiving programs, and families. However, according to O'Brien (1991, p. 10):

> . . . Our current intervention approaches put the burden for adaptation and accommodation on the *child,* whose performance is then evaluated for success or failure. The model of early school success strongly indicates that it is not the child alone who is responsible. Teachers must accept the responsibility of educating *every* child in the early years of school, regardless of the child's skill level, maturity, or family background.

Some Solutions One way to promote continuity during transition is for educators, administrators, and parents to meet both to discuss the problem of disjointed early childhood curricula and subsequently to work together to create more continuous, developmentally appropriate learning experiences for children throughout their early childhood years. The National Association of Elementary School Principals (1990) has called upon its members to convene such workgroups in each community. Therefore, early childhood educators—including special educators—serving children from birth through age 8 will come together with administrators and parents to define and implement more developmentally appropriate ways of: teaching children in groups (Goffin & Stegelin, 1992; Murphy & Goffin, 1992; Peck, McCaig, & Sapp, 1988), allowing for individual differences (Finger, 1992; Safford, 1989), and ensuring success for a variety of children (Bredekamp & Rosegrant, 1992; Wolery, Ault, &

Doyle, 1992). Strategies for coordinating such workgroups include the following:

- Schedule regular meetings and sharing sessions.
- Plan classroom visitations.
- Learn new skills together.
- Study and discuss policy statements and new publications.
- Attend early childhood conferences and inservices together.
- Visit classrooms that are already working toward being developmentally appropriate and inclusive.
- Work together with a consultant in developing a local philosophy and a curriculum that provides continuity for young children.
- Use peer coaching to support and assist one another (Robbins, 1991).
- Evaluate and share information with parents, colleagues, and the public.

Communities where such workgroups are active report that, although change is slow, it is extremely well received by participants as well as by the children and families served (Drew & Law, 1990; Goffin & Stegelin, 1992).

Caldwell (1991) cautions such workgroups in her discussion of the national study of early childhood programs in public schools that was conducted by Mitchell, Seligson, and Marx (1989). Mitchell et al. found that some communities have attempted to improve transitions between preschool and kindergarten by extending the practices of elementary schools downward to the preschool levels. Although continuity was established, the services were not developmentally appropriate for many of the young children receiving them. Caldwell (1991) noted: "This pattern should be viewed with alarm. Both prekindergarten and kindergarten should focus on an upward extension of earlier development rather than a downward extension of schooling" (p. 83).

While working to change their local early childhood system to provide continuity by linking curricula and instituting developmentally appropriate practices, professionals must work with fellow teachers as well as classrooms as each currently exists. Indeed, despite the professional cooperation that occurs, some differences between classrooms will always remain. That means that steps must be taken to bridge various differences and subsequently to ensure children's success in new classrooms.

Respective visits to the receiving program by sending teachers and to the sending program by receiving teachers reveal routines, patterns of communication, and activities that can be implemented to promote continuity for children. The checklist shown in Figure 8.2 can be used as a guide during such observations. Although classroom interactions and routines are likely to be similar from day to day, observers should note that particular events observed during a visit may or may not represent *typical* occurrences in that classroom. Indeed, elements like the time of year may affect both the extent of explanation offered and the modeling provided to children.

Children benefit when receivers as well as senders alter their usual routines a month or so before or after the transition to make them more like those of the other program. This, in turn, eases the challenges of transition for young children. Familiar books, records, toys, or games can be introduced into the sending program and continued in the receiving program in order to convey a sense of sameness in the midst of change.

For instance, one preschool had a "teddy bear shelf" in the library corner containing bears that could be read to by the children. After his visit to the preschool, the kindergarten teacher instituted a teddy bear shelf in his classroom as well. Many of the children starting kindergarten on the first day of school went immediately to the library corner and began to read to a bear; it was a moment of continuity on a day filled with change.

Similarly, a sending teacher can incorporate songs, transition cues, activities, or learning materials that children are likely to encounter in the future environment.

Conversations, interviews, or surveys of teachers (Beckoff & Bender, 1989; Blaska, 1989; Hains et al., 1989) also provide clues regarding teacher expectations and subsequently aid in program planning. For example, one such conversation revealed that, unlike the family-style meals provided by Head Start, the kindergarten program served milk in individual cartons. Consequently, every fall, the kindergarten teacher was teaching her students to open milk cartons. The Head Start teacher then decided that opening milk cartons was a useful fine motor skill. Thus, she spent the month of May helping her class to master the skill. When school started in the fall, most of the Head Start graduates were adept at this task—a confidence booster for the incoming children and much appreciated by the kindergarten teacher.

Similarly, a preschool teacher learned that several entering 3-year-olds attended the same childcare center where there were no

Checklist for Classroom Visits

SCHEDULE (note activities and times)

DURATION
- Length of session?
- Number of days per week?
- Additional opportunities for home visits and parent conferences?

MEMBERSHIP
- Number of children in class?
- Number of children with disabilities in class?
- Number of adults interacting with children during various activities?
- Teacher : child ratio?

SEATING ROUTINES
- Do children play or work while sitting:
  - On the floor?
  - As a cluster for group discussions?
  - In individual spaces (e.g., carpet squares or taped spots)?
  - In chairs?
- Do children ever sit at desks?
- Do children ever sit at small tables?
- Do children sit in assigned places at any time during the day?

CLASSROOM INTERACTIONS
- To what degree does instruction reflect children's individual developmental levels?
- To what degree does the environment encourage children's choices?
- In what ways does the classroom environment encourage children to engage with learning materials?
- What evidence is there that children are actively involved in learning?
- To what degree are activities cooperative? Individualistic?
- When is group problem-solving evidenced?
- When and how do children receive feedback on their accomplishments?
- For how long are children expected to listen and converse in a large group setting?
- What kinds of opportunities are provided for children to interact with one another?
- Is there a posted schedule that is followed daily?
- Is there a defined system for behavior and guidance? What is that system?
- Does the teacher describe and demonstrate how to do a task after assigning it?

INDEPENDENT PLAY AND WORK ROUTINES
- To what degree are children allowed and expected to play or work without an adult guiding the activity? For how long?
- Are children expected to devise in advance a plan for work or play? Cooperative planning? Independent planning?
- How frequently are children expected to follow sequential directions given in advance of the task?
- What terms (e.g., write your name, go to your area) are children expected to understand in order to work or play independently?
- What are children expected to do when an assigned activity is finished?

FREE PLAY ROUTINES
- Is there a scheduled *choice* time? How long is that time?
- Are activity choices solely at the children's discretion or are they restricted to a certain area(s) or type(s) of equipment chosen by the teacher?

(*continued*)

Figure 8.2. Checklist for classroom visits. (Adapted from Fowler [1982] and the National Academy of Early Childhood Programs [1985].)

Figure 8.2. (*continued*)

Are teachers available for assistance and encouragement during chosen activities?

ATTENTION AND ASSISTANCE-SEEKING ROUTINES

In group discussions, are children allowed to respond without being called upon?
Do children ever raise their hands to answer questions in a group situation?
Are there other acceptable ways for children to seek the teacher's attention?
Is it acceptable to ask peers for help with written tasks?
Is there evidence of planned cooperative learning?
How do children address adults?

MATERIAL MANAGEMENT ROUTINES

Do children manage a schoolbox or other personal supplies?
Do children get and return classroom materials independently?
Do children have cleanup responsibilities? What are they?
What kinds of self-care tasks are children expected to perform independently?
What tasks are children expected to manage independently during eating times?
What are children expected to manage independently during toileting times?

MOVEMENT ROUTINES

Is movement structured or unstructured?
Do children move in lines? When?
Do children hold hands with a partner while moving?
When is movement cued by a direction from the teacher to the whole class?
How many different instructions are given at one time during group directions?
What types of external cues are given to initiate movement?

RESTROOM ROUTINES

Where is the restroom in relation to the classroom?
Do children go in a group or singly to the restroom?
Do children ask permission before using the restroom?
Are there any unique routines for using restrooms?
Do boys and girls use the same restroom?
What visual symbol identifies the restroom?

SERVICES PRESENTLY AVAILABLE

Speech therapy?
Occupational therapy?
Physical therapy?
Music therapy?
Art therapy?
Adaptive physical education?
Vision therapy?
Hearing therapy?
Bus transportation to and from school?
Child care?
Library (on premises)?
Lunch program?
- In familiar classrooms or in a special lunchroom?
- With classmates or with children from other classes?

Other special services?

WHAT OTHER ROUTINES MIGHT BE TAUGHT TO HELP CHILDREN BRIDGE SERVICE PROGRAMS?

stairs or ladders. But, the loft in the preschool reading corner featured a ladder. Thus, the teacher knew that he would need to help incoming children learn how to use the ladder safely upon their entrance into preschool.

Pre-transition visits and conversations are especially valuable for teachers whose classes include children with disabilities (Hains et al., 1988). During such activities teachers can convey the characteristics and preferences of individual children, effective methods of teaching them, and suggestions for supporting their families. The sending and receiving teachers can also form a personal relationship that facilitates ongoing consultation as questions arise in the days following the transition.

What about large communities, where children are often placed in different schools too late in the year to arrange pre-transition visits or conversations between sending and receiving teachers? In these instances, a local goal must be to coordinate earlier, more systematic placements. Until that goal is achieved, teachers may still benefit from classroom visitations and discussions with their counterparts in other schools.

When classroom visits are simply not possible, however, videotapes can provide glimpses of a child and his or her peers that may convey information about both the classroom's routines and the amount of progress made by a child since the inception of intervention services. Other materials that benefit young children experiencing transitions and their teachers can also be shared between programs. Indeed, exchanging curricula, newsletters, unit plans, teaching materials, and phone calls helps teachers in building strong foundations for transition planning.

Finally, informal visits to new programs prior to enrollment may help ease the strangeness of unfamiliar surroundings for children and their families. Indeed, families can take children to visit the new school's playground repeatedly before the first day of school (Gwost, 1992). Some kindergartens sponsor "kindergarten round-ups" to orient incoming children to their new environment. Love et al. (1992) reported that only 47% of American schools have formal programs for pre-enrollment visits, yet 81% of schools said that at least half of all incoming children visit the school before they begin kindergarten. Careful planning in this regard can increase young children's anticipation and reduce stress related to starting school (Logue & Love, 1992). Indeed, visits to the lunchroom, gymnasium, library, playground, and restrooms help children to become familiar with their new setting prior to enrollment.

Small and Large Groups

The Challenges Class sizes typically grow as children get older. In fact, the National Association for the Education of Young Children (1984) estimates 1:6 as the teacher–child ratio in programs serving 2-year-olds and 1:10 in programs serving 3- and 4-year-olds. Kindergartens average one teacher per 23 children, nationally (Boyer, 1991).

The size of a particular class does make a difference. Smaller groups tend to have fewer rules, less regimentation, more individualization, more child contact with adults, and less "business" to transact (Carta et al., 1990; Fowler & Ostrosky, in press). Conversely, larger groups may require more independence and self-monitoring on the parts of young children, more sensitivity to group cues and peer models, and more child responsibility in caring for clothing and work materials (Hains et al., 1988).

New expectations regarding group behavior may challenge young children with special needs if they have not yet learned required behaviors such as moving in a group, responding to explanations or instructions intended for large groups, or participating in large group discussions. Transition planning should address these issues.

Some Solutions As stated previously, many localities have expanded elementary school practices downward to the primary grades and even into preschool (Shepard & Smith, 1988). In places where group size has become an excuse for such developmentally inappropriate practices, new guidelines must be implemented (Love et al., 1992; U.S.D.O.E., 1992). However, a class of 25 students necessarily operates differently from a class of eight students. Children must be *taught* to function in larger as well as smaller groups, for they may be unable to negotiate new systems on their own.

Teachers aware of an imminent shift from a smaller to a larger group can provide more group instruction—including demonstrating for children how to sit in groups for brief periods, how to ask questions or make comments while in groups, and how to work together with children to accomplish a common goal. Special skills that may be needed for a particular placement—such as lining up, making quiet transitions between activities, or responding to group cues rather than to individual names—can be introduced during the weeks prior to the time they will be needed in the new environment. Of course, this can be done in developmentally appropriate ways (e.g., by encouraging children to traverse obstacle courses with partners as a prerequisite to learning to walk in a line later in elementary school). The underlying skill needed for "lining up" is accommodating the child's body position to that of his or her peers while moving toward a goal. That skill can be practiced in many enjoyable, developmentally appropriate ways during daily routines.

Carta et al. (1992) have developed a curriculum for teaching young children with special needs to be more independent as they enter kindergarten. The curriculum has been validated in both urban and suburban schools and has been shown to be effective in increasing children's success in kindergarten (cf. control group children who were not taught these skills performed poorly compared to children exposed to the curriculum). The skills taught include such things as participation in a large group, working independently, and making smooth transitions between activities.

Schools having classes larger than those previously experienced by children may provide attention to individual needs by exposing children to partial classes upon initial entry into the new service program. Indeed, the McPherson, Kansas, school system begins kindergarten with one third of the children attending on each of the first 3 days; on the fourth day, the entire class attends. This procedure allows the teacher to interact personally with each child on his or her first day of school. Thus, it helps to reduce the tumult and crowding typically inherent in the first days of preschool or kindergarten. Finally, it allows for a calm introduction of new routines and the formation of a buddy system that may help slower children to learn new group skills.

Some schools employ an alternative procedure whereby the length of class sessions is shortened during the early weeks of school. They may even provide additional adult helpers to assist children in acquiring competence as well as confidence as they begin to interact within their new surroundings.

Receiving schools with larger classes also help children adjust when they: 1) minimize whole group activities during the early months of school; 2) use aides, volunteers, or family members to assist small groups of children at centers; and 3) specifically teach necessary group behaviors rather than assuming that children will learn them spontaneously from their peers.

Changes in the Nature of Adult Leadership and Attention

The Challenges Teachers of classes comprised of more than 15 children speak more to the group as a whole and less to individual children than do teachers of smaller classes. Indeed, the incidence of individual prompts, cues, and responsive comments decreases as class size increases (Blaska, 1989; Rosenkoetter & Fowler, 1986). Teachers of older children may become more group-oriented and directive with the increasing ages and larger numbers of students being supervised (Fowler, 1982; O'Brien, 1991). In fact, large group, teacher-directed instruction continues to be the norm in many places, especially during kindergarten and beyond (Love et al., 1992).

Some Solutions Published curricula guide teachers of preschool and primary-age children in providing less formal, more interactive small group learning experiences that are more responsive to individual interests and abilities (Brinckerhoff, 1987; Dodge, 1991; *High Scope Resource*, 1993; Mitchell & David, 1992; Murphy & Goffin, 1992; Nebraska and Iowa Departments of Education, 1993; Trostle & Yawkey, 1990). These approaches as well as others based on similar philosophies merit serious study, for they attempt to accommodate children at various developmental levels within a single classroom.

Sending teachers with very small classes also can help in promoting continuity by systematically reducing the frequency of comments to individual children just prior to their moving into larger classes (Hains, 1992). Furthermore, they can teach children to follow directions given to the entire class without individual prompts from the teacher. To the maximum extent possible, sending teachers should teach children to care for their own work materials and clothing, dress and undress independently, and clean their own play and work areas (Chandler, 1992; Hains et al., 1988).

Many children at home as well as in preschools, childcare centers, Head Starts, and kindergartens are allowed to choose their own activities for much of the day. Thus, receiving teachers promote continuity when they provide many opportunities for child choice and spontaneous child–child interactions (Love et al., 1992). Incorporating more time for these activities also allows the receiving teacher greater opportunities to: 1) make personal comments to individual children, 2) hear new students' expressions, and 3) provide individual encouragement that is often overlooked in large group situations.

Rules

The Challenges In every classroom, there are stated as well as unstated rules—a hidden curriculum that children must master to succeed in school (Rule et al., 1990). That which is initially introduced as a routine (e.g., how to use the restroom in the school building) may become a rule after children have had enough time to master it. In other cases, teachers often use competent children as peer models and hope other children will imitate them (Rosenkoetter, 1990b).

Children with special needs are more likely to have difficulties in learning new rules, applying old rules to new situations, and extracting unstated rules from everyday situations (Chandler, 1992). They may also be less likely to watch and learn from more competent peers if they become confused regarding precise expectations.

Some Solutions Transitions require the specific teaching of new rules. Teachers usually realize this and subsequently spend a great deal of time during the first days of school in explaining expectations and demonstrating how certain activities should be accomplished (Rosenkoetter, 1990b). General rules that may be needed in new settings (e.g., hand raising) may be taught just prior to the transition. Conversely, practices specific to a classroom or building are best taught upon a child's arrival in that setting.

Potentially helpful strategies include: 1) verbal rehearsal (i.e., when a child is taught to repeat steps for accomplishing a task as a guide for performing it) (Vygotsky, 1962, 1978); 2) peer modeling (trained or untrained) (Goldstein & Kacsmarek, 1992; Kohler & Strain, 1990); 3) time delay (Schuster & Griffen, 1990); 4) graduated guidance (i.e., waiting for a child to perform a skill independently, providing assistance as needed, and systematically reducing aid) (Wolery, Ault, & Doyle, 1992); and 5) partnering (Sainato, Strain, Lefebre, & Rapp, 1987). Role plays, joint action routines, and puppetry may also help young children to apply rules in new situations (Goldstein, Wickstrom, Hoyson, & Jamieson, 1988; Snyder-McLean, Solomonson, & McLean, 1984; Wallace, 1992). In addition, cue cards in obvious places may remind children to follow classroom rules and routines (Cantor, 1976; High Scope, 1992).

Roles for Families and Relationships Between Parents and Program Staff

The Challenges As discussed in Chapter 6, the frequency and intensity of family–professional interaction is likely to diminish as children grow older. Although opportunities for meaningful participation may exist, parents may not know how to take advantage of those opportunities. Indeed, there may be rules governing parental involvement that are unknown to parents (e.g., "phone ahead for an appointment"; "register first in the school office"). These rules are often related to the large numbers of children being served in a new setting, but parents who are unaware of this may view the

rules as being designed to exclude them from meaningful involvement in their children's education. Therefore, families who felt comfortable and welcome in previous programs may feel uneasy in new surroundings and uncertain about how to communicate effectively with new service providers (Epps, 1992).

Focus groups made up of parents regularly elicit comments regarding the fear of authority figures in schools (perhaps these reactions developed when parents were themselves children). Ironically, similar focus groups conducted with teachers elicit comments concerning fears of interacting with assertive parents. The challenge is thus to move beyond such issues in forming a parental–professional partnership to nurture children's development.

Some Solutions Chapter 7 provides suggestions for encouraging parental involvement before as well as after transition. It is essential that schools and other service providers: 1) regard parents as the primary caregivers for their children, 2) invite parents to observe and assist in the classroom, and 3) develop channels of communication that respect parents' concerns as they meet teachers' time constraints. This active valuing of parents begins with their full inclusion in the interagency as well as intra-agency aspects of transition planning. It continues with actively encouraging them to participate both in the preparation of their child for future program placements and in the efforts to help him or her to prosper there. Indeed, parents are instrumental in creating continuity for children during transitions.

Funding Arrangements

The Challenges In early intervention programs, parents may be billed for services rendered. This is not the case with special preschool or elementary school services, where special education and other related services are the financial responsibility of the school system. However, early intervention programs are likely to provide a greater array of services for children and their families than do public school systems.

These differences may have positive *or* negative effects on children. Nutrition counseling provides a good example. Although it was drafted as part of Sylvia's IFSP and has therefore been provided as part of her early intervention services, nutrition guidance will not be provided by the school system after Sylvia's third birthday. Thus, prior to Sylvia's transition, her parents must arrange for nutrition services elsewhere in the community and subsequently determine how to pay for those services. The new arrangements will likely mean that a different nutritionist is employed to work with Sylvia and her family. This will, of course, affect Sylvia directly.

Some Solutions Some issues regarding funding are specific to individual families, whereas others are relevant to many children and families within a community. Funding for family service coordination and case management, nutrition counseling, family life education, and assistive technology devices and services are but a few of the services likely to be needed by many families beyond their child's third birthday, when school districts are responsible only for "educationally related" services. These funding needs are transition issues that should be addressed by state and local interagency coordinating councils. The policies developed for one family may subsequently aid many families who face similar situations. The goal here is to promote continuity in the midst of change.

Parents and teachers in Elkhart's Head Start program became concerned that some of their children were falling behind in kindergarten after doing quite well in their preschool program. They contacted an elementary school principal who had already been alerted to relevant issues regarding transition by articles in professional magazines. This principal formed a community taskforce—including representatives from the local special education cooperative—that set out to identify transition issues for all of Elkhart's children. The following issues were identified:

- Differences in the roles of parents in sending and receiving programs, respectively
- Differences in curriculum and philosophy
- Staff from the two levels of programs were not familiar with one another and consequently were not working together to ease transitions for children and families
- Costly health, social, and family support services available in Head Start were not available through the school system upon entry into kindergarten
- Change in the delivery of therapies from in-class, integrated therapy in Head Start and the special preschool program to one-to-one pull-out therapy in kindergarten

The taskforce decided that fostering relationships among all early childhood personnel in Elkhart was a high priority. Several inservice sessions were planned for gathering people from various agencies to take part in structured, small group discussions.

Administrators of both kindergarten and preschool/Head Start programs arranged for release time designed to provide teachers with the opportunity to visit each others' classrooms. In addition, an outside facilitator was enlisted to help teachers in discussing commonalities and differences across classrooms.

A year-long study of developmentally appropriate practices eventually grew out of these discussions. This study has, in turn, led to an ongoing effort to develop a curriculum for young children in Elkhart. In fact, a preliminary curriculum is currently being field tested.

Parental involvement was deemed to be another high priority. A committee comprised of parents and professionals studied opportunities for parent education in Head Start and the Elkhart preschools and subsequently worked with the elementary schools in improving the information available to, as well as the welcoming procedures for, incoming families. The parent education program that resulted is being run solely by parents who have already experienced the transition to kindergarten with their children. Through this program, parents are invited to participate in the kindergarten's classroom activities, just as they had in Head Start.

Service models for therapy also merited study. It appears that the new curriculum will make it easier to deliver integrated therapies throughout the early childhood years.

Finally, Elkhart's planners wrestled with the question of funding for "wrap-around services"—services that are "wrapped around" the core school program. These services are used to support children and families (and education), but are not the responsibility of the local school system. The Elkhart Interagency Council wrote a grant proposal in an effort to gain funding for providing more services to families. This may provide an adequate short-term solution, but the problem remains unsolved for the long-term. Planners determined that some needed services were already available, but that families were unable to obtain them. The new community services directory, produced by the Interagency Council, will hopefully be helpful for both professionals and families as they attempt to continue to meet the needs of individual children and their families.

Elkhart has been looking at its system in order to improve transitions for all local children, including but not limited to those with disabilities. Evaluations of this effort are presently commencing by observing the progress of the children for whom the Elkhart system was designed in the first place.

IMPLICATIONS

This chapter describes various challenges to both children's development and families' well-being that are presented by transitions between programs. It also presents some creative ways that communities can successfully deal with those challenges. Indeed, local communities must identify the issues that hinder continuity for young children and their families and subsequently work to overcome them. The primary goal is to maximize the continuity experienced by children and families as they move between intervention programs.

9

Preparing Young Children for Transition

Packing for the Trip

Children adjust most readily to unfamiliar situations if they possess the information and skills necessary to cope with new expectations. Parents and early childhood personnel can do a great deal to help individual children move successfully into a new program.

The realistic goal is not to establish a uniform standard to evaluate individual readiness. Indeed, some children with special needs will not meet "average" standards at any time during their early childhood years, if ever. In all likelihood, some students without identified exceptionalities will also lag behind, whereas others will out perform any "standard" measure. Schools must, therefore, be ready to initiate successful beginnings for all children who enroll (Peck et al., 1993; Salisbury & Vincent, 1990; U.S.D.O.E., 1991). For each child, the experience of transition must provide a positive foundation for future learning (NAEYC, 1990). The goal here is not to make sending programs into carbon copies of receiving programs. Rather, it is to include preparatory activities in transition planning to minimize surprise and increase continuity for all children (Bredekamp, 1987). A planned orientation program coupled with an organized sequence of learning activities can make a difference for every child (Chandler, 1992).

Sylvia's family has informed the Daisy Center's early intervention program that they want their daughter to begin preschool at the parochial school attended by their other three children. Although many arrangements will have to be made, both the family and the home visitor want to prepare Sylvia to make her move into preschool a positive event.

* * *

Joey's move to the city and enrollment in the employer-supported childcare center meant that he had to adjust to new surroundings, unfamiliar people, and different expectations. This was difficult for a shy child with a severe language delay. Soon Joey will move into kindergarten and face additional changes. The staff at the childcare center, in collaboration with the transition coordinator and a special educator appointed by the school system, and the hospital's speech-language pathologist, have taken many steps toward helping Joey learn to make friends and develop other essential skills that may ease his transition.

Preparing a child for future environments includes two important elements:

1. *Providing the child with accurate information, concrete experiences, anticipatory comments about the new school, and opportunities to ask questions and express reactions* These activities will help the child make sense of the upcoming move. Indeed, they will reduce his or her stress as they augment anticipation regarding the new program.
2. *Teaching the child coping skills and routines that will be useful in the new program* These strategies will help the child to feel more comfortable in an unfamiliar place as they allow him or her to capitalize readily on new learning opportunities.

STRATEGIES TO HELP CHILDREN PREPARE FOR TRANSITION

Change is an essential component of life. The successful navigation of each of life's transitions prepares us for future changes. Indeed, strategies that children develop to cope with change may help in easing future transitions. Thus, activities such as planned (though brief) separations from the family; exploring a new house, store, or park; getting acquainted with a new neighbor; and spending time with other children in a church nursery or during Mom's Morning Out all serve to prepare children for later program transitions. This chapter discusses specific actions that families, care providers, teachers, and therapists can take both to alleviate the concerns that children have prior to transition (see Table 9.1) and to promote successful adjustment to new environments.

Anticipate

Concerned adults should speak with anticipation regarding preschool or kindergarten. They can equate transition with the child's "getting to be a big girl or boy" and subsequently show pride in the child's increasing maturity and independence.

For instance, parents and early interventionists can build confidence by calling attention to small similarities between present and future environments: "This is a trampoline like the one at preschool" or "During kindergarten, you'll have a storytime just as we do here in preschool." A new item of clothing can even be tied to transition: "Your new coat will keep you warm on the playground at Head Start" or "You'll wear these shoes to play games in the gym in kindergarten." Similarly, adults can introduce other children who will be attending the same program: "That's Holly; she's going to be in your class." Holly could even be invited to play. Anticipation depends on positive forecasting. Thus, it is important to avoid negative expectations such as, "Your teacher won't like it if you suck

Table 9.1. Common questions and concerns of children prior to transition

Why do I have to go to a new school?
Will my old teacher come with me to my new school?
Will I get to play with my friends again?
I want to be big.
I want to be little.
Will my new teacher be nice?
What happens if I get lost?
What will happen if I miss the bus?
Do I have to be quiet all the time at school?
What if I need to go to the bathroom?
Will I be able to sleep at school?
Where will I sleep at school?
Will there be big kids on the playground?
What if I don't like the food at lunch time?
How do I get home?
What if my mom doesn't come to pick me up from school?
What will the teacher do if the kids aren't good?
Do I get to play at school?
Can I bring my toys to school? What about my blanket?
Can my mom stay with me at school for awhile?
Where will my mom and dad be while I'm in school?

your thumb at Head Start," or "You will have to work very hard in kindergarten."

Read

Reading books about other children in transition reduces the stress of being placed in a new environment (see Table 9.2). Similarly, role plays or joint action routines can provide relevant practice with transition events (Goldstein et al., 1988; Snyder-McLean et al., 1984).

Table 9.2. Books to prepare children for transition

Author	Title
Alexander	Sabrina
Allard	Miss Nelson is Missing!
Anderson	Carlos Goes to School
Arnold	Where Do You Go to School?
Barkin	I'd Rather Stay Home
Barkin	Sometimes I Hate School
Behrens	What I Hear in My School
Berenstain	The Berenstain Bears Go to School
Boyd	I Met a Polar Bear
Bram	I Don't Want To Go to School
Breinburg	Shawn Goes to School
Buchmeier	I Know a Teacher
Burningham	The School
Calmenson	The Kindergarten Book
Cassidy	We Like Kindergarten
Caudill	A Pocketful of Cricket
Charles	Calico Cat at School
Cohen	First Grade Takes a Test
Cohen	The New Teacher
Cohen	No Good in Art
Cohen	See You Tomorrow, Charles
Cohen	When Will I Read?
Cohen	Will I Have a Friend?
Cole	What's Good for a Five-Year-Old?
Delton	The New Girl at School
Elliott	Grover Goes to School
Frandsen	I Started School Today
Gordon	Crystal is the New Girl
Haas	A Special Place for Johnny
Hamilton-Meritt	My First Days of School
Harris	The School Mouse
Hillert	Who Goes to School?

(continued)

Table 9.2. *(continued)*

Hoffman	Steffie and Me
Holland	First Day of School
Horvath	Will the Real Tommy Wilson Please Stand Up
Hurd	Come with Me to Nursery School
Isadora	Willaby
Jones	Going to Kindergarten
Lenski	Debbie Goes to Nursery School
Lexau	I Hate Red Rover
Lystad	Jennifer Takes Over P.S. 94
Mann	The 25 Cent Friend
Marino	Where Are the Mothers?
Marshall	Fox at School
Marshall	Miss Nelson Is Back
Mason	I Go to School
Matthias	Out the Door
McInnes	Goodnight Painted Pony
Meshover	The Monkey that Went to School
Nichols	Big Paul's School Bus
Oppenheim	Mrs. Peloski's Snake
Ormsby	Twenty One Children
Oxenbury	First Day of School
Parish	Jumper Goes to School
Quackenbush	First Grade Jitters
Relf	The First Day of School
Relf	Show and Tell
Rockwell	My Nursery School
Rogers	Mr. Rogers Talks about . . .
Schick	The Little School at Cottonwood Corners
Schwartz	Bea and Mr. Jones
Simon	I'm Busy Too
Stein	A Child Goes to School
Steiner	I'd Rather Stay with You
Steptoe	Jeffrey Bear Cleans Up His Act
Thwaite	The Chatterbox
Tobias	The Dawdlewalk
Udry	What Mary Jo Shared
Welbar	Goodbye, Hello
Wells	Timothy Goes to School
Wisema	Morris Goes to School
Wittman	The Wonderful Mrs. Trumbly
Wolde	Betsy's First Day at Nursery School
Wolf	Adam Smith Goes to School
Wooley	Gus Was a Real Dumb Ghost

This list is reprinted by permission from *Transition,* published by the Head Start Bureau, U.S. Administration for Children, Youth, and Families, Washington, D.C.

For example, a preschool class could pretend to be riding a school bus, eating in a school cafeteria, meeting a new teacher, or asking for the location of the restroom. Indeed, "playing school" may become a dramatic play theme for several weeks prior to a child's transition.

Children possessing more advanced skills might create imaginary stories about children who are going to new schools. Individual children may even dictate stories to be read back to them and later shared with friends, teachers, or parents.

Visit

Many children participate in general orientation sessions (e.g., "Play Preschool" or "Kindergarten Round-up"; see Appendix D for additional examples). However, children with special needs will additionally benefit from visiting the new classroom in the company of a parent or other family adult on a day when the receiving class is engaged in appealing activities. Such visits help the child to become familiar with the new setting and to feel comfortable with program personnel. For children with visual impairments or other issues that present mobility problems, it may be wise to visit the new school when crowds of people are not present. The child can then be introduced privately to the main classroom areas and shown the best routes to restrooms, lockers, and eating areas. Extra practice on navigating major routes will help young children to feel more confident in their new environments. A preliminary ride on a school bus also can be scheduled as part of this visit for those children who have not previously ridden on a bus. Similarly, during the weeks preceding school entry, parents, siblings, or teachers can take one child or a group of children to play on the playground at the new school.

Dramatic play before and after visits to the new school can expand opportunities for learning as children experiment with possible behaviors relating to the new situation. For instance, play storytime or art will help the child to anticipate future group activities.

Substitutes for "real" visits to the destination classroom may be necessary if a child is hospitalized or the placement schedule is inflexible. For example, an older sibling or neighborhood peer may take the incoming child on a general tour of the school. Alternatively, children from last year's "graduating class" may return to describe the fun offered at the school, or a parent or teacher who knows the new school well—perhaps even the actual receiving teacher—may be willing to share stories about it. If most of the children in a particular preschool class will be attending the same kindergarten, the kindergarten teacher might write them "welcome letters" in the spring and then again just before school starts in the fall; photographs are sometimes enclosed with such letters. A kindergarten class might even produce a videotape (to be shared with the local Head Start and preschool classes) that documents typical daily activities and events.

Of course, each of these strategies shares the common goal of reducing the strangeness of and increasing children's familiarity with new placements.

Change the Schedule

Sometimes children are forced to adjust to a significant schedule change as they enter a new program. Indeed, after a transition, they may be required to get up earlier, eat lunch later, or skip an afternoon nap. In such cases, it is important to introduce schedule changes prior to the first day of school, when additional stressors will be present. Parents can introduce a new bedtime or phase out naptime several weeks prior to the actual transition (see also Murphy & Corte, 1985; N.E.A., 1983; and Paulu, 1992 for home activities to "get ready for school").

Encourage Separation

Because of the close relationships that often develop between professionals and families, it may be difficult for teachers and therapists to separate themselves from vulnerable students with special needs and their families. As a transition approaches, professionals need to evaluate their own attitudes and behaviors and subsequently eliminate mannerisms that may encourage further dependency for either families or their children. For instance, it may be detrimental to the new family–teacher (or family–therapist) relationship if members of the sending staff imply that the new program is unsatisfactory, less adequate, or more impersonal than their own. However, expressions of confidence regarding the new program and its staff help facilitate a smooth transition for children as well as their families.

TEACHING SKILLS AND ROUTINES NEEDED DURING TRANSITION

Demonstrating competence in an activity or custom that is valued by the receiving teacher helps incoming children to feel in control during a period of relative powerlessness. Such feelings promote positive, empowering attitudes that facilitate good beginnings in new settings. Parents and teachers can encourage competence and self-confidence by teaching children to perform well a few developmentally appropriate skills and routines that are useful during transition.

Individualized Planning

The initial vehicle for transition planning is the IFSP or IEP. The IFSP and IEP are based on family preferences, assessments of a child's performance, and analysis of the environment(s) the child is likely to experience. Relevant outcomes or goals must be included in the IFSP prior to the age 3 transition and should also be included in planning documents during preparation for future transitions.

The IFSP or IEP team designates professionals, family members, and community personnel who will provide service and support for the child and family during the transition period. This team should discuss the steps comprising the transition process—including child preparation—and subsequently make them available both to families and to professionals—orally as well as in writing—about 9 months prior to the actual transition. The IFSP or IEP team also delineates a small number of specific skills that will enhance the child's opportunity for a smooth transition into the new program. The team also determines what, if any, special resources may be needed to achieve desired outcomes, and it sets timelines for those outcomes. To the greatest extent possible, outcomes should be designed for and monitored in natural settings with groups of children similar to those to be encountered in future placements (Safford, 1989). The transition portions of Sylvia's and Joey's IFSP/IEP are outlined in Figures 9.1 and 9.2 respectively.

Target Skills

Making friends and continuing to learn in new environments depends on developing coping and so-called "learning-to-learn" skills as well as on becoming competent in the more traditional developmental domains (Chandler, 1992; Conn-Powers, Ross-Allen, & Holburn, 1990; Rule et al., 1990). Some of the important transition skills culled from research literature are outlined in Tables 9.3 and 9.4.

Few children will have mastered all of these skills by the ages of 3 or 5, and they are certainly *not* prerequisite to school entrance. Rather, these lists are intended to aid parents and staff in including in the IFSP or IEP some outcomes that will help the child with special needs to adjust in new settings (Murphy & Vincent, 1989; Salisbury & Vincent, 1990). Indeed, certain skills important for transition should be taught and subsequently practiced frequently in

IFSP for *Sylvia Schmidt*
Date of birth: September 12, 19--
Today's date: September 1, 19--

Outcomes	Strategies	Timeline			Evaluation
		Start	End	Check off	
1. According to their expressed wishes, Mr. & Mrs. Schmidt will learn about the transition process and participate in it in order to make informed transition decisions.	1.a. The family service coordinator (FSC) will meet with the Schmidts to share information about the process, the timeline, and parental rights; to seek permission to exchange information with the school district; and to learn how the Schmidts want to be involved in transition planning.	9-7	9-15		Meeting occurs—case log
	1.b. The FSC will answer questions or locate information to assist the Schmidts in their transition planning.	9-1	9-30		Questions are answered—parent report
	1.c. The Schmidts and the FSC will meet with a representative from the school district to learn the legal context and the local history of services provided to children eligible for special education whose parents chose to enroll them in parochial schools. They will also obtain information about possible placements for Sylvia.	9-15	10-15		Meeting occurs—case log
	1.d. The Schmidts and the FSC will meet with a representative of the diocese to	9-15	10-15		Meeting occurs—case log

(*continued*)

Figure 9.1. Sylvia Schmidt's IFSP transition plan.

Figure 9.1. (*continued*)

IFSP for *Sylvia Schmidt*
Date of birth: September 12, 19--
Today's date: September 1, 19--

Outcomes	Strategies	Timeline			Evaluation
		Start	End	Check off	
	learn about its policy about serving children with disabilities.				
	1.e. The Schmidts and the FSC will meet with the principal at St. Patrick's to discuss Sylvia's possible attendance there next year.	10-15	11-15		Meeting occurs—case log
	1.f. The Daisy Center will share with St. Patrick's any information requested by the Schmidts.	9-15	8-30		Information is shared—parent report
	1.g. Since Sylvia's 90-day transition planning period occurs during the summer, the family and the FSC from the Daisy Center will meet in early spring with a representative from the school district to devise a transition plan for their family and to explore placement options for Sylvia.	2-15	3-15		Meeting occurs—case log; plan is formulated and distributed
	1.h. Mr. & Mrs. Schmidt will attend the state Parent Center's discussion group explaining the IEP process.	9-15	12-15		Schmidts attend class—parent report
	1.i. The FSC will help the Schmidts to locate other families whose children with disabilities are attending parochial schools.	11-15	12-15		Families are located—parent report
2. With parental permission, the Daisy Center will share information, including evaluation results, with the school district in order to ease Sylvia's transition.	2.a. Initial meeting	9-15	10-15		Information is shared—case log
	2.b. 90-day meeting	2-15	3-15		Information is shared–case log

	2.c. Timely exchange of requested information over 12 months	9-15	8-30		Information is shared—case log
3. Sylvia will learn to separate from her mother in order to attend preschool successfully.	3.a. Sylvia and Mrs. Schmidt will attend the toddler playgroup with Mrs. Schmidt absenting herself for longer and longer periods at a time.	9-15	5-25		Note attendance, separation behaviors by mother and Sylvia, and length of separation—parent report
	3.b. Mr. & Mrs. Schmidt will begin to leave Sylvia with a babysitter approximately 4 times per month.	11-1	8-30		Checkbook history of babysitting occasions; parents' anecdotal reports
4. Sylvia will cease using her pacifier in order to gain greater acceptance from other children in preschool.	4.a. The Schmidts and the early interventionist will develop and implement a 9-month plan to eliminate Sylvia's use of the pacifier.	10-15	7-15		Pacifier is no longer used—parent report
5. Sylvia will increase eye contact and engagement with objects in order to complete more tasks successfully.	5.a. The Schmidts and the early interventionist will develop a list of activities that Sylvia favors.	9-10	9-20		List developed
	5.b. The interventionist will record data on how often and how long Sylvia gazes at play objects.	9-10	9-30		Data gathered
	5.c. They will plan together how to use these favored activities to increase eye contact and engagement.	9-30	10-20		Plan developed

(*continued*)

Figure 9.1. (*continued*)

IFSP for *Sylvia Schmidt*
Date of birth: September 12, 19--
Today's date: September 1, 19--

Outcomes	Strategies	Timeline			Evaluation
		Start	End	Check off	
	5.d. They will implement the plan.	10-20	4-1		Sylvia makes eye contact with objects and plays with them more frequently and for longer periods, according to the interventionist's data
6. Sylvia will comply with four one-step directions in order to perform preschool class routines.	6.a. The early interventionist and the Schmidts will teach Sylvia to obey the "look at me" request.	9-15	10-15		Sylvia complies in a natural situation four of five times in a 2-day period.
	6.b. The early interventionist and the Schmidts will teach Sylvia to obey the "come" request.	10-15	11-20		Sylvia complies in a natural situation four of five times in a 2-day period.
	6.c. The early interventionist and the Schmidts will teach Sylvia to obey the "stop" request.	11-30	2-1		Sylvia complies in a natural situation four of five times in a 2-day period.
	6.d. The early interventionist and the Schmidts will teach Sylvia to obey the "wash hands" request.	2-1	4-1		Sylvia complies in a natural situation four of five times in a 2-day period.

Note: Joey began receiving special education services late in the school year. He will continue to attend the childcare center and work toward these objectives throughout the summer months.

GOAL 1: Increase strategies for classroom learning and coping.

1. By April 1, Joey will play or work cooperatively with at least 2 peers for at least 4 minutes, on 3 of 4 days.
2. By May 1, Joey will observe a more competent peer and imitate his or her actions in an unfamiliar situation, on 3 of 4 days.
3. By June 1, Joey will respond to a group cue to move between activities without requiring an individual cue, 3 days in a row.
4. By July 1, Joey will clean up his craft or play materials without an individual prompt, 3 days in a row.
5. By August 15, Joey will write his name in the kindergarten style on his art papers without a prompt, 3 days in a row.

GOAL 2: Improve communication skills

1. By April 1, Joey will maintain a 3-turn verbal interaction with a peer, daily for a week.
2. By June 1, Joey will, in an appropriate manner, verbally express feelings of anger, disagreement, sadness, and puzzlement to a peer, three times each, respectively.
3. By August 15, Joey will request assistance from an adult using appropriate words, four times during one week.

Figure 9.2. Two goals of Joey's IEP.

natural environments. Some of these skills may be worked on over the course of the school year, whereas others should be introduced in the few months immediately prior to the child's transition. For instance, 5-year-olds may be taught throughout the preschool year to pre-plan and to later describe their play or work activities. Conversely, walking in lines or raising hands for recognition may be introduced in April or May if the local kindergarten expects children to adhere to such procedures. Toddlers can be taught to carry small school bags and remove their jackets before hanging them on hooks. Basic concepts that are already included in the curriculum can be applied in situations likely to be encountered in the new setting. For example, a program for teaching the use of prepositional phrases can be assimilated into a lesson incorporated into general classroom directions or in a learning center or at small group time.

At some point, all children need to care for their possessions; to learn in a group setting; to understand and follow directions; to handle variety in formats, routines, directions, and reinforcers; to meet new people; to monitor their own behavior; and to move toward independent self-care. Indeed, these are important transition skills

Table 9.3. Skills that ease preschool entry

NOTE: The following skills may be useful in defining desired outcomes if they are developmentally appropriate for a given child. They should *never* be used as entrance criteria or to exclude any child from a classroom.

SOCIAL SKILLS

1. Separates from parents for short periods of time
2. Communicates with adults who are not family members
3. Responds positively to social recognition by nonfamily members
4. Expresses emotions appropriately for his or her developmental level
5. Tries new activities
6. Imitates other children's actions
7. Initiates contact with adults as well as other children

COMMUNICATION SKILLS

1. Uses a signal either to gain attention or to obtain objects
2. Communicates wants and needs such as eating, drinking, or toileting
3. Makes eye contact with speakers
4. Attends to speakers for at least brief periods
5. Responds to adults when called by name
6. Seeks help from adults, as needed
7. Follows some one-step directions
8. Responds to questions

ADAPTIVE SKILLS

1. Feeds oneself
2. Responds to warnings
3. Puts on or removes some garments
4. Recognizes his or her own belongings

COGNITIVE SKILLS

1. Recognizes relatives and other significant people
2. Explores objects and places
3. Demonstrates an awareness of cause and effect
4. Combines parts of toys or sets of materials
5. Avoids obvious dangers

for all children. A list of curriculum aids for building transition skills appears in Table 9.5.

For children whose physical or mental impairments hinder complex skill development, the goal becomes partial participation (Baumgart et al., 1982; Brown, Nietupski, & Hamre-Nietupski, 1976; Brown & Lehr, 1989). A child who will never be able to dress herself independently (due to physical impairment) may, nevertheless, learn to assist as she is being dressed. Similarly, a child unable to run around the circle during a game of Duck, Duck, Goose may nevertheless participate by tapping other children on the head while

Table 9.4. Nonacademic skills useful for transition into kindergarten

NOTE: The following skills may be useful for goal writing, if they are developmentally appropriate for a given child. They should *never* be used as entrance criteria or to exclude any child from a classroom.

PLAYING AND WORKING INDEPENDENTLY AND COLLABORATIVELY

1. Plays and works appropriately with and without peers
2. Completes activities approximately on time
3. Stays with an activity for an appropriate amount of time
4. Plays and works with few individual prompts from the teacher

INTERACTING WITH PEERS

1. Imitates peers' actions when learning new routines
2. Initiates and maintains contact with peers
3. Responds to peers' initiations
4. Learns and uses names of peers
5. Shares objects and takes turns with peers
6. Plans activities with peers

FOLLOWING DIRECTIONS

1. Responds to adults' questions
2. Responds appropriately to multi-step verbal directions
3. Responds appropriately to verbal directions that include common school-related prepositions, nouns, and verbs
4. Complies with group as well as individual instructions
5. Modifies behavior as needed when given verbal feedback
6. Recalls and follows directions for tasks previously discussed or demonstrated
7. Watches others or seeks help if he or she doesn't understand directions

RESPONDING TO ROUTINES

1. Learns new routines after limited practice
2. Moves quickly and quietly from one activity to another without individual reminders
3. Reacts appropriately to changes in routine
4. Cares for personal belongings

CONDUCTING ONESELF ACCORDING TO CLASSROOM RULES

1. Waits appropriately
2. Lines up if teacher requests that he or she do so
3. Sits appropriately
4. Focuses attention on the speaker, shifts attention appropriately, and participates in class activities in a manner that is relevant to the task or topic
5. Seeks attention or assistance in acceptable ways
6. Separates from parents and accepts the authority of school personnel
7. Expresses emotions and feelings appropriately

See also Hains et al., (1989) and Rosenkoetter (1990b).

Table 9.5. Curriculum aids in teaching for transition

Bredekamp, S. (Ed.). (1987). *Developmentally appropriate practice in early childhood programs serving children from birth through age 8.* Washington, DC: National Association for the Education of Young Children.

Bredekamp, S., & Rosegrant, T. (Eds.). (1992). *Reaching potentials: Appropriate curriculum and assessment for young children.* Washington, DC: National Association for the Education of Young Children.

Byrd, R. (Ed.). (1987). *Project STEPS: Helpful entry level skills and instructional strategies.* Lexington, KY: Child Development Centers of the Bluegrass.

Carta, J.J., Elliott, M., Orth-Lopes, L., Scherer, J.B., Schwartz, I.S., & Atwater, J.B. (1992). *Project SLIDE: Skills for learning independence in diverse environments.* (Teacher's Manual). Kansas City: University of Kansas, Juniper Gardens Children's Project.

Carta, J.J., Schwartz, I.S., Atwater, J.B., & McConnell, S.R. (1991). Developmentally appropriate practice: Appraising its usefulness for young children with disabilities. *Topics in Early Childhood Special Education, 11*(1), 1–20.

Foyle, H.C., Lyman, L., & Thies, S.A. (1991). *Cooperative learning in the early childhood classroom.* Washington, DC: National Education Association.

Goldstein, H. (1993). Use of peers as communication intervention agents. *Teaching Exceptional Children, 25*(2), 37–40.

Hains, A.H., Fowler, S.A., Schwartz, I.S., Kottwitz, E., & Rosenkoetter, S. (1989). A comparison of preschool and kindergarten teacher expectations for school readiness. *Early Childhood Research Quarterly, 4*(1), 75–88.

Head Start. (1989). *Transition.* Washington, DC: Administration for Children, Youth, and Families. Available from Chapel Hill Training-Outreach Project, 800 E. Town Drive, Suite 105, Chapel Hill, NC 27514.

Killoran, J., Rule, S., Stowitschek, J.J., Innocenti, M., & Levine, L.M. (1982). *Let's be social: Language-based social skills for preschool at-risk children.* Tucson, AZ: Communication Skill Builders.

Kohler, F.W., & Strain, P.S. (1993). The early childhood social skills program: Making friends during the early childhood years. *Teaching Exceptional Children, 25*(2), 41–42.

Odom, S.L., Bender, M., Stein, M., Doran, L., Houden, P., McInnes, M., Gilbert, M., DeKlyen, M., Speltz, M., & Jenkins, J. (1989). *Integrated preschool curriculum.* Seattle: University of Washington Press.

Paulu, N. (1992). *Helping your child get ready for school with activities for birth through age 5.* Washington, DC: U.S. Department of Education, Office of Educational Research and Improvement.

Rosenkoetter, S.E., & Fowler, S.A. (1986). Teaching mainstreamed children to manage daily transitions. *Teaching Exceptional Children, 19,* 20–23.

Rule, S., Feichtl, B.J., & Innocenti, M.S. (1990). Preparation for transition to mainstreamed post-preschool environments: Development of a survival skills curriculum. *Topics in Early Childhood Special Education, 9,* 78–90.

Sainato, D.M., & Strain, P.S. (1993). Integration success for preschoolers with disabilities. *Teaching Exceptional Children, 25*(2), 36–37.

Sainato, D.M., Strain, P.S., & Lyon, S.R. (1987). Increasing academic responding of handicapped preschool children during group instruction. *Journal of the Division for Early Childhood, 12,* 23–30.

being carried. Thus, transition skills include not only those pertaining to learning and coping, but also to behaviors that help children to achieve greater acceptance in new classroom communities (York et al., 1992). Transition planning provides a good opportunity to examine children's routines and subsequently to seek further opportunities for at least partial participation.

Another aspect of skill development relevant to transition involves decreasing adult support. Teachers in early childhood programs, especially those in special education classrooms, sometimes forget to reduce the levels of assistance provided to their students. A study (Hains, 1992) examined the effects of reducing teacher support during the on-task reading activities of 11 young children with disabilities in three self-contained early childhood special education classrooms. The results indicated that, when the teacher's attention was reduced, the children in two of the classrooms continued to work appropriately. The children in the third classroom did not, however, maintain on-task behavior with such minimal teacher support. But, when a simple checksheet self-monitoring procedure was implemented, the performance of three of the four children improved. This study shows that not all children need elaborate programs to improve transition skills. Systematic alterations in their environments are often sufficient for most children to work or play more independently.

Carryover of Familiar Skills

Young children with special needs often have difficulty in performing a familiar skill in new locations with different people, various cues, and unfamiliar materials (Fowler, 1982) (e.g., a boy who had been saying his name upon request refuses to do so in his new preschool; a girl who shares toys freely in preschool will not do so in kindergarten; a child who had been toilet trained for several months regresses in a new environment). Skill carryover thus becomes an important goal in transition planning because transition into a new program requires both the modification of existing routines and the assimilation of extensive new learning.

The primary way in which to promote skill carryover is to "teach loosely" (Stokes & Baer, 1977; Vaughn, Bos, & Lund, 1986) (i.e., to teach new skills and practice familiar ones in multiple settings, with multiple people, using a variety of natural cues and consequences). Rather than relying on pre-determined lesson plans, the use of children's interests and chosen activities coupled with incidental teaching effectively builds skills that transfer to new environments (Bricker & Cripe, 1992; Hart & Risley, 1975, 1980; Kaczmarek, 1985). For example, a child who regularly identifies himself by name when addressed by his teacher can be encouraged to do so when addressed by peers, the school janitor, the cook, and other people encountered during regular school and family routines like riding the school bus, eating in the snack area, listening at library storytime, and learning in Sunday School.

The checklist in Figure 9.3 may be useful in evaluating how effectively a child applies a skill or skills throughout a day and across settings. Systematic efforts to promote carryover should be undertaken during the months prior to transition.

Intentionally increasing the variety of practices and routines employed in special classrooms will encourage skill carryover. In turn, this will make these classrooms more comparable to inclusive classrooms, which tend to have a broader array of options regarding daily routines (Hains, 1992; Rosenkoetter & Fowler, 1986; Sainato et al., 1990; Trostle & Yawkey, 1990). Skills taught in clusters during natural activities rather than individually during contrived tasks will be more likely to carry over into other environments (Bricker & Cripe, 1992; Holvoet, Mulligan, Schussler, Lacey, & Guess, 1984).

Some children behave in very routinized ways and consequently resist change—an urgent problem when approaching transition. For such children, an IEP goal might be "to increase the variety of stimuli to which [he or she] responds appropriately." Specific IEP objectives should delineate the benchmarks for the child's progress in adjusting to change. Accompanying instructional plans should outline strategies and activities designed to increase the child's tolerance for change. Indeed, for a considerable number of children, attention to this issue is vital for their successful transition into a new program.

A matrix outlining a family's or classroom's daily activities on one axis and a child's individual objectives on the other can be used to plan when instruction will occur to maximize adaptability of skills (McCormick, 1985). The matrix may also indicate who will oversee planned intervention activities and subsequent performance probes. This approach is illustrated in Figures 9.4 and 9.5.

Some families and teachers resist matrix planning because they fear that they will be unable to implement the plan perfectly each day. Even imperfect implementation, however, will cause personnel to attend to their efforts and will achieve more progress than complete dependence on instructional spontaneity.

	SKILLS									
FACTORS IN SKILL CARRYOVER	Plays/ works alone	Plays/ works with peers	Stays on task; completes on time	Plays/ works without close super-vision	Imitates peers to learn new routines	Initiates contact with peers	Responds to peers' initiations	Uses names of peers	Shares objects and turns with peers	Seeks assistance from adults
Support needed Physical and verbal assist										
Verbal or visual assist										
Independently										
Cues needed Many cues										
Single cue										
No cues										
Reinforcement needed Tangible plus social										

(continued)

Figure 9.3. Checklist to assess the carryover of skills.

Figure 9.3. *(continued)*

FACTORS IN SKILL CARRYOVER	SKILLS: Plays/ works alone	Plays/ works with peers	Stays on task; completes on time	Plays/ works without close super- vision	Imitates peers to learn new routines	Initiates contact with peers	Responds to peers' initiations	Uses names of peers	Shares objects and turns with peers	Seeks assistance from adults
Privilege plus social										
Social alone										
Reduced social										
Internal reinforce- ment										
Duration of performance Performs momentarily										
Performs for brief period										
Sustained perfor- mance										
Location One location/ present setting										
Several locations/ present setting										
Several settings										
Novel settings										

Distraction tolerated during performance None										
Some										
Many, or especially salient, distractions										
Monitoring of performance In response to directions										
In response to "What do you do next?"										
Self-monitoring										
Time One time of day only										
Throughout day										

DAILY ACTIVITIES	TARGETED OBJECTIVES						
	Sylvia will separate from mom	Sylvia will cease using pacifier (Step 1)	Sylvia will increase eye contact and engagement with objects	Sylvia will "look at me"	Sylvia will "come"	Sylvia will "stop"	Sylvia will "wash hands"
Breakfast				X			X
Bath	Every Tuesday morning and approximately 1 evening per week	X	X		X	Whenever hazards are encountered	
Diapering #1			X				
Dressing			x				
Lunch				X			X
Diapering #2			X				
Nap					X		
Dinner				X			X
Play with dad and sister		X	X	X			
Put away toys			X				
Undressing							
Storytime			X		X		
Errands with dad and mom					X	X	

Figure 9.4. Sylvia's daily intervention plan.

Staff responsible for oversight and data collection: TP, DS, SS, MR

	TARGETED OBJECTIVES							
CLASS-ROOM ACTIVITIES	Play/work cooperatively 4 minutes (probe 1 X per week per activity)	Observe and imitate peer (probe 2 X per week per activity)	Respond to group transition cue (probe 1 X per week per activity)	Clean up craft or work materials (probe 1 X per week per activity)	Write name on papers (probe 1 X per week per activity)	Maintain verbal interaction (probe 1 X per week)	Express feelings: anger, disagreement, sadness, puzzlement (anecdotal report daily)	Request assistance from adult (anecdotal report daily)
Arrival								
Play	DS			DS		DS		
Bathroom								KC
Breakfast		TP						TP
Play	DS, MR		DS	MR		DS, MR, SS	DS, MR, SS	DS
Small groups				DS	DS			SS
Outside play	DS, MR		DS				DS, MR, SS	SS
Art				DS, TP	DS, TP			
Story, music								
Bathroom								KL
Lunch		TP						TP
Music								
Nap								
Bathroom								KL
Snack		TP						TP
Play	MR							
Leave taking								

Figure 9.5. Joey's classroom intervention plan.

Preparing a Class of Children

The strategies discussed earlier in this chapter comprise an important element in preparing children for new environments. Skill development activities can also occur classwide. From the matrices developed for individual children, a class matrix can be prepared (see Figure 9.6) showing which skills are being targeted during a routine activity and which staff members are responsible for implementing instruction and overseeing probes for data collection (Bricker & Cripe, 1992).

Learning centers as well as play and small group activities may be designed to augment transition skills (Snyder-McLean et al., 1984). Some typical activities include playing school, riding a pretend school bus, putting on gym shoes for gym class, and cleaning up after art or construction activities. Also helpful in skill acquisition and carryover is the introduction prior to transition of materials (e.g., schoolboxes), family/home communication practices (e.g., daily home–school notebook), sitting positions (e.g., on the floor, with or without boundaries; at tables), and games similar to those to be found in future environments. If only one or two kindergartens receive graduating preschool children, a class field trip to the playground(s) allows both discussion regarding the concept of recess and the opportunity to practice outdoor play skills that may be helpful.

BEGINNING CHILD PREPARATION

The previous pages have outlined a number of strategies for preparing young children with special needs for transition into new classrooms or programs. But, how does a teacher or early interventionist get started? What tasks need to be accomplished to ensure that each child is adequately prepared for upcoming transitions?

A four-step action sequence will accomplish this goal of child preparation for transition. The early interventionist(s) or preschool teacher(s) guides the process with suggestions, feedback, and assistance from parents, team members, and the receiving staff. The process runs as follows.

Assess

- Assess the receiving program(s) to which "graduates" may go, utilizing materials distributed to parents as well as classroom visits and interviews to learn which skills are appreciated in children who enroll there (see Figure 8.2; Carta et al., 1990; Hains et al., 1989).

- Assess the present program to facilitate a comparison of practices and suggest ways to adapt present practices in helping children bridge to other programs (see Table 8.3; Carta et al., 1988; Vincent et al., 1980; Walker & Rankin, 1983).
- Assess the child regarding both coping and learning-to-learn skills that are important for transition (see Tables 9.3 and 9.4) and subsequently probe the child's understandings about the upcoming move (Chandler, 1992).
- Assess the entire class or caseload to determine which practices may be altered to facilitate the preparation of every child for his or her future environment(s) (Fowler, 1978; Vincent et al., 1980).
- Assess parents' preferences regarding transition skills to be emphasized (see Chapter 7).
- Assess community resources to determine which can be enlisted in helping to prepare children for transition (NASBE, 1991). A community resource directory, like the one illustrated in Appendix E, can aid in this effort.

Plan

- Plan parent–professional partnership in preparing children for transition while honoring individual family differences (Lynch & Hanson, 1992). If parents wish, plan to incorporate intervention activities into daily routines at home.
- Plan with the team (including involved parents) IFSP or IEP outcomes and goals relating to transition for each child and family. These can then be inserted into a daily class and home schedule via matrix planning, as shown in Figures 9.4 and 9.5.
- Plan activities and strategies to accomplish transition goals for individual children as well as the entire class or caseload (Figure 9.6).
- Plan (with families) to use community resources in accomplishing transition-related goals.
- Plan to evaluate the preparatory activities for each child in order to learn whether they have been effective. Such activities may include: testing for general development, assessing children's progress with regard to IFSP or IEP goals, identifying the impact of preparatory activities on the overall class or caseload, evaluating parental satisfaction, and seeking reactions of both sending and receiving teachers.

Implement

- Implement transition activities for the entire class or caseload, including activities to: 1) help children understand change, and

Staff responsible for oversight and data collection: MR, TP, DS, SS

TARGETED OBJECTIVES

CLASSROOM ACTIVITIES	Greet adults/peers; make eye contact	Play/work cooperatively	Independence in toileting	Independence in hand washing	Attention to task	Express feelings appropriately	Initiate to peer	Request assistance from adults	Clean up play or work space
Arrival	Pippa, Paul, Sammy-TP								
Play		Joey, Jenna, Jody-DS				Joey, Kate-DS	Phillip-DS		
Bathroom			Josh, Jacob, Shawndell-SS	Ramon, Megan-MR				Joey-SS	
Breakfast							Phillip-DS	Joey-DS	
Play		Joey, Jody, Peter-DS				Joey, Kate-MR		Joey-DS	Joey-MR
Explore small group					Sammy, Alexander-MR				Joey-MR
Build small group					Tisha, Anthony-TP			Joey-TP	Joey-TP
Science small group					Susan, Todd-DS			Joey-DS	Joey-DS

Outside play		Joey, Peter, Samantha-SS				Joey, Kate-SS	Roger-SS		Joey-SS
Art					Randy, Alexander-DS				Joey-DS
Story, music									
Bathroom			Josh, Jacob, Shawndell-TP	Ramon, Megan-TP			Roger, Stephen-TP	Joey-TP	
Lunch								Joey-TP	
Music									
Nap									
Bathroom			Josh, Jacob, Shawndell-TP	Ramon, Megan-TP					
Snack							Stephen	Joey	
Play		Joey, Samantha, Peter-SS					Stephen-SS	Joey-SS	
Leave taking	Pippa, Paul, Sammy-SS								

Figure 9.6. Classroom intervention plan.

2) teach a few chosen skills such as cooperative learning and asking for help.
- Implement intervention regarding particular skills that are identified in individual children's IFSPs or IEPs.
- Assist families in implementing activities designed to support transition skills training at home.
- Provide assistance to adults in other community programs who are involved in transition activities.

Evaluate

- Follow the previously specified evaluation plan.
- Assess whether planning occurred for every child making a transition.
- Determine whether each IFSP and IEP adequately addressed transition planning.
- Collate and analyze the results obtained by evaluating all child preparation activities and recommend improvements for the following year.

A PRACTICAL APPROACH

Applying the ***assess-plan-implement-evaluate*** framework in transition planning will help teachers and early interventionists structure preparatory activities for each child as well as for the class or caseload as a whole. It will help to ensure that pre-transition activities continue as part of transition planning and that these activities are relevant to individual needs. Sharing information regarding children after their future placements have been determined is important for promoting continuity. With parental permission, the sending staff forwards to the receiving staff both a summary report regarding the child and a copy of his or her current IFSP or IEP. The community's transition plan should include a procedure as well as a timeline for this information exchange. It is imperative that the report be made available to the staff members who will be assuming direct responsibility for the child; this should be accomplished prior to the child's arrival in the new program. Table 9.6 on page 160 outlines a format and contents suggested for inclusion in the summary report. This report describes steps that have been taken in preparing the child for his or her new environment as it outlines transition skills mastered and delineates others for which continuing support and instruction will be necessary.

Sylvia's parents are working with school district personnel to ensure ongoing physical and speech therapy for their daughter who has Down syndrome after she enrolls in preschool at St. Patrick's.

In the meantime, the family's early interventionist is coordinating the transition activities that are outlined in Sylvia's IFSP. She has talked at length with the family regarding the transition process and has arranged for Sylvia's parents to meet with the parents of a child with an orthopedic disability who are also trying to work with both the diocese and the school district. Ninety days prior to Sylvia's third birthday, a meeting will be held with representatives from Sylvia's family, the early intervention program, the school district, and St. Patrick's Preschool.

The family along with the home visitor are working toward the learning outcomes identified as important for Sylvia's transition. In addition to outlining specific strategies to accomplish these goals, they devised a matrix (see Figure 9.3) to determine how learning activities could be assimilated into the family's daily routines. For instance, they planned a routine in which Mrs. Schmidt places a variety of small toys near the changing table and moves them into position for Sylvia to manipulate as her diaper is being changed. The home visitor has also modeled ways for Mrs. Schmidt to reinforce Sylvia's engagement with a toy during diapering.

Because Sylvia has difficulty being separated from her parents and siblings, she and her mother are participating in a neighborhood playgroup with other toddlers and their mothers. In time, Sylvia will learn to play in the playgroup without her mother being present.

The family is also working with their early interventionist in helping Sylvia to give up her pacifier. They believe that the use of a pacifier at St. Patrick's Preschool would cause other children to call Sylvia a "baby." Obviously, they want to prevent this.

Now, only halfway through the pre-transition year, Sylvia's family is already grateful that a good plan is guiding the upcoming transition.

* * *

Joey will move next month from the local hospital's childcare center to a kindergarten that offers continuing intervention for his language and social needs. David Scott, Joey's childcare teacher, consulted with the early childhood special educator and used the *assess-plan-implement-evaluate* system in preparing Joey and his classmates for transition.

David visited the classroom that Joey was likely to enter and took note of the teacher's expectations and routines. He then assessed his own program and compared the two. Both programs featured an organizational structure that provided significant opportunities for children to choose their own activities. That similarity would, in turn, ease students' transition. David noticed that the kindergarten teacher required children to take complete responsibility for their own work materials, to carefully replace chairs under tables after use, and to sit on the floor during large group activities without carpet squares or any other type of individual boundary marker. He also noticed that the kindergarten teacher emphasized cooperative learning, with children frequently problem-solving in pairs. Similarly, he noted that the teacher asked children to write their names in the upper, right hand corner of their papers.

After visiting the kindergarten classroom, David thought about what Joey and the other children would need to learn in order to take care of their materials, sit on the floor without boundary markers, and work cooperatively for paired problem-solving. He planned activities to teach children the necessary skills and provided many opportunities for practice. He talked with the kindergarten teacher about ways in which the kindergarten classroom could be adapted to be more familiar to the incoming children. After she visited David's childcare class, the kindergarten teacher decided to provide a taped "X" on the floor for each child. Although Joey was not yet able to write his name using conventional letters, David began writing Joey's name in the upper, right hand corner of his papers and encouraged Joey to copy it. Without pressuring him, this practice would acquaint Joey with both the correct shapes of and the desired locations for the letters of his name.

Mimi Shrove—the school's special educator—administered the Battelle Developmental Inventory to Joey. She also evaluated Joey's performance with regard to the "Skills Which Ease Kindergarten Entry" checklist, excepting "walking in line" and "hand raising" because they were not required in the kindergarten classroom. As a result of the evaluation, David learned of Joey's developmental age as well as strengths and needs in various traditional areas. He also discovered that Joey needed to learn how to ask for help and how to move from one activity to another without creating a disturbance in the classroom. In a conversation with Joey's mother, David learned that she wanted Joey to do a better job of putting away his clothes and toys at home. Because these skills are also expected in kindergarten, Joey's mother was pleased to work with the childcare staff in teaching them to Joey; they even showed her how to get started. David himself was eager for the 4-year-old to learn how to zip his coat and put on his mittens independently because the childcare center was intending to begin taking the children to a gymnastics program at a local church on a daily basis. Indeed, Joey's independence in self-care would make the trips easier during the late winter months.

David planned to work with Joey's mother and the special educator to introduce and develop the skills that Joey would need next year. Together, they wrote IEP objectives for Joey's particular transition needs.

David and the special educator ascertained that most of the children in Joey's class had difficulty moving between activities, that cooperative toy pick-up was a need expressed by many of their parents, and that, with cold weather approaching, most children had limited zipping skills. David planned both classroom activities and routines to teach targeted skills to all his students and a systematic sequence to teach specific ways in which Joey could ask for assistance during natural classroom activities. He planned some ways for Joey's mom to promote work on the transition objectives at home, and he consulted her regarding how these methods could be assimilated into the family's daily activities. Since Joey wears thick glasses, David called the school's vision specialist and enlisted suggestions for teaching Joey to zip. He then shared these ideas with the rest of the childcare staff and Joey's mother.

David determined specific dates and delineated ways for evaluating Joey's transition preparation. He also made long-term plans for reading books on transition and doing transition-related activities that will help Joey and his classmates to anticipate moving into their new kindergarten programs.

In cooperation with other members of Joey's IEP team, David carried out his plans for the entire class, integrating critical transition skills into daily routines. He used more capable peers to model classroom behaviors that would be valuable in kindergarten. He showed children how to watch others for cues if they didn't understand directions given to groups of children.

David taught Joey how to ask for help when he didn't understand instructions and subsequently set up classroom situations that made assistance-seeking necessary. A great deal of guided practice was required for Joey to learn this and similar skills. Later, David set up situations elsewhere in the center that required Joey to ask the cook, janitor, and secretary for help on various occassions. Joey initially progressed well with his new skills, but ultimately plateaued. David used the "Evaluating Children's Progress in Carrying Over Skills Important for Transition" checklist to refine his instructional plan, and Joey again improved.

David next invited Joey's mother to observe the way in which children were taught to pick up toys at school. He helped her in developing a workable system of toy retrieval for the family. He subsequently visited with Joey's mother periodically, noting Joey's progress on each of the targeted skills.

With David's leadership, the childcare staff evaluated Joey's achievement regarding his transition objectives. They also discussed the impact of transition planning on the entire class. Use of the matrix planning system brought David's present class closer to attaining their targeted goals than any previous class. Working with individual pupils on critical transition skills did not harm other students because it was integrated into daily routines. Indeed, Joey typically worked on assistance-seeking during snack, restroom, and freeplay periods, as planned in his individual matrix. David found that Joey's mother was pleased with her son's progress and thus was eager to work with David on additional skills that Joey may need in kindergarten.

When he first moved to the city, Joey needed individual cues, a high degree of physical assistance, and frequent hugs and individual praise after accomplishing tasks. However, as the year progressed, David reduced (but did not eliminate) the individual attention given to Joey. Indeed, group cues, verbal rather than physical guidance, group encouragement, or perhaps a grin from across the room are more typical practices in kindergarten.

After the decision regarding Joey's placement was reached, David arranged for him and his mother to visit the new school in the company of the special educator whom they already knew. Joey was delighted to hear the kindergartners reciting *Brown Bear, Brown Bear,* which was one of his favorite books in preschool.

Joey is eager to begin kindergarten. In addition to his positive attitude, Joey is fortunate to have learned many of the important transition skills that will help him to succeed. Both of these outcomes occurred because Joey's childcare provider, parent, therapist, vision specialist, special education consultant, and future kindergarten teacher worked together to prepare Joey for his transition into kindergarten.

Table 9.6. Elements of a summary report

Child and family demographic information
- Child's name, address, birth date, chronological age, present placement, present disability/area of exceptionality (if identified in current program), parents' names and address(es)

Initial referral information

Medical information related to the child's ability to function in future environments

Description of current program
- List of special services received
- Names of program staff members who have worked with the child
- Names of resource persons who have been especially helpful to family and school in planning for the child

Developmental skills: a general summary
- Current skills (preacademic/academic, motor, language, self-help, coping, and learning to learn) and conditions under which they are demonstrated
- Curriculum materials used
- Degree of teacher guidance required
- Amount of reinforcement needed and specific type(s) of reinforcement that is most effective
- Some recent tasks performed well (to be introduced on the first day of the new program to promote security) and suggestions of future tasks in the sequence
- List of preferred and disliked topics and activities (academic and play); preferred activities may be used as rewards after difficult tasks in the new classroom

Social skills summary
- Current social skills
- Degree of initiations to peers (familiar and unfamiliar)
- Degree of maintenance of interactions

(continued)

Table 9.6. *(continued)*

Problem behaviors and effective prevention and management strategies for them
Social situations that are especially difficult

Summary of IEP or IFSP goals and tasks completed
Include relevant dates

List of current classroom goals

Recommendations for future goals

Summary of IEP or IFSP

Parental concerns and suggestions

General comments and recommendations

Date report prepared: name, position, address, and phone number of person who prepared the report and/or whom to contact for more information

IMPLICATIONS

This chapter describes the roles of the early interventionist, teacher, family (if they choose), therapists, and other adults in preparing young children to move successfully into new service settings. Such preparation comprises two elements: 1) providing children with information, concrete experiences, positive comments regarding new schools, and opportunities to ask questions and express reactions prior to transition; and 2) teaching children routines and coping skills that will be useful in new programs. These activities are based on information gathered from receiving programs and are carefully planned to accomplish children's transition goals. The IFSP or IEP developed during the year prior to transition should include plans to prepare children for movement between and into service programs.

This chapter also presents a framework to be used by early childhood professionals to organize preparatory activities for every child as well as to share information between sending and receiving programs.

10

Receiving the Child

Moving In

Planned or not, transitions occur; ready or not, children and their families move into new programs; prepared or not, program personnel enroll and teach new children with disabilities.

Sylvia, a child with Down syndrome, is entering St. Patrick's Preschool next week. The preschool staff is preparing to welcome Sylvia along with all the other incoming 3-year-olds.

* * *

Joey will start at the Highpoint School kindergarten tomorrow. The kindergarten teacher and speech-language therapist at Highpoint are ready to receive Joey from the local hospital's childcare center and launch him in elementary school. Some modifications have been planned in advance that should help Joey to learn. Others will be implemented as necessary.

* * *

Micah is eager to attend pre-kindergarten just like his friend who lives next door. He will spend half the day in a class for children with hearing impairments and half the day in the regular pre-kindergarten classroom with his neighborhood friends. Micah's parents and the early intervention staff have done all that they can to initiate Micah's schooling. Now it is up to the receiving staffs to carry the transition forward.

* * *

Twelve 3- and 4-year-olds with special needs will begin in the Somerset Children's Center next week. Somerset's parent organization and school board have decided to provide more inclusive services. Seven children previously served in a segregated pre-

school will attend the Children's Center along with 80 other preschool-age children, including some with special needs, already enrolled there. A special education teacher and a paraprofessional will join the staff at the Center and will participate on teams in classrooms where the children with special needs will be served. Careful planning has guided each of these transitions, and everyone is eager for the new children to arrive. Regardless, several perplexing issues may arise.

* * *

Lexi transferred to the local preschool from another state earlier this week. She brought no records or previous IEPs with her, though her mother says that Lexi attended a special education preschool before they moved. Observations of Lexi in her wheelchair suggest that she will qualify for special education services in this state as well. The Concordia school district has some quick work to do to ease the transition for Lexi's family and to start Lexi in services as soon as possible.

It is certain that the issue of continuity in the early years extends beyond preparatory activities for children and their families. Accommodation and adaptation by receiving personnel are extremely important for smooth transitions between services. Receiving programs must promote and support continuity for children and their families by examining potential activities at both the interagency and intraagency levels. This chapter discusses several practical suggestions for serving individual children and their families after transition.

THE INTERAGENCY TRANSITION AGREEMENT

As discussed in Chapter 4, the development of local transition agreements facilitates transitions for children and their families. These agreements combine the responsibilities of the receiving staff with those of the sending staff and parents in joint transition planning. They subsequently minimize stress and decrease the number of last-minute adjustments necessary for the receiving staff. The community's interagency transition agreement should delineate individual responsibilities for promoting the successful assimilation and adjustment of children to new programs and classrooms.

Administrators

The administrators of receiving programs should:

- Ensure that assessment is complete, eligibility determined, IFSPs and/or IEPs written, and transportation and other arrangements

finalized so as to allow children to begin services on appropriate days.
- Expedite (prior to the entry dates) both the purchase of special equipment and materials and the provision of necessary staff training to support children's learning.
- Provide release time for staff to attend IFSP and/or IEP conferences, to visit sending programs, and to confer with parents as well as personnel from sending programs.
- Ensure that families know whom to contact for information prior to entry and subsequently are properly welcomed into new programs.
- Ensure that classroom teachers and therapists receive reports from sending staff prior to children's arrival.
- Ensure that transitions are evaluated properly.

Teachers

Similarly, teachers in receiving programs have transition-related responsibilities:

- Learn about the curricula and philosophies with which incoming children and families have been served.
- Observe children with special needs functioning in their respective sending environments.
- Attend the IFSP and/or IEP meetings prior to transitions, when outcomes, goals, and objectives are planned.
- Welcome children and their families to pre-transition visits in the new classrooms and learn about interests and preferences.
- Meet children's parents prior to the transitions and learn about their values and priorities.
- Work with the sending programs, families, school systems, and outside agencies to ensure that needed equipment, furniture, and assistive technology are available for use on children's first days in their new programs.
- Develop expertise in addressing any unique needs of children.
- Obtain and carefully review records of children's development in previous programs.
- On children's first days in new programs, plan activities that promote continuity and encourage self-confidence, security, and friendship among all children in the class.

Therapists

Likewise, therapists in receiving programs benefit from conversations with sending therapists and parents regarding:

- The nature of children's disabilities
- Effective intervention strategies
- Children's preferences and fears
- Past IFSP outcomes or IEP goals and objectives for individual children
- Proven ways of including therapy both in families' daily routines and in classroom routines

The information gained can be immediately applied in making children's first days in new programs successful and in continuing their progress in learning.

The interagency collaboration prompted by activities such as these does, however, require time and expense. Therefore, these activities must be included in local interagency agreements that have been endorsed by agency administrators.

GRADUAL INTRODUCTIONS

On occasion, a child will benefit greatly from gradual introduction into a new program (i.e., reduced lengths of time or days in attendance per week, or split attendance between sending and receiving programs). If one of these approaches is likely to promote success for a child in a less restrictive manner, then the local interagency agreement should allow for deviations from standard enrollment practices. Such individualized approaches may be necessary (for some children) in addition to the routine transition activities like toddler transition playgroups (see Appendix D).

INFORMATION SHARING

Parents and children benefit most when the entire staff—including paraprofessionals, aides, and assistants—receive factual information and an orientation to the particular characteristics of children's abilities and disabilities as well as the families' preferences. Sending program personnel and participating parents may contribute significantly to an orientation such as this (see Chapters 8 and 9). This information sharing should disclose any potential restrictions or necessary health procedures. Regarding procedures for children with complex health care needs, training in health management should be provided by certified personnel according to prescribed protocol. Subsequent practice should be supervised and monitoring procedures must be developed (see Chapter 11). If key staff members have no previous experience with children with a specific disability, they may need more lengthy orientation and perhaps active support from special education personnel during the first weeks of school. Resource libraries in most states provide print as well as multi-media materials to introduce the characteristics of specific disabilities, aid novice teachers in the management of particular conditions, and guide in the development of effective instruction for an atypical learner within a group setting. Again, personnel from the sending agencies may share valuable expertise. As an increasing number of childcare programs, Head Start centers, and community programs serve children with special needs, they should stand ready both to seek and to share information and training with early intervention and special education personnel.

Resistance to Information Sharing from Parents

Parents occasionally want their children's records to be withheld in order that new teachers may form opinions independently. Whenever records are exchanged, they should always be evaluated carefully with regard to their relevance for present educational decision-making; new teachers should always look at children's current levels of performance, not merely at historical data. With every child, however, the patterns and challenges observed in earlier development can be very useful to new teachers in understanding present behaviors. Therefore, careful explanations of developmental continuity and differences in learning styles may cause parents to embrace the wisdom of information sharing. Of course, parents have the right to examine any information to be shared, and information cannot be shared across agencies without parental permission.

Resistance to Sharing from Sending Personnel

When transitions from special education to community-based programs are underway, staff members from the sending program may hesitate to share information with non–special educators, even if parental permission is obtained. Relevance is an appropriate issue here as well. However, in order to implement intervention activities, everyone working on a daily basis with the child should be aware of his or her goals and objectives. Obtaining parental permission to share information with the community-based team should therefore allay agency concerns about confidentiality.

Receiving Professionals' Resistance to Reading the Reports of Others

Receiving teachers and therapists occasionally wish to remain "unbiased," not wanting to know anything about a child's previous learning patterns or goals. However, current levels of performance certainly provide critical information (included in the sending program's report), as does a summary of each child's individual learning style. Data can be discounted if evidence from the receiving program suggests such action, but every piece of information that could potentially be useful in understanding and teaching the child should be considered.

Receiving personnel should freely contact personnel from the sending program to arrange consultations to facilitate joint problem-solving during the first months in a new program. Sending staff members have worked with children and their families for many months or even years and therefore often have valuable insights regarding program planning and suggestions for aiding children's adjustment to new settings. Telephone conversations between sending and receiving teachers after a child has begun a new program can be useful in answering questions and resolving minor dilemmas before they become major problems.

STARTING TO TEACH

Even if interagency planning does not occur, the receiving staff can take steps to promote continuity for children and their families (Balaban, 1985; Caldwell, 1990; Golant & Golant, 1990). Some of the most unsettling elements of transition are obvious and are thus rather easy to analyze (Jervis, 1984; McCracken, 1986). Leaving good friends—adults as well as children—and meeting strangers in a new setting causes uncertainty for children as well as their parents. The new building may look different; it may be larger, more crowded, and noisier; the rules may even be different. Most of the children are bigger than the incoming child, and many of them seem to know where they are going and why. In many cases, parents wonder if their child will be able to measure up to the expectations of the new program (Gwost, 1992). Anxiety for young children and their families often results from these changes. The poem on page 169 addresses some concerns of children that need to be addressed either directly or indirectly.

Certainly, a positive orientation and generous explanations are required here. A child's arrival at a new school entails an introduction to a large number of new routines, rules, and locations. Some rules and regulations require immediate introduction, whereas others may be gradually explained, as real life situations necessitate. A study by Rosenkoetter (1990b) shows that kindergarten teachers spend as much as 2 hours on the first day of school introducing classroom rules, in all likelihood conveying more information than most young children are able to process at one time.

The First Day of School

Will they let me go when I need to
  go to the bathroom?
And what if I get lost on my way
  back to class?
And what if all of the other kids are
  a hundred, a thousand, a million
  times smarter than I am?
And what if we have a spelling test,
  or a reading test, or an . . .
  anything test, and I'm the only
  person who doesn't pass?

And what if my teacher decides
  that she doesn't like me?
And what if, all of a sudden,
  a tooth gets loose?
And what if I can't find my lunch,
  or I step on my lunch, or I (oops!)
  drop my lunch down someplace
  like the toilet?
Will they just let me starve or will
  somebody lend me a sandwich?
A cookie? A cracker? An apple?
  Some juice?

And what if they say, "Do this,"
  and I don't understand them?
And what if there's teams, and
  nobody picks me to play?
And what if I took off my sneakers,
  and also my socks, and also my
  jeans, and my sweatshirt and
  T-shirt,
And started the first day of school
  on the second day?

Presenting classroom practices through stories, modeling, role playing, simulations, or other tangible supports assists children with special needs in coping with both the strangeness of a new situation and the wealth of new information to be learned in the new classroom (Safford, 1989).

Differences Between Home and School

Somewhat more challenging to address are the cultural and curricular elements to which children and families must adjust during transition. Rich histories, experiences, and learnings accompany children and their families when they enter new service programs. In some families, many of these experiences are congruent with a school's expectations. In others, early childhood experiences are rich in stimulation but employ different activities, alternative relational patterns, and perhaps different languages and child-rearing practices than schools typically use with young children (Fillmore, 1992; Heath, 1983). The challenge for receiving teachers is to learn enough about the child's home environment to bridge the gap between it and the new one at school (Lynch & Hanson, 1992). As discussed in Chapter 8, home visits, conversations with parents, and written surveys help teachers to learn about individual family values and priorities and subsequently promote ongoing parental involvement in their children's schooling.

Cultural and Curricular Differences Between the Sending and Receiving Programs

Similarly, the milieu of the previous child care, preschool, or Head Start may be congruent with that of the new environment, or it may differ dramatically (Caldwell, 1990; Love et al., 1992). Without question, effective transitions require curricular bridge-building by receiving as well as sending program personnel (NAESP, 1990; USDOE, 1991). The challenge for the receiving staff—administrators, teachers, therapists, and paraprofessionals—is to make the child's first weeks in the new program congruent with previous experiences. The classrooms of preschool programs and the early grades, respectively, "should look different but should not feel so terribly different to young children" (Kagan, 1991a, p. 8).

Increasingly, local areas (e.g., Greenville, SC, and Miami, FL) and even entire states (e.g., Nebraska and Missouri) are promoting the adoption of a common curricular approach across the early childhood years so that preschool and primary-age children may learn without major changes in instructional approaches (Barbour & Seefeldt, 1993; SERVE, 1992). This approach requires that both the organization and presentation of learning activities and the ways in which children are expected to respond remain constant, thus contributing significantly to feelings of familiarity and competence during transition (Barbour & Seefeldt, 1993).

Similarly, a single receiving teacher or therapist may act independently in promoting continuity. This receiving professional may observe a sending program in operation or solicit suggestions from its personnel regarding ways to promote continuity for children. For instance, if a teacher or a therapist can find out which materials, routines, books, songs, or games a child was working with in his or her previous environment, these items can be used to facilitate transition into future programs.

ASSESS-PLAN-IMPLEMENT-EVALUATE

Receiving teachers attempting to incorporate one or more children with special needs into their classrooms can use an ***assess-plan-implement-evaluate*** approach similar to the one recommended (in Chapter 9) for sending programs. Such a system—adapted for receiving programs—is outlined as follows.

Assess

- Observe the program(s) from which students have come, read materials distributed to parents, and interview staff members regarding their respective curricula and practices.
- Observe one's own program to compare curricula and practices. This will suggest ways for adapting the present classroom to help incoming children.
- Observe children both directly during a classroom visit and indirectly through reports from professionals and parents. Include observations of coping and learning-to-learn skills important during transition (see Chapter 9).
- Analyze information about the rest of the class to determine what practices might be altered to facilitate the successful inclusion of all incoming children.
- Solicit parents' preferences regarding which transition skills to emphasize (see Chapter 7).
- Consider community resources, such as recreation programs or childcare providers, that may help to support children's developing competence and confidence in the new environment. Use of a community resource directory such as the one shown in Appendix E of this volume may be helpful.

Plan

- Plan partnerships with parents to help children succeed in the new school; include communication plans and home–school carryover (see Chapter 7).

- Plan to teach to the entire class classroom procedures and learning-to-learn skills.
- Plan to continue or expand the IFSP outcomes or IEP goals that are related to successful adjustment in new settings. These can be inserted into a daily class plan via matrix planning, as shown in Figure 9.6.
- Plan activities to accomplish transition goals for individual children as well as the class as a whole.
- Plan to use community resources in accomplishing transition-related goals.
- Plan how to evaluate to determine whether transition activities have been effective.

Implement

- Welcome children and their families (see Chapter 8 for relevant suggestions).
- Implement transition activities for the entire class, including activities to introduce new people and new practices, and teach selected transition skills such as gaining the teacher's attention and putting identifying marks or names on papers.
- Implement intervention to target the objectives identified in individual IFSPs or IEPs.
- Assist families in implementing activities that they request to support skills learning at home.
- Assist adults involved in other community programs who are helping with individual transition plans.

Evaluate

- Carry out the evaluation plan.
- Determine whether planning occurred for every child making a transition.
- Determine whether local IFSP and IEP development adequately included transition planning.
- Collate and analyze the results of evaluating local orientation activities.
- Recommend improvements in the transition process for the following year.

ADAPTING THE CLASSROOM TO FIT THE CHILD

The ***assess-plan-implement-evaluate*** approach involves attending to the characteristics of individual children while considering the demands of the classroom environment (i.e., physical, social, cognitive/pre-academic, and behavioral characteristics; resources for assistance and coping; and performance expectations). The goal is to facilitate a match between each child's developmental level and the readiness of a school to teach him or her in various domains (Graue, 1993).

Some common ways to achieve this match include the following modifications:

- Changing instructional methods and/or materials (Cook, Tessier, & Klein, 1992)
- Providing additional peer and/or adult support (Allen, 1992; Stainback & Stainback, 1992)
- Changing expectations (Baker & Brightman, 1989; Baumgart et al., 1982; Orelove & Sobsey, 1991)
- Adapting the physical environment (Mulligan et al., 1992)
- Instituting assistive technology (Church & Glennen, 1992)
- Altering the daily schedule (Spodek, Saracho, & Lee, 1984)

Any of these modifications can apply to the class as a whole, to a small group of children, or to an individual child. They can be applied singly or in combination. A modification may be temporary (instituted only while a child adjusts to new surroundings) or permanent (maintained for as long as he or she remains in a particular classroom). Many of these modifications will also assist peers who are not students receiving special education (Safford, 1989).

Tabitha is a 3-year-old who was born without arms. Her hands extend from the sides of her shoulders. Tabitha is becoming quite skillful in using her legs and feet; she even performs some fine motor tasks like drawing with her toes. In developmental areas not affected by her physical disability, Tabitha excels. Her language, problem-solving, and preacademic skills are more than 2 years above levels expected for her chronological age.

Tabitha's parents didn't want her to attend a special education program. Instead, they enrolled her in Somerset's Children's Center. The teachers consider Tabitha's special needs in planning every activity, but their plans are most often modified to allow children greater latitude in completing tasks. For example, children may choose to do puzzles and art activities either at a table or on the floor *(changed expectations);* Tabitha and several other children always choose the floor. When an activity requires cutting, children may use scissors independently or ask for help *(additional peer support);* Tabitha always requests assistance. As the

only reader in her class, however, she reads books to friends during story time, thereby helping them to enjoy that activity more. Although Tabitha wants to be independent in hand washing, she is unable to reach the faucets. Thus, she now has a "pusher stick" *(assistive technology)* that allows her to activate the faucets.

Because Tabitha tires easily, her *schedule has been altered* so that she may take a 15-minute mid-morning rest each day. In subtle ways, the *physical environment has also been changed* to allow Tabitha to reach various toys and books that she chooses. The staff and students also try to keep the floors tidy because Tabitha often walks on them barefoot.

Deciding whether to *change instructional materials or methods* is a dilemma frequently faced by Tabitha's teachers. However, they often opt to provide physical support to Tabitha as needed because she is becoming self-reliant in ways that the staff had never anticipated. For instance, she feeds herself finger food with her toes when she tires of stretching to use her hands. In fact, after a discussion of Tabitha's "amazing" skills last week, other children attempted—unsuccessfully—to eat with their toes.

Her classmates like Tabitha. They accommodate her special needs and spend little time noting her differences. She is thus learning to cope successfully in the "real" world.

Activity Profile

A profile of a typical day in an early childhood classroom may elicit any of the following four types of structures for each time slot (Giangreco, Cloninger, & Iverson, 1992):

Same All the children participate in the same activity with the same curricular emphasis and objectives. For example, everyone verbally greets the teacher each morning with the goal of practicing a valued social skill.

Multi-level All the children participate in the same activity or lesson but at different levels. For example, although everyone greets the teacher each morning, some do it by signing, some by using a communication board, and some by speaking. Some speakers use single words, whereas others use longer utterances; alternatively, some speak without prompts, and still others speak only after being prompted.

Curriculum Overlapping All children participate in the same activity, but each has a different objective. For instance, one child has the objective of making eye contact (rather than greeting) during the arrival routine.

Alternative One or more children participate in an alternative activity, rather than in the general class activity; they in turn have different objectives than their classmates. For example, one child may go directly to the gymnasium for physical therapy on Mondays and not participate in the greeting routine with her peers.

Desirable Skills

Certain skills (see Tables 9.3 and 9.4) are highly valued during transition because they aid children's adjustment to and learning in new settings. However, many children entering new programs, including some without identified disabilities, lack some or all of these skills. The ***assess-plan-implement-evaluate*** approach provides a way for the receiving staff to promote individual as well as group development of these transition skills while achieving more traditional curricular goals. Each type of goal should be targeted for intervention, written into the new IFSP or IEP, taught individually as well as in groups, and subsequently evaluated. The so-called "learning-to-learn" skills are extremely important here because they allow children to build relationships with adults and other children and subsequently to profit from the educational interactions that result (Carta et al., 1992).

COUPLING INTERVENTION WITH CLASSROOM ACTIVITIES

Teachers can use a matrix such as the one described in Chapter 9 in planning how IFSP and/or IEP objectives can be taught and practiced during group activities throughout the school day. Activity-based intervention (Bricker & Cripe, 1992) and an integrated approach to curriculum development (Hohmann & Buckleitner, 1992; Trostle & Yawkey, 1990) will help children to apply and practice transition skills in various settings. Table 10.1 contains a list of strategies that are effective in providing additional support to children with special needs who are moving into less restrictive environments.

Some Transitions Are Lengthy

Although some children separate easily from their parents, not every 3-year-old can manage that developmental task in short order (Balaban, 1985; Cooper & Holt, 1982). Teaching a skill, procedure, or rule one time does not necessarily mean that all incoming children will master it immediately. Although most kindergarten teachers who were interviewed (Hains et al., 1989) tolerated children's incompetence on a host of skills upon initial entry into school, those same teachers expected most of those skills to be learned by December,

Table 10.1. Strategies that assist children in moving to less restrictive environments

Explanation—The teacher tells children what to do and why, and redirects inappropriate actions or prompts incomplete ones (Grusec, 1979; Kostelnik, Stein, Whiren, & Soderman, 1993; LeBlanc, 1982).

Direct demonstration or modeling—The teacher performs desired actions while verbalizing each step (Lovaas, 1977; Meichenbaum, 1977; Rowbury, 1982).

Reinforcement of desired behaviors with contingent praise—Through environmental manipulation, actions, or words, the teacher rewards a desired action while verbalizing that which has been accomplished (Essa, 1990; LeBlanc, 1982).

Task analysis—When a new routine or task is complex and thus difficult for a child to learn, the teacher breaks the desired skill into parts and teaches each part in sequence (Rowbury, 1982; Smith, Smith, & Edgar, 1976).

Role play—Children and adults "act out" appropriate as well as inappropriate actions for the class to discuss and/or emulate (Goldstein et al., 1988; Snyder-McLean et al., 1984; Wallace, 1992).

Verbal rehearsal—An adult repeats a sequence of tasks to be accomplished and encourages the child to do the same in order to self-prompt and self-monitor (Vygotsky, 1962, 1978).

Contracting/checksheets—A child and his or her teacher agree to adhere to a certain course of behavior in advance, and the child self-monitors using a checksheet; rewards follow successful completion (Cooper, Heron, & Hewerd, 1987; Hains, 1992).

Prompting or cuing—The teacher employs environmental and/or verbal reminders to the child to encourage desired actions; reminders may be verbal, visual, tactile/kinesthetic, or oral (LeBlanc, 1982; Rowbury, 1982; Snell & Zirpoli, 1987; Wolery et al., 1992).

Picture stimulus cards or icons—Color codes, photographs, line drawings, or pictographs cue the child regarding which materials should be used and/or what should be done with them (Curl, Rowbury, & Baer, 1985; High Scope, 1992).

Peer modeling—Either spontaneously or with training, a peer performs a desired action as the child's attention is called to the peer's movement (Goldstein & Kacsmarek, 1992; Kohler & Strain, 1990; Peck, Apolloni, Cook, & Raver, 1978).

Partnering—The child is paired with a more competent peer to carry out activities (Sainato, Strain, Lefebre, & Rapp, 1987).

Cooperative learning—Children with differing abilities and disabilities are grouped to work together in accomplishing learning goals (Cooper & Holt, 1982; Foyle, Lyman, & Thies, 1991; Johnson, Johnson, Holubee, & Roy, 1984).

Affection training—The teacher modifies typical early childhood games, songs, and activities to include affectionate responses; this brings children with disabilities together with those without disabilities during enjoyable activities (McEvoy, Twardosz, & Bishop, 1990).

Community building—Teachers employ a number of strategies that delineate the classroom as a caring community and subsequently promote the values, attitudes, and skills that make communities function effectively (Sapon-Shevin, 1990; Schaps & Solomon, 1990; Snow, 1991).

Grouping—Children are grouped across ages in attempts to facilitate peer teaching, the development of leadership skills, and the de-emphasis of uniform expectations regarding performance for all children of the same chronological age (Hunter, 1992; Katz, Evangelou, & Hartman, 1989).

and nearly all of them mastered by June. In some cases, satisfying such expectations requires an astounding rate of learning for children previously slow in acquiring new skills. Thus, teachers with uniformly high expectations are bound to be disappointed. Receiving teachers must remember that patience and continued effort results in eventual learning. Indeed, for some children, transition takes a very long time.

However, developing IFSP/IEP goals and instructional plans that target transition skills and coping (see Tables 9.3 and 9.4) can help in speeding transitions. Similarly, systematic attention as the result of IEP objectives will hasten the acquisition of skills useful for future transitions.

Supporting Families

A major change for families as their children grow older is the decrease in communication between home and school. The trend leads children and their families from home-based to center-based programs. In the latter, parents may transport children, volunteer frequently in the classroom, or visit regularly with the teacher by phone. Indeed, a small caseload often allows the teacher time to communicate regularly with all families. However, when the child reaches elementary school, class size grows larger, parental transportation is often not needed, and parent–teacher contact becomes less frequent. Parents' concern nonetheless continues; it may even increase during the early days after a child's transition into a new program.

This scenario helps to underscore the importance of sharing both general and child-specific information with parents regularly during periods of transition. As described in Chapter 7, it is also valuable to inform parents when and how the receiving teacher prefers to be contacted, what means will be used for communication, and which "rules" govern parents' navigation of the school system. For example, Joey's new teacher informed his mother that a class newsletter would be sent home on a weekly basis, that she would write a "Joey note" once a week, and that she would welcome the opportunity to have Joey's mother visit the classroom. She requested that phone calls be made to the school between 3:30 and 4:00 P.M. if Joey's mother had a particular question. The teacher also emphasized the importance of checking in at the school office prior to coming to the classroom. She explained that checking in serves as a security precaution designed to monitor who is in the school building at all times. It is intended to keep children safe from intruders. Every receiving teacher needs to communicate such guidelines to parents (in a friendly manner) in order to prevent confusion after transition.

Marcia Mullen, Sylvia's new teacher at St. Patrick's Preschool, has read the reports from Sylvia's early intervention program, met with her parents and previous teacher, and talked with a physical therapist regarding positioning. Marcia has also read several books and articles about Down syndrome, and was very eager to work with bright-eyed Sylvia.

After several weeks of school, Marcia commented that Sylvia is a "character, just like each of the other children." The little girl obviously loves coming to preschool and is "a joy" to have in class. The housekeeping area is her favorite place.

Modifications? Sylvia is very active and needs frequent activity changes. She needs "hands on" with everything; but, so do several other children. The hospital's speech therapist, whom Sylvia was seeing once a week, taught Marcia how to model short sentences designed to expand Sylvia's comments. Marcia now tries to work on language expansion every day in the housekeeping area. Sylvia has recently been toilet trained. Marcia therefore makes sure that the child gets to the bathroom at least once each hour, and then Marcia or her helper works with Sylvia on pulling up the child's pants.

Because Sylvia's family opted not to have an IEP, there are no formal goals or objectives. Marcia, nevertheless, designed a matrix to remind herself what is important for Sylvia at different times of the day.

* * *

Joey is doing well at the Highpoint School kindergarten. The group participation skills (included in the IEP that was developed during his last few months at the childcare center) have helped him enter kindergarten successfully. A speech-language therapist comes to the kindergarten regularly to work with Joey and several other children. She also consults with both Joey's teacher and mother regarding interactions to stimulate Joey's language development. In order to increase his social competence, the teacher often arranges for Joey to work with a partner in class. The teacher and Joey's mother have even worked out an efficient system of communication. Joey's mother likes his teacher and the new school. She feels welcome there.

* * *

Micah transferred from home-based services into a half-day prekindergarten program for children with hearing impairments. The program is highly structured, with its primary purpose being communication development. In the afternoon, Micah attends a play-based pre-kindergarten in his neighborhood school. His attendance there is designed to promote interactions with typically developing children. Micah and his family have thus had to adjust to two new programs, each being very different from the other.

Each program is quite clear regarding the primary purpose of its pre-kindergarten experience, which in turn helps Micah to cope with a tremendous amount of change. Both teachers stress the objectives that govern the purposes of their respective programs, and each meets with the parents twice per month in addition to frequent telephone conversations. A notebook is also circulated among the home and each classroom to share observations that may help in teaching Micah.

IMPLICATIONS

This chapter lists the roles of receiving programs in promoting positive transitions for incoming children and their families. Some of these roles are delineated in the interagency agreement and its transition timeline. Others are defined within classrooms as receiving teachers seek both to develop positive relationships with children and their families and to provide effective instruction by incorporating children with special needs into groups of typical peer learners. Transition planning requires that staff members of receiving programs work closely with those of sending programs as well as with families to ensure smooth program changes.

11

Creating Successful Transitions for Children with Complex Health Care Needs

New Friends on the Journey

Dianne Koontz Lowman
Sharon E. Rosenkoetter

Some of the terms that have been used to identify students with complex health care needs include children who are technology-dependent, children who are medically fragile, children with special health care needs, or children with chronic illnesses (American Academy of Pediatrics, 1990; Council for Exceptional Children, 1988; Koop, 1987; U.S. Congress, 1987). For the purposes of this chapter, however, the following definition will be utilized:

> Children with complex health care needs are children between the ages of birth and 21 years who have a chronic illness, who require technology or ongoing support to survive, and/or who require health-related procedures during the school day. Children with complex health

Dianne Koontz Lowman, M.S., is the Part H Training Coordinator at the Commonwealth of Virginia Early Intervention Office, Post Office Box 1797, Richmond, VA 23214.

care needs may or may not require special education (Bruder, 1990; Mulligan-Ault, Guess, Struth, & Thompson, 1988; Sirvis, 1988).

"Health-related procedures" refers to such things as conducting clean intermittent catheterization, administering nasogastric or gastrostomy feedings, oxygen monitoring, or tracheostomy care.

Scott will be entering Head Start at age 3. Services have been carefully planned and delineated in a cooperative agreement between Concordia's Special Education Division and the local Head Start. The family service coordinator from Scott's early intervention program and the staff at Head Start have been working together with Scott's father to ensure a smooth transition. Indeed, parents of participating children are always encouraged to be actively involved in their early childhood programs.

Scott was born after only 26 weeks gestation and as a result, had a very difficult first year of life. He will continue to need oxygen support after reaching the age of 3. Scott has a complex seizure condition (that is partially controlled by two medications), as well as cerebral palsy. Although his speech is limited to two-word utterances, he has made great progress during the past 6 months. Scott is fed through a gastrostomy tube, and moves by means of a travel chair. He is highly sociable and makes friends wherever he goes. He has visited the local Head Start with his father and is eager to begin.

Not so long ago, Scott's early education would have been provided at home, in a hospital, in a special classroom, or possibly even in a special school for children with "severe and multiple handicaps." Now, however, Scott will receive special preschool services while learning alongside typical peers at his neighborhood Head Start. Indeed, regulations disseminated by Head Start's national administration encourage the enrollment of children like Scott (Administration for Children and Families, 1993).

The Head Start staff has received training in order to accommodate Scott's medical needs. The school nurse, in consultation with Head Start's health coordinator, will oversee the administration of his medication. The teacher and the disabilities coordinator will oversee Scott's educational program as well as related services to be provided through special education. A paraprofessional will be near Scott throughout the day to support his needs and those of the children with whom Scott is playing.

Other children are a very important component of Scott's developmental plan. The staff at Head Start will work to help Scott learn just as other children do—through play and exploration with peers.

For children like Scott with complex health care needs, transition planning must begin very early to ensure that services are available to make the placement both safe and developmentally appropriate. If too little time is allotted for transition planning, the child with complex health care needs may be forced to accept a more restrictive placement simply to ensure his or her safety. Conversely, allowing adequate time during transition planning facilitates the preparation of both personnel and environments to meet individual children's needs as well as to address the concerns of families and professionals (Caldwell & Kirkhart, 1991).

IMPORTANT ISSUES TO BE CONSIDERED

Issues that must be addressed during transition planning for children with complex medical needs are listed in Table 11.1.

Concerns regarding children's safety are paramount in the minds of both parents and professionals (Lowman, 1992). Use of the health services plan discussed later in this chapter will help to ensure that individually appropriate health-related services are available to support the education and maintenance of children with complex health care needs during transition.

Administrators' concerns regarding possible litigation relating to liability for children with complex health care needs is the primary deterrent to providing services in less restrictive environments (Caldwell & Kirkhart, 1991). Table 11.2 provides a checklist of elements (for administrative consideration) designed to reduce the risks of placing children with complex health care needs in the least restrictive environments possible.

Table 11.1. Educational issues to consider in the transition of children with complex medical needs

1. Determining eligibility for special education services.
2. Providing related and non-educational services.
3. Assuring equal access to appropriate educational settings in the least restrictive environment.
4. Promoting a safe learning environment.
5. Assuring that health care services are delivered by appropriate and adequately trained personnel.
6. Establishing support systems for staff, students, and families.
7. Including appropriate information about students with specialized health care needs in inservice, preservice, and continuing education programs.
8. Providing appropriate and safe transportation.
9. Promoting research that assesses current and future delivery models.

From *The Report of the Council for Exceptional Children's Ad Hoc Committee on Medically Fragile Students* (pp. 2–6). Copyright 1988 by The Council for Exceptional Children. Reprinted with permission.

Table 11.2. Steps to ensure safety and to reduce the risk of liability litigation related to children with complex medical conditions

1. Obtain individualized prescriptions and protocols for procedures to be performed.
2. Review protocols approved by the physician with parents and have them sign the form indicating their agreement with the procedures outlined in the protocol.
3. Document that appropriate training based on protocols has occurred. Include persons' names, specific procedures demonstrated, and dates of scheduled rechecks.
4. Train anyone who will be involved in the child's care (e.g., the bus driver).
5. Establish contingency plans. Train other personnel who will take over when the major caregivers are not available and who will be available to assist the major caregiver in an emergency situation.
6. Include maintenance and emergency procedures in your training.
7. Develop plans with physicians and parents for the transport and provision of services in the local emergency room.
8. Inform agencies providing services to the school (i.e., electric and telephone companies) of the need for priority service restorations.
9. Provide information to agencies that will interact with the school during natural disasters (i.e., fire department, Red Cross) to inform them of the student's participation in that particular school and the needs that he or she will have during an emergency.
10. Effectively document needs and how they will be met in the IEP.

Adapted with permission from Caldwell, Todaro, & Gates (1989).

Administrative Issues

Training Training regarding daily routines as well as emergency procedures for everyone who will have contact with the child is a very significant element in the transition process. In fact, the key to increased competence and comfort for all staff members is typically training (Lehr, 1990). In addition to those who will share the primary responsibility of carrying out health-related procedures, at least one back-up person must also be trained for each relevant duty. Both professional and nonprofessional staff (e.g., bus drivers, monitors, and cafeteria personnel) are likely to require training (or retraining) based on individualized prescriptions and protocols for procedures to be performed (Caldwell, Todaro, & Gates, 1989). Specific information about this training is included in each child's health services plan. Both major and seemingly minor issues regarding the performance of a procedure should be addressed in a timely manner to avoid difficulties. For example, one team of educators was taught to administer medication through a gastrostomy tube, but ran into problems when faced with converting milliliters (the unit of measure on their directions) to cubic centimeters (the unit on their syringes).

A health care professional should oversee all training regarding the administration of health-related procedures. This professional may be a physician, a nurse from the hospital, the case manager from the health department, or the school nurse coordinator. It may also be helpful for parents to participate in the staff's training sessions. In this capacity, parents are able to monitor the training and personalize instructions for their child (Lowman, 1992). Indeed, effective training acknowledges the characteristics of both the child and the persons being trained. A list of training resources appears in Table 11.3.

Table 11.3. Resources for training persons to work with children with complex health care needs

Beckett, J. (1989). *Health care financing: A guide for families.* Iowa City, IA: The University of Iowa, National Maternal and Child Health Resource Center (Intended for families; valuable also for professionals).

Bilotti, G. (1984). *Getting children home: Hospital to community.* Washington, DC: Georgetown University Child Development Center.

Caldwell, T.H., Todaro, A.W., & Gates, A.J. (Eds.). (1989). *Community providers' guide: An information outline for working with children with special health needs.* New Orleans, LA: Children's Hospital, National MCH Resource Center.

Cohen, S., Bull, N., Bernheimer, C., & Breitenback, C. (1990). *A guide for planning for the psychological needs of the young chronically ill child and family: Post hospitalization.* Los Angeles: University of California, Department of Pediatrics.

Epstein, S.G., Taylor, A.B., Halberg, A.S., Gardner, J.D., Walker, D.K., & Crocker, A.C. (1989). *Enhancing quality: Standards and indicators of quality care for children with special health care needs.* Boston: New England SERVE.

Finnie, N.R. (1975). *Handling the young cerebral palsied child at home.* New York: E.P. Dalton.

Graff, L.C., Mulligan-Ault, M., Guess, D., Taylor, M., & Thompson, B. (1990). *Health care for students with disabilities: An illustrated medical guide for the classroom.* Baltimore: Paul H. Brookes Publishing Co.

Haynie, M., Porter, S.M., & Palfrey, J.S. (1989). *Children assisted by medical technology in educational settings: Guidelines for care.* Boston: The Children's Hospital, Project School Care.

Heller, K.W., Alberto, P.A., Schwartzman, M.N., Shiplett, K., Pierce, J., Polokoff, J., Heller, E.J., Andrews, D.G., & Kana, T.G. (1990). *Suggested physical health procedures of students with special needs.* Atlanta: Georgia State University.

Katz, K.S., Pokorni, J.L., & Long, T. M. (1989). *Chronically ill and at risk infants: Family centered intervention from hospital to home.* Palo Alto, CA: VORT Corporation.

Quinn, J., & Jackson, B. (n.d.). *Case coordination: The project continuity model.* Omaha: University of Nebraska Medical Center, Meyer Rehabilitation Institute.

Urbano, M.T. (1992). *Preschool children with special health care needs.* San Diego, CA: Singular Publishing Group.

Videotapes and accompanying training manuals from Learner Managed Designs, 2201-K West 25th Street, Lawrence, KS 66047, 913-842-9088, on CPR and emergency choking procedures, positioning, feeding, use of home oxygen procedures, gastrostomy and tracheostomy care, clean intermittent catheterization, and apnea monitoring.

Planning Environmental Arrangements Environments must be accessible and free from hazards. Running water and special electrical outlets may need to be provided, and temperature and allergen control may require consideration in many cases. Materials commonly found in many early childhood special education classrooms (viz., sand, oil-based lotion, powder, styrofoam pieces) must be carefully monitored around children with tracheostomies. Provisions must be made for the storage of special equipment, such as an oxygen canister, a back-up ventilator, or the suction machine. Similarly, a private area should be designated for performing procedures such as catheterization or diapering. Environmental adaptations such as these must be planned in advance (Caldwell et al., 1989).

Delivering Appropriate Education Considering the careful attention that is required to ensure the health and safety of children with complex health care needs, it is easy to de-emphasize the delivery of developmentally appropriate early childhood education. However, effective administrative leadership can help to support efforts toward play-based, peer-referenced learning activities that are enjoyable to children.

Collaboration with and Support for Parents During numerous hospitalizations, children with complex health care needs are exposed to and cared for by many different professionals (e.g., multiple shifts of nurses; physicians; surgeons; and physical, occupational, respiratory, and speech therapists). It is important to remember that the parents are constant in the child's life (Hains et al., 1991; Katz, 1992; Shelton et al., 1989). Collaboration with the parents of children with complex health care needs is therefore critical.

It is also important to remember that parents of children with complex health care needs may have experienced numerous life-threatening episodes and/or extensive hospital stays. Moving from the home into an early childhood intervention program may be especially difficult for these parents. Indeed, parents of children with more severe disabilities tend to have more concern regarding transition than do parents of typically developing children or even of children with milder impairments (Kilgo et al., 1989; Rosenkoetter & Rosenkoetter, 1993). As with developmentally appropriate education, administrative leadership can alleviate some parental anxiety by: 1) encouraging the inclusion of parents in all aspects of the transition planning process; 2) providing families with the names and telephone numbers of contact persons to answer questions; and 3) developing procedures to ensure frequent and individually appropriate communication among families, teachers, and other service providers.

Service Issues

The Health Services Plan Two types of team-developed plans are recommended for children with complex health care needs: the usual IFSP and/or IEP as well as an attached health services plan. The latter is a separate plan that should be developed before the child begins school to ensure that all team members are in agreement and that an emergency plan is in place prior to the child's arrival. The needs of children with complex health care needs will change frequently; the health service plan is a document that can be reviewed and perhaps revised many times throughout the course of the year. The important elements for inclusion in the health services plan are listed below.

Members of the Planning Team Effective planning must involve a team effort; no single person or discipline can satisfy all of the many and varied needs of children with complex health care needs. The following individuals (as well as others, as appropriate) should be included in the planning team: parents, the new program's lead teacher, the paraprofessional who will spend the most time with the child, the school administrator, support staff such as therapists, the transition nurse from the discharging hospital or the local health department, the school nurse, the Medicaid waiver case manager, a representative from the medical equipment company, and the previous childcare provider or early interventionist. Names of these people and their telephone numbers should be included in the health services plan.

Description of the Child's Medical Condition This section should contain a complete description of the child's current medical condition, including relevant medical history as well as his or her requirements for growth and development. Potential warning signs that indicate either developing concerns or potential side effects of medication should also be discussed.

Limitations for the Child in a School Setting This section specifies any activities in which the child may not participate (e.g., field trips) or any necessary restrictions (e.g., substances to be avoided).

Transportation Arrangements In this section, detail arrangements for transportation. If the child will be riding a school bus, describe any special resources that may be necessary (e.g., support personnel or equipment, temperature controls, and/or special training for transportation workers).

Feeding and Nutritional Needs Describe the child's current diet, including allergies, likes and dislikes, his or her feeding plan(s), and oral-motor interventions. Also, list staffing responsibilities for each intervention.

The Amounts of Medication, as well as the Schedule and Persons Responsible for its Administration These factors are delineated along with a procedure for record-keeping. Detailed records regarding the child's behaviors as well as the administration of medication may help to determine cycles that may be helpful to his or her physician. The plan for who will administer medication must comply with state law; regulations differ across states (Orelove & Sobsey, 1991).

Procedures To Be Performed by School Personnel This section outlines the child's medical needs and specifies which health-related procedure(s) will *necessarily* be performed at school. Each procedure should be described in detail, and record-keeping practices should be established.

Location for Performance of Procedure(s) In addition to the physical location, the frequency and the times of day for the administration of each health-related procedure should be established.

Persons Responsible for Performing the Procedure(s) The names of a back-up as well as a primary person responsible for each health-related procedure, as well as their respective qualifications, are delineated.

Training To Take Place Prior to the Child's Entrance into the Class This section lists in detail who will provide training and how often that training will be monitored and reviewed. Note that the training should be provided either by a health care provider, or by a health care provider in collaboration with the parent(s), but not by the parents alone.

Schedule for Review and Monitoring of Training This section includes timelines for the monitoring and regular review of required health-related procedures. Because the needs of the child will change, it is important to monitor and review training on a regular basis. Retraining may be necessary if the child's condition changes significantly.

Emergency Procedures Describe any expected emergency(ies) in terms of the child's typical behavior(s), if known. List specifically what to do, whom to call (phone numbers should be included), and the order in which people should be notified. Specify who will have a copy of the emergency plan, and where it will be filed or posted. In addition, notify the local emergency squad regarding the procedures to be followed in the event of an emergency and describe the location of the child within the school building.

Plan for Absences Two types of absences are discussed here: those of the caregiver and those of the child. The first section outlines a plan for training substitute(s) to take over whenever a teacher and/or paraprofessional is absent. Because children with medically complex conditions often experience illness and/or hospitalization, their absences should also be anticipated and planned for. Outline a plan for home-based instruction if the child becomes too ill to attend school. Be sure to include this plan in the child's IFSP/IEP as well as in his or her health services plan. Also, outline a plan for receiving current medical information prior to the child's return to school after an extended illness or hospitalization.

Dates in Effect and Plans for Change Although the health services plan should encompass a single year at most, it should be monitored continually by the case coordinator, reviewed frequently, and revised as needed to ensure adequate coverage. This is the reason for its being a separate document and not part of the child's IFSP or IEP. The plan is likely to require revision after a major illness or hospitalization. Dates for planned reviews should thus be stated.

Intervention For children with complex health care needs, intervention is planned and delivered just as it is for other children. Appropriate intervention should balance developmental appropriateness with the child's special needs. As for all young children, collaboration among sending and receiving programs and families during transition will ensure that appropriate education and care are provided as disjunctions in learning are minimized.

However, it is important to consider the demands inherent in current and subsequent environments (Brown et al., 1979) and the principle of *partial participation* (Baumgart et al., 1982). The latter emphasizes the child's involvement—to the maximum extent possible—in activities performed by other children, even if the child with a disability may never be able to perform the activity independently. Given the child's medical history as well as his or her necessary dependence on at least some health-related services, it is important for all staff members to foster independence wherever possible (Campbell, Garner, Cooper, & Wetherbee, 1986).

The child's history of involvement with adults in medical settings, coupled with any unusual equipment or procedures that may be required, may serve to isolate the child from other children in the classroom. As a result, teachers and therapists may need to implement special procedures to stimulate social interaction with peers (Fauvre, 1988). Table 11.4 lists several resource directories for serving children with special health care needs.

FOSTERING COLLABORATION AMONG HEALTH, EDUCATION, AND SOCIAL SERVICE AGENCIES

Coordinating services among health, education, and social service agencies is in the best interests of both the child with complex health care needs and that child's family. However, the process may be time consuming and challenging (Morse, 1990; Quinn & Jackson, n.d.).

The challenge is heightened because different agencies inhabit "different conceptual worlds . . . [which] slice up the social world differently" (Skrtic, 1986, p. 6). Gilkerson (1990) describes education and medicine as being two different "cultures" that need to develop sensitivity to each other's values, diagnostic terms, approaches to learning, communication patterns, and uses of time. Indeed, even the same words can have alternative meanings in different settings (Morse, 1990). Similarly, terms such as milliliter or cubic centimeter that are familiar in one culture may be foreign to another.

Thus, it makes sense for early childhood teams and their family service coordinators to develop appropriate strategies for communi-

Table 11.4. Resource directories for serving children with special health care needs

Center for Children with Chronic Illness and Disability. (1991). *Compendium 1989–91: A research resource manual.* Minneapolis: Author.

Holman, A., Hochstadt, N.J., & Yost, D.M. (1991). A nationwide directory of resources for medically complex children. In N.J. Hochstadt & D.M. Yost (Eds.), *The medically complex child: The transition to home care.* Chur, Switzerland/New York: Harwood Academic Publishers.

National Center for Education in Maternal and Child Health. (1990). *Children with special health needs: A resource guide.* Washington, DC: The National Maternal and Child Health Clearinghouse.

Tamari, P., Kempf, B., & Woodward, E. (Eds.). (1991). *Information and resource directory for children with special health care needs.* Selden, NY: Starting Early. Childhood Division of Developmental Disabilities Institute.

Table 11.5. Reports: research, technical, proceedings

Bureau of Maternal and Child Health and Resources Development. (1989). *Guidelines for the care of children with chronic lung disease.* New York: Alan R. Liss, Inc.

Caldwell, J.H., Sirvis, B., Todaro, A.W., & Accouloumre, D.S. (1991). *Special health care in the school.* Reston, VA: Council for Exceptional Children.

Joint Task Force for the Management of Children with Special Health Needs. (1990). *Guidelines for the delineation of roles and responsibilities for the safe delivery of specialized health care in the educational setting.* Reston, VA: Council for Exceptional Children.

Koop, C.E. (1987). *Surgeon General's report: Children with special health care needs* (DHHS Publication No. HRS/D/MC 87-2). Rockville, MD: U.S. Department of Health and Human Services.

National Center for Education in Maternal and Child Health. (1990). *Children with special health needs: A resource guide.* Washington, DC: The National Maternal and Child Health Clearinghouse.

U.S. Congress, Office of Technology Assessment. (1987). *Technology-dependent children: Hospital v. home care—A technical memorandum* (OTA-TM-H-38). Washington, DC: U.S. Government Printing Office.

Williams, B.C., & Miller, C.A. (1991). *Preventive health care for young children: Findings from a 10-country study and directions for United States policy.* Arlington, VA: National Center for Clinical Infant Programs.

cating regularly with the medical and social service professionals who serve children with complex health care needs. The reports and newsletters listed in Tables 11.5 and 11.6, respectively, may be helpful in this regard. Sending programs may be able to offer to receiving programs valuable suggestions regarding workable strategies to facilitate communication with the multiple agencies serving a child and his or her family. Active participation by a nurse employed by the school or local health department may also ease the process (Lowman, 1992).

Table 11.6. Newsletters

ACCH News Published bimonthly by the Association for the Care of Children's Health, 7910 Woodmont Ave., #300, Bethesda, MD 20814, 301-654-6549

Families and Disability Newsletter Published three times a year by the Beach Center on Families and Disability at the University of Kansas, 3111 Haworth Hall, Lawrence, KS 66045, FAX 913-864-5323

The Medical Home Newsletter Published by the Hawaii Medical Association, 1360 South Beretania, Honolulu, HI 96814, 808-536-7702

The Networks Published by the National MCH Center at Children's Hospital, 200 Henry Clay Ave., New Orleans, LA 70118

Springboard Published by the Center for Children with Chronic Illness and Disability, Box 721-UMHC, Harvard Street at East River Road, Minneapolis, MN 55455

Health Services Plan

Student: ***Scott Bascom***

Parent: ***David Bascom***

This health services plan will be in effect from January 4, 1994 through April 30, 1994.

Members of the Planning Team

Name	*Phone*	*Role*
David Bascom	296-1020(W) 294-9100(H)	Father
Emily Gomez	294-7561	Family Service Coordinator
Jonnie Graves	294-1400	Director, Early Childhood Special Education
Milli Keck	294-1400	Teacher, Head Start
Pat Ward	294-1400	Paraprofessional
Penny Hoffmeister	241-4000	Disabilities Coordinator, Head Start
Joseph Smerga	241-4000	Health Coordinator, Head Start
Johnnie Pappas	241-4000	Family Involvement Coordinator
Virginia Walker	241-4000	Director, Head Start
Mary Gallano	294-1400	School Nurse
Laura Clark	295-6428	Director, Special Education
Max Overman	294-9273	Building Principal
Harrison Cole	370-7184	Cole Home Health Services
Polly Ortega	289-8981	School Social Worker

Description of Child's Medical Condition

Scott was born after 26 weeks gestation and was hospitalized for the first 6 months of his life. He currently requires oxygen supplementation on a 24-hour basis. He has a complex seizure condition that is partially controlled by two medications as well as cerebral palsy. He currently speaks two-word utterances. Nutrition is provided through a combination of bolus gastrostomy feeding and simultaneous oral feeding, and he moves by means of a travel chair. Scott is a very sociable young man who makes friends wherever he goes.

Limitations for the Child in School Setting

Scott's oxygen cylinder must be secured in an upright position with reasonable proximity to Scott during all of his activities. Because oxygen supports combustion, the danger of fire always exists when oxygen is used. Do not place the cylinder near heaters or radiators. Similarly, remove any highly combustible materials from the classroom. Don't permit oil or grease to come into contact with the cylinders, valves, regulators, or fittings, and never drape anything over the cylinder.

The team will develop a written plan prior to each field trip that might require extra equipment, medications, and so forth.

Transportation Arrangements

Because of his dependence on oxygen, the team decided not to transport Scott on the regular school bus. Instead, a car will pick him up at home. The driver of the car will be trained in both managing a seizure, if one occurs, and handling the oxygen cylinder and nasal cannula. The car will be equipped with a CB radio in case emergency communication becomes necessary.

Feeding and Nutritional Needs

Scott's nutrition is provided through a combination of bolus gastrostomy feeding and simultaneous oral feeding. Scott's father will send the nutritional formula to the school in cases. Because Scott has very specific food preferences for oral intake, the special educator will send Mr. Bascom the weekly menu. If Scott is unable to tolerate a specific meal, his father will send a substitute lunch for that day's oral feeding. Records of amounts consumed will be kept by the paraprofessional and shared with Scott's father on a weekly basis.

Medication To Be Dispensed, Amount, Time, and Person Administering

The school nurse will administer Scott's medications. She will keep a record of doses, days, and times in a file at the program office.

Procedure(s) To Be Performed By School Personnel

Oxygen: School staff members will monitor Scott's oxygen flow. Scott's father will conduct routine maintenance of the equipment and make sure that Scott begins each day with a full cylinder. The school staff will be trained to change cylinders during the school day (i.e., wash hands, attach tubing to oxygen source, set flow on the flowmeter as prescribed by the doctor, check cannula prongs to ensure that oxygen is coming out, insert prongs into the child's nose).

Seizures: School staff members will be trained in first aid to handle Scott's seizures (i.e., gently ease Scott to the floor; clear area of hazards; put something flat and soft like a pillow or folded jacket under his head; turn him carefully to one side to keep his airway clear; *do not* try to put anything into his mouth). Scott's father will describe for the staff what Scott's seizures are typically like. They usually last less than 5 minutes. However, if a seizure lasts more than 5 minutes, the school nurse should be called.

Gastrostomy feeding: The paraprofessional responsible for Scott's care will prepare and administer the G-tube feedings, care for the equipment, and conduct Scott's simultaneous oral feedings.

Where the Procedure(s) Should Be Performed

Scott receives oxygen on a continuous basis; it must therefore go wherever he goes. If the cylinder requires changing, the procedure will be performed in the teacher's office where the replacement cylinder is stored. Scott will eat with the other children.

Who Will Perform the Procedure(s)

The paraprofessional who works directly with Scott will have the primary responsibility for monitoring his oxygen and conducting feedings, although the early childhood special education teacher and the lead teacher also have been trained. All school staff should be prepared to perform first aid in the event of a seizure.

Training that Is To Take Place Prior to the Child's Entrance into the Class

Training will be provided by the school nurse and will include procedures for the assembly and maintenance of equipment, as well as for changing cylinders and conducting tube feedings. The staff will also be alerted to any problems that will require immediate attention. Scott's father will participate in the training in order to describe Scott's unique needs. All school staff will be trained in performing both first aid in the event of a seizure and CPR.

Schedule for Review and Monitoring of Training

The performance of procedures will be monitored on a weekly basis by the school nurse. Retraining will take place every 6 months (or sooner if Scott's needs change).

Emergency Procedures

The contact person from the home oxygen supply company is a member of this team. His telephone number will be posted on the bulletin board mounted above the teacher's desk. Spare oxygen will be readily accessible and stored in a secure place. Extra tubing and tank equipment will also be available if needed.

The local fire department and rescue squad will be notified regarding the use of oxygen in the school. The principal will also send them a map indicating the location of Scott's classroom.

Observations regarding breathing: Note if Scott shows any of the following signs of respiratory distress:

- Increased work to breathe, harder to catch breath
- Agitation
- Blueness or pallor of the lips, nails, or ear lobes
- Nasal flaring
- Pulling in of muscles in the neck or chest
- Confusion, dizziness, or headache
- Rapid or pounding pulse

Action:

- Check oxygen flow.
- Check equipment.
- Ensure that tubing is not blocked or kinked.
- Call the school nurse; if the nurse is unavailable, call the local rescue squad; begin CPR if needed.
- Notify Scott's father.

Observations regarding feeding: Note if Scott's color changes or feeding becomes difficult.

Action:

- Terminate feeding immediately and call the school nurse.

Note other possible problems:

- Nausea and/or cramping
- Vomiting
- A blocked tube
- Bleeding, drainage, redness, or irritation in area of the stoma
- Leaking of stomach contents
- Tube or button comes out

Actions:

- Check rate of feeding.
- Check temperature of formula.
- Check the tube for blockage and flush it with water.
- Clean stoma site.
- Call the nurse or parent to reinsert the tube.

Plan for Absences

A substitute will be trained to care for Scott when the paraprofessional is absent. In the rare instance that both the paraprofessional and the substitute are unavailable, the early childhood special educator will provide direct care for Scott. If all three are absent—which is extremely unlikely—Mr. Bascom has offered to keep Scott at home with his home childcare provider. The team also outlined a plan for providing appropriate home-based instruction if Scott becomes too ill to attend school. This plan has been included in Scott's IEP.

Scott's father will request that his physicians send formal written reports containing current medical information when Scott returns from an extended illness or hospitalization. To ensure that school personnel have the appropriate information prior to Scott's return, Mr. Bascom will also: 1) provide discharging physicians with short memo forms (designed by the school) to summarize and forward recommendations prior to sending their formal reports, and 2) ask physicians to converse by phone with the school nurse regarding any major changes.

Plan for Change

This plan will be revised after any major illness or hospitalization.

The following team members agree on the components described in this plan:

____________________ ____________________

____________________ ____________________

____________________ ____________________

____________________ ____________________

____________________ ____________________

IMPLICATIONS

This chapter outlines transition procedures for children with complex health care needs. Administrative leadership is necessary both to ensure that a safe, developmentally appropriate environment is provided to receive the child and to encourage family participation. The most critical element in this regard is the preparation of a health services plan, in addition to an IFSP or IEP, prior to the child's entrance into his or her new school program. This additional plan: 1) outlines procedures for the training and subsequent monitoring of personnel who manage health-related procedures, 2) specifies practices for medication distribution, and 3) delineates emergency procedures. The goal of transition planning for children with complex health care needs is to ensure safety while providing appropriate intervention in the least restrictive environment possible.

12

Evaluating the Transition Process

How Did It Go?

There are many and varied reasons for evaluating early transitions. For sending as well as receiving programs, the purpose of evaluation is to determine how well they meet the needs of children and their families.

> Evaluation is an objective, systematic process for gathering information about a program or set of activities that can be utilized for the following purposes:
> (a) to ascertain the program's ability to achieve the originally conceived and implemented goals,
> (b) to suggest modifications that might lead to improvement in quality and effectiveness, and
> (c) to allow well-informed decisions about the worth, merit, and level of support a program warrants.
> (Bickman & Weatherford, 1986, p. ix)

With this information in hand, programs can improve specific transition activities. At the system level, evaluation of the transition process indicates how responsive the interagency transition agreement and the transition timeline have been to the individual needs of children, families, professionals, and agencies. Similarly, evaluation reveals whether or not a coordinated, comprehensive system of support and services is being provided by the community as a whole. With proper planning, evaluation may also suggest an alternative, more efficient strategy for allocating resources during future transition efforts.

HOW DO WE FOCUS EVALUATION?

The first step in the evaluation process is to determine its focus (Stecher & Davis, 1987). Questions (like those listed in Table 12.1) guide decision-making regarding which people and what information should be considered. Regardless of who actually makes these decisions—the local interagency coordinating council, the transition policies team, and/or an individual program—the results should elicit improvements in transitions between programs. In order to ensure that the most relevant questions are asked, family members as well as direct service providers and administrators should be involved in developing an evaluation plan.

Table 12.1. Consider these issues for evaluation

ATTAINMENT OF THE TRANSITION PLAN: Process

1. How many children and families made the transition?
2. Did personnel and agencies adhere to the transition timeline?
3. Where and why did breakdown(s) occur?
4. How should the timeline or personnel responsibilities be changed for next year?
5. Should the interagency agreement be changed in any way before next year? If so, how?
6. Are there additional agencies that should be included in the interagency transition agreement (i.e., programs that sent or received children and/or families that are not part of the existing agreement)?

SUCCESS OF THE TRANSITION PLAN: Outcomes

1. Was each child appropriately placed?
2. Does each child appear to be happy in his or her new environment?
3. Were you satisfied with the transition process and its participants?
   - Parents
   - Sending staff members
   - Receiving staff members
   - Sending program administrators
   - Receiving program administrators
4. How did the transition timeline work for each participant?
5. How might the transition process be changed?
6. What additional information do families and professionals need to improve the transition process?
7. What suggestions do participants have for improving the transition process?

RESOURCES USED IN TRANSITION PLANNING: Costs

1. How much time was spent in implementing the transition plan?
   - By families
   - By professionals in each agency
2. Should time requirements be changed for next year? If so, how?
3. What were the actual costs of implementing the transition plan?
4. Should funding for next year's transition planning efforts be increased, decreased, or remain the same?

HOW DO WE DESIGN THE EVALUATION?

The plan's design is determined largely by the resources (including available time) that local planners bring to the task (King, Morris, & Fitz-Gibbon, 1987). Greater resource investment may answer more questions with greater certainty. Fitz-Gibbon and Morris (1987) delineate several broad-based evaluation designs that can be employed. Although some communities are forced to choose simple, more cost-effective approaches due to their limited resources, every evaluation should begin with specific question(s) and should produce information that is useful in improving the transition process.

System-Level Evaluation

Here, evaluators seek information regarding the transition plan's accomplishments as they relate to the entire community. Personnel from various agencies as well as families are likely to be involved (Swan & Morgan, 1993). A variety of relevant evidence pertaining to the transition questions should be considered. A subsequent plan for responding to each question is then specified as part of the interagency transition planning process (described in Chapter 4 of this volume).

Program-Level Evaluation

Feedback from parents and staff members often improves in-house transition practices. A wide range of evidence is collected from interviews, records, notations of parents and/or staff members, surveys, and observations. Evaluation planning as part of the intraagency transition plan (described in Chapter 5) can provide suggestions for improving individual transitions as it assists in agency improvement from year to year.

WHO IS EVALUATED BY WHOM, AND HOW?

The next step in evaluation is to identify the participants in the transition event (Stecher & Davis, 1987). The evaluation may comprise the entire group of staff, families, and children recently involved in the transition process, or it may include only a random sample of these populations. Most obviously, consumers—the children and family members who move from one program to the next—can provide valuable information regarding the success of the transition just experienced. Indeed, they may speak knowledgeably about specific activities that were particularly helpful or especially difficult. Most often, questionnaires measuring children's progress and families' satisfaction are used to document the effectiveness of transitions (Hanline, 1993). Although these products represent standard program evaluation strategies (Hupp & Kaiser, 1986), equally important is evaluation of the transition process conducted by the direct service staff and administrators from both sending and receiving agencies. Indeed, their perspectives often provide guidance for the improvement of transition activities. It is quite surprising (albeit unfortunate) that direct service providers are often omitted from community efforts to develop effective evaluation processes.

Ideally, one or more outside evaluators designs the evaluation plan and gathers desired information. This "team" may include parents and professionals with expertise in early intervention working in consultation with program staff and parents from the sending and receiving agencies. Parental representation is critical to ensuring that the evaluation process is family-centered. Similarly, enlisting evaluators not affiliated with either the sending or receiving programs should minimize concerns regarding bias. For instance, if a sending program's service coordinator contacts a parent several months after a transition occurs, the parent may feel uncomfortable communicating problem areas directly to the agency's representative. Conversely, that parent may be more willing to discuss problem areas with someone not associated with either the sending or receiving agency (perhaps with another parent involved with the local interagency coordinating council). The same suggestion applies for staff and administrators. Indeed, professionals are frequently hesitant to criticize colleagues when program evaluation may serve as a basis for budgetary or employment decisions. Some communities participate in a self-assessment/program evaluation process facilitated by parents and professionals from nearby communities (Bailey, McWilliam, & Winton, 1992; Jesien & Tuchman, 1992). In fact, the evaluation of transition practices can be integrated into the more general program evaluation plan as part of such a self-assessment process.

In the absence of an outside evaluator, surveys, questionnaires, anecdotal information, and/or observations of children can be compiled anonymously. Indeed, the absence of an outside evaluator should never preclude evaluation of the transition process.

WHEN DO WE EVALUATE?

Evaluation may take place before, during, and/or after transitions occur, as determined by the type(s) and source(s) of information to be collected. For children, formal as well as informal measures of behavior recorded both before and after transition(s) may be useful in determining the success of specific preparatory activities (Carden-Smith & Fowler, 1983). For instance, if "walking up and down steps" is identified as a goal designed to teach a child to negotiate the new school's main entrance successfully, observation of the child both before and after the transition could be planned. It may be valuable for staff members to conduct simple surveys and/or focus group meetings when either receiving or sending children and their families into or out of their programs. Transition coordinators are likely to evaluate their agencies' practices and subsequent costs as well as their local interagency transition agreement on a yearly basis.

WHAT TOOLS ARE USEFUL FOR GATHERING EVALUATION INFORMATION?

The proper evaluation of transitions may produce a wide range of information. Each piece of information that is collected may provide a unique perspective regarding service delivery. Consequently, not all tools for gathering evaluation information (e.g., questionnaires, observations) are appropriate for all transitions. The selection of tools depends on: 1) the evaluation question(s) being considered; 2) the size and characteristics of the community; and 3) individual staff, family members, and children. For example, the question, "How many children made a transition?" simply requires a records search and subsequently yields a numerical answer. However, answering the question, "How well did the transition go for your family?" may require the use of a variety of both descriptive and quantitative evaluation tools to obtain an accurate cross-section of families who differ with regard to race, ethnicity, language, age (e.g., primary caregivers who are teenage parents, grandparents), literacy, and/or children's disabilities. If the program seeks information directly from parents about the transition process, several strategies may be employed. The transition satisfaction scale for parents shown in Figure 12.1 may be appropriate for some families. For others, similar questions can be modified and asked during a telephone interview or home visit (with an interpreter, if necessary).

Research has identified several family preferences regarding informal ways of gathering information (Summers et al., 1990; Winton & Bailey, 1993). However, little information exists delineating the best way in which to ascertain families' satisfaction after transition (Hanline, 1993). At present, studies report parents' general satisfaction with transition planning (Fowler, Chandler, Johnson, & Stella, 1988; Hanline & Knowlton, 1988; Johnson et al., 1986; Kilgo

How did your child's transition go? Check the box that best describes your feelings about the following items.	Needs improvement	OK	Very well
The amount of time you had when you began planning your child's transition to the next program			
Available program options			
Pre-transition visits you or your child made to the new program			
The preparation provided by the sending program to ease your child's transition			
The information and support provided by the receiving program to welcome you and your child			
The adjustment your child has made to the new program			
The adjustment your family has made to the new program			
The way your child's teachers shared information with you about your child			
Opportunities for discussions you had with other parents about your child's transition			
Decisions you made regarding your child's transition			
Decisions others made regarding your child's transition			
The whole transition process			
The amount of time you spent helping prepare your child at home			
The decisions you made in selecting the new program for your child			

Figure 12.1. Transition satisfaction scale for parents. (Adapted from Johnson, unpublished manuscript). (See also Johnson et al., 1986.)

et al., 1989; Spiegel-McGill et al., 1990), although this research does not reflect the changing ecology of families, particularly for families from minority populations in a variety of settings (Vincent et al., 1990).

Evaluation research on the specific effects of participation in integrated programs by children, families, and staff has, however, received some attention (see Odom & McEvoy, 1988; Peck, Carlson, & Helmstetter, 1992). More broadly, observational systems for examining the behaviors of children as well as staff in various early childhood environments have been discussed at length in research literature (see tools suggested by Bricker & Cripe, 1992; Carta et al., 1988; Hupp & Kaiser, 1986; Meisels & Shonkoff, 1990).

A procedure recommended for examining the transition process at the system level requires transition coordinators to determine the degree to which both the interagency agreement and the transition timeline govern the process as a whole and subsequently to evaluate the efficacy of each. Some communities may find it helpful to revisit periodically the Transition Planning Self-Assessment Tool (discussed in Chapter 4) and document their progress over time. McLaughlin and Covert (1984) also provide suggestions for evaluating the interagency elements of transition.

HOW DO WE COMMUNICATE EVALUATION FINDINGS?

Data are gathered according to the evaluation plan developed in response to specific questions posed by parents and professionals—the transition consumers. For this information to be useful, it must be analyzed and shared with those charged with actually carrying out transitions. Morris, Fitz-Gibbon, and Freeman (1987) suggest three priorities:

1. *Information must be communicated to appropriate potential users.* This means that evaluation results must be shared with the interagency and intra-agency transition planners as well as with families and service providers. Each person responsible for any element of transition should have access to this information.

2. *Reports must address issues that users perceive to be important.* Busy people won't take time to decipher esoteric data. They simply want to know how they or their agency can better facilitate transitions the following year.

3. *Reports must be delivered in a timely manner and in a form that is clearly understood by intended users.* Regardless of how graphically data are presented, the report should also contain an executive summary as well as a list of recommendations for program improvement. Both oral and (perhaps more detailed) written reports are valuable.

Parents, teachers, and agency directors were concerned about the lack of inclusive, community-based preschool programs in Somerset. The children with special needs had few options for services upon reaching age 3. Although special education services were provided in a special education classroom at a local elementary school, few opportunities existed for preschool-age children to interact with their peers. The early childhood classroom served the entire county, which in turn meant that a number of children traveled 30–40 minutes each day by bus from their home com-

munity. For parents, coordinating child care for their children was extremely difficult, in Somerset as well as in their home towns.

The county leaders recognized a growing need for quality child care in communities throughout the county. Therefore, early intervention and preschool staff members as well as parents advocated for a more community-based approach to special preschool services. A proposal to address these issues was subsequently passed by the county board, and the Children's Center was selected as the pilot site.

The Children's Center is a new early childhood facility supported by county, community, and school district funds; a child-care block grant; federal funds; parent fees; and private donations. Its long-term goal is to provide comprehensive services for all children and families in the local community (including those children with special needs and their families). The involved administrators, teachers, and parents naturally wanted this experience to be successful.

They carefully designed an in-depth evaluation plan to document the program's impact on children, their parents, and relevant staff members. In addition to considering children's pre- and posttest scores and the degree to which IEP objectives were achieved, the evaluators planned to videotape children both before and after their transitions into the Children's Center in order to compare and analyze their language and play skills. Comprehensive interviews and surveys were designed to gather information from parents and staff members of both special education and the Children's Center before the children with special needs were enrolled at the Children's Center, 3 weeks after their initial arrival, and again 6 months after that. The purposes of this evaluation were:

1. To ensure that the new program met the needs of all involved children and families
2. To identify needed changes in the approach
3. To decide whether or not to expand this new model for special education service delivery throughout the county (examples of tools used in this comprehensive evaluation plan may be found in Appendix F of this volume)

* * *

The Concordia Local Interagency Coordinating Council decided to adopt a standard procedure for evaluating all local early childhood transitions. Because the Council wanted to obtain parallel information for each transition (and since it had limited time to spend on this project), it designed two postcards—one for families, and one for sending and receiving staff—to be sent 1 month subsequent to each child's transition. The Council determined that a variety of resources could be used to support this effort. The transition coordinator from the sending program would then be responsible for collecting the data and reporting to the Council during quarterly meetings. Examples of the postcards used may be found in Figure 12.2.

Parent Transition Survey

Please circle your response and mail within 3 days. Thank you!

1. I was satisfied with the preparation activities for my child and family before the transition to the new program.
   Strongly Disagree | Disagree | Neutral | Agree | Strongly Agree | COMMENTS:
2. Our family's concerns, priorities, strengths, and resources were considered throughout the transition process.
   Strongly Disagree | Disagree | Neutral | Agree | Strongly Agree | COMMENTS:
3. My child's strengths as well as needs were addressed during the transition process.
   Strongly Disagree | Disagree | Neutral | Agree | Strongly Agree | COMMENTS:
4. My child's current program meets his or her needs.
   Strongly Disagree | Disagree | Neutral | Agree | Strongly Agree | COMMENTS:
5. Please make any comments that might enhance the transition process.

If you wish to discuss this further, please provide your name and phone number here.

Program Transition Survey

Please circle your response and mail within 3 days. Thank you!

1. I am satisfied with the preparation activities for children and families before transitions to new programs.
   Strongly Disagree | Disagree | Neutral | Agree | Strongly Agree | COMMENTS:
2. Families' concerns, priorities, strengths, and resources were considered throughout the transition process.
   Strongly Disagree | Disagree | Neutral | Agree | Strongly Agree | COMMENTS:
3. Children's strengths and needs are addressed during the transition process.
   Strongly Disagree | Disagree | Neutral | Agree | Strongly Agree | COMMENTS:
4. The current transition process works well in our community.
   Strongly Disagree | Disagree | Neutral | Agree | Strongly Agree | COMMENTS:
5. Please make any comments that might enhance the transition process.

If you wish to discuss this further, please provide your name and phone number here.

Figure 12.2. Sample postcards for evaluation.

IMPLICATIONS

Evaluation is essential if transitions are to be effective. This chapter presents a practical approach to gathering information from children, families, staffs, and agencies that are involved with transition. Using appropriate tools, evaluation seeks to answer those questions that are relevant to the participants in the transition process. It ultimately yields a summary of views expressed by those participants as well as a list of recommendations for improving local practices. Thus, findings are directly beneficial to future participants in the transition process. Clearly, this information is inextricably linked to that obtained through the broader program evaluation activities that ascertain impact and effectiveness at the program level.

13

Transitions Among Early Childhood Services in the 1990s

The Larger Context

Services for young children with special needs are provided within a broad landscape of national policies and trends regarding young children in general. When programs for children with special needs can be linked with these broader agendas, necessary changes may occur at a faster rate (National Conference of State Legislatures, 1991; Odom & Warren, 1988).

The era between 1988 and 1998 has been dubbed "the decade of the child" (Cuomo, 1988) due in great part to the amount of attention being given issues affecting children and families during the early childhood years. Transition planning is a key element in providing quality services for young children and their families (Bredekamp, 1987). In fact, it is becoming increasingly prominent and is even receiving some limited resources at the national level.

GOVERNMENT-SPONSORED TRANSITION INITIATIVES

The federal government has sponsored many projects throughout the 1980s and 1990s regarding early childhood transitions.

America 2000

Recommendations made by United States governors to former President George Bush resulted in the creation of the America 2000 program, which was designed to improve educational opportunity in the United States. Goal 1 of this plan states, "By the year 2000, all children in America will start school ready to learn." Among the recommendations of the U.S. Department of Education (1991) for implementing this goal are two that directly support transition planning:

- *Collaborative planning:* Initiate collaborative, community-based planning to ensure that children who are disadvantaged or who have disabilities have equal access to quality early childhood education and care. (p. 5)
- *Transitions:* Build connections among parents, preschools, and elementary schools to ensure smooth and coherent transitions. (pp. 5–6)

America 2000 urges individual communities to commit to their educational goals and subsequently to devise local plans to marshal their resources in achieving those goals. Ideally, America 2000 would have all local community agencies working together to facilitate more effective transitions for all young children.

Head Start

Some early collaborative efforts between Head Start and the public school system were funded in the late 1970s under the title *Project Developmental Continuity.* In 1986–1987, the Administration for Children, Youth, and Families—Head Start's parent agency under the U.S. Department of Health and Human Services—funded 30 demonstration projects designed to provide more coordinated educational experiences for children and their families. It then specified four components of good transitions:

- Providing program continuity through curricula that are developmentally appropriate for preschool- and kindergarten-age children
- Maintaining ongoing communication and cooperation among preschool and kindergarten staff members
- Preparing children for transition
- Involving parents throughout the transition process

In 1991, 32 additional projects were funded to study and promote continuity for children in Head Start through grade 3. Each of these projects has a strong evaluation component whose commendable goal is to obtain clear data regarding the impact of sound transition practices on children and their families. A list of these projects appears in Appendix A of this volume.

In 1993, Head Start issued new regulations governing the services it provides for children with disabilities and their families (Administration for Children and Families). These new policies help to minimize adjustments regarding eligibility of and service delivery for children with special needs who are moving into or out of Head Start.

Follow Through

Developed in the late 1960s, Follow Through introduced and validated a variety of instructional models regarding transitions into primary school and subsequently supported the replication of those models on a national scale. The Follow Through effort was based on the premise that graduates of Head Start require continuity and follow-up to ensure continued success beyond their early programming (Southwest Educational Development Laboratory, 1992).

National Policy Forum and Regional Meetings

Continuity has also been a major theme of the National Policy Forum on Transition as well as of various regional meetings convened between 1991 and 1993 by the U.S. Departments of Education and Health and Human Services. The first National Forum identified the following needs:

- The need to realign structures at federal, state, and local levels to ensure collaboration, placing children from birth through age 8 and their families at the fore of program concerns
- The need to restructure funding to promote versatility
- The need to establish comprehensive interagency agreements and initiatives that require and/or reward collaboration
- The need to provide additional resources for research and dissemination, professional training, and the development of assessment models (National Policy Forum, 1991)

Publications are also being produced by many regional education laboratories to aid in local transition efforts (SERVE, 1992). The focus of these and other efforts has been to ease the transition from preschool, Head Start, or child care into kindergarten for all children.

Many strategies recommended for promoting smoother transitions for all children entering kindergarten are consistent with the

Bridging Early Services Transition model espoused in this book. Some of these strategies include: establishing a community team approach, setting transition goals and outcomes, involving parents in the transition process, improving communication among relevant staff, and focusing on children's needs rather than on system requirements in promoting success for all children.

National Transition Study

As kindergartens have grown larger and more academic in nature (Elkind, 1981; Freeman & Hatch, 1989; Karweit, 1988), concern has increased regarding their ability to successfully accommodate the increasing diversity of children (Goffin & Stegelin, 1992). Some policy-makers additionally ponder a related concern, the transition from home or preschool into kindergarten, especially for those children who are at risk of failure in school (Love et al., 1992).

Accordingly, the U.S. Department of Education commissioned a major study (Love et al., 1992) to survey a nationally representative sample consisting of 830 school districts and 1,169 schools midway through the 1989–1990 school year. This study evaluated transition policies and practices between preschool and kindergarten, as well as the characteristics of pre-kindergarten and kindergarten programs housed in public schools. Results showed that transition activities are not widely utilized in U.S. schools; in fact, schools most often provide only a few of those activities that are actually possible. Indeed, only 13% of the elementary schools surveyed have formal transition policies. Although such policies do not necessarily ensure effective practices, they do indicate a commitment to bridging services for children and their families.

Regarding coordination and/or communication, this national study also found that very little effort is devoted to transition activities such as:

- Coordinating pre-kindergarten and kindergarten curricula
- Establishing communication among staff members at both levels regarding either the incoming (or outgoing) students and/or their respective instructional programs
- Providing joint training for staff at both levels

However, the study found more widespread implementation of those specific transition activities that are comparatively easy to establish, especially those involving parents:

- Welcoming incoming children and their parents with special orientations and visitations
- Informing the parents of incoming students about their rights and responsibilities in the school
- Involving parents in classroom activities designed to facilitate smooth transitions

Researchers later stated that the relatively low emphasis placed on transition may be attributable to the belief of school personnel that most children do not experience difficulty in adjusting to kindergarten. When problems do occur, however, adjusting to the academic demands of kindergarten is seen as posing the greatest difficulty. This, in turn, is viewed as a deficit affecting individual children rather than as a system deficiency. However, 18% of all schools and 33% of schools serving children from high poverty backgrounds reported that children often have difficulty in adjusting to academic demands, thus invalidating such a conclusion.

This study also revealed that smooth transitions are often obstructed by the instructional orientation espoused by many kindergartens. "Most schools consider their kindergarten programs to be 'developmental,' yet they rate themselves relatively low on some of the key classroom activities that early childhood educators define as developmental practice" (Love et al., 1992, p. 124). Thus, curricular discontinuity appears to be a major challenge to bridging services between preschool and kindergarten for children and their families.

The study did nevertheless report four conditions relevant for the transition between preschool and kindergarten that result in greater continuity for children: 1) administrative support and leadership, 2) a school climate that includes positive attitudes toward children and their parents, 3) structural connections between prekindergarten and kindergarten programs, and 4) an increase in poverty level among families whose children are enrolled in that school (Love et al., 1992).

STATEMENTS OF PROFESSIONAL ORGANIZATIONS

Numerous policy statements advocate local interagency planning in meeting the needs of all children and families experiencing transition in a given community.

National Association of State Boards of Education

In its 1988 taskforce report *Right from the Start,* NASBE stated that programs serving children preschool through grade 3 should "include parents in decision making about their own children and on the overall early childhood program [and] provide a gradual and supportive transition process from home to school for those young children entering school for the first time" (p. 19). Furthermore, schools should make "provisions for young children to make an incremental transition from home to school when entering for the first time" (p. 20). NASBE is thus

> concerned about the lack of planning and collaboration to ensure a smooth transition for children between early childhood programs in the community and programs in the schools. Such transitions occur annually as children move between program types, and they occur daily as children move from school to child care. We believe there is greater continuity for children and parents when both types of programs are developmentally appropriate. Schools can facilitate this transition by helping to ensure such programs both in the school and the community, by maintaining ongoing communication with community services, and by collaborative planning to prepare children and involve parents in these transitions. (pp. 27–28)

More recently, in its 1991 National Task Force on School Readiness report titled *Caring Communities: Supporting Young Children and Families,* NASBE advocated integrated and comprehensive services: "Services should be conveniently located, promote continuity and respond to the comprehensive needs of both children and families" (NASBE, 1991, p. 25).

In 1992, NASBE published *Winners All: A Call for Inclusive Schools,* which advocated major changes in service systems such that all children, including those with disabilities, attend their neighborhood school(s) with peers of the same age and grade, and that they each receive appropriate in-class support to succeed there. These recommendations obviously have major implications for transition planning for all children entering school.

National Association of Elementary School Principals

NAESP published *Early Childhood Education and the Elementary School Principal: Standards for Quality Programs for Young Children* in 1990. One standard clearly states, "The principal works with preschool and day-care providers to assure a smooth transition into the public school" (p. 31). Indicators of quality regarding this standard include such items as the following:

- The principal has initiated communication and cooperation with the various groups in the community that serve young children.
- The principal has arranged opportunities for joint staff development with these organizations and institutions.
- The principal invites parents and their children to visit the public school prior to enrollment.

- When a transfer is to occur, the principal and the school staff familiarize themselves with what that particular child has been learning and strive to provide continuity between the two educational programs.

According to NAESP, "continuity between programs and services can make a significant contribution to the success and security of students and parents alike" (p. 31).

National Association for the Education of Young Children

NAEYC, with a membership of more than 80,000 early childhood professionals, has emphasized transition planning as part of its *Developmentally Appropriate Practice in Early Childhood Programs Serving Children from Birth through Age 8* (Bredekamp, 1987). Four key elements are recommended for easing transitions (pp. 60–61):

1. Ensure program continuity by providing developmentally appropriate curricula for all age levels in all educational settings.
2. Maintain ongoing communication and cooperation between staff members in different programs.
3. Prepare children for transition.
4. Involve parents in transition planning.

Four position statements of NAEYC are also relevant for transition planning. Its *Position Statement on Standardized Testing of Young Children 3 through 8 Years of Age* (1988b) discusses appropriate as well as inappropriate practices in screening children for developmental delays prior to entry into kindergarten. Similarly, the NAEYC *Position Statement on Developmentally Appropriate Practice in the Primary Grades* (1988a) delineates early elementary environments that nurture all children, including those who are developing at a slower rate than their peers. The NAEYC *Position Statement on School Readiness* (1990) urges that schools be responsive to the needs of individual children, thus rejecting the use of uniform timelines or standards in determining eligibility and/or development. Finally, NAEYC's *Guidelines for Appropriate Curriculum Content and Assessment in Programs Serving Children Ages 3 through 8* (1991) discusses curricular issues that are significant both to decisions regarding placement for young children and to broader school reform.

National Association of Early Childhood Specialists in State Departments of Education

NAECSSDE published a position statement in 1987 supporting developmentally appropriate kindergartens that "welcome" all children "as they are" (p. 3). However, it rejected retention at a specific grade level as a viable option for young children. NAECSSDE co-sponsored the 1991 curriculum statement with NAEYC (discussed above).

IMPLICATIONS

Each of the position statements described in this chapter is the work of many individuals who are nationally recognized leaders in providing services for young children and their families. Each statement is intended to guide state and local planners as they develop transition programs that promote success for all children, including those with special needs.

Government agencies and professional organizations at the highest levels have recommended that systematic transition planning occur for all children and their families. In this regard, they suggest increased local communication, coordination, and planning; greater parental participation in decision-making; prevention of children's adjustment problems through preparation; instructional continuity via developmentally appropriate practices that consider individual needs; open admissions into kindergarten; and recognizing children's failures as shortcomings of the system as a whole—as wake-up calls for local action.

These recommendations are consistent with the Bridging Early Services Transition model. Parents and professionals alike are urged to: 1) support interagency efforts in their communities, 2) encourage community efforts that help programs to serve a growing diversity of children, and 3) join with other local efforts to make schools and agencies more responsive to parents during transitions. Individual communities can initiate collaboration by addressing either a particular transition (e.g., entry into kindergarten) or the local early services system as a whole.

The vision seen by a variety of national agencies and organizations is one in which families and children move comfortably within a single community support system—one that provides family-centered services and appropriate learning environments for all children from birth through their early school years. With hard work and understanding, this vision can be realized.

14

Future Directions for Transition Planning

Build More Bridges!

Each year, several hundred thousand young children with special needs and their families undergo significant transitions between service programs. Local communities, in attempts to facilitate these transitions, are sharing and implementing effective ways of supporting the various participants in transition planning. These efforts, which are targeted for infants, toddlers, and young children with special needs, are part of the larger effort in the United States to improve early transitions for all young children and their families.

CHALLENGES AND RESPONSIBILITIES

A variety of challenges confront transition planners, both now and in the future:

- To develop trusting relationships and appropriate procedures to accomplish early childhood transitions in a timely and effective manner
- To involve all transition participants—families and sending and receiving programs—in information sharing and decision-making
- To place and appropriately serve children with special needs in natural environments among typically developing peers, to the maximum extent possible

- To prepare children and their families for transition and to support their success in new surroundings
- To evaluate transition practices in efforts to improve them.
- To train personnel (professionals as well as families) in planning effective transitions locally in their communities

As with most other facets of early childhood intervention, the responsibility for transition planning is shared among states, local program leaders, service providers, families, and researchers.

Challenges for the States

Develop One Statewide Plan for Transition This action begins when representatives from various sending and receiving agencies, parents, and local program personnel come together to develop a comprehensive state plan for each significant transition. This plan should outline responsibilities, timelines, funding options, schedules for review, and dissemination plans. Participating agencies should commit to the plan through an official memorandum of understanding; its implications should be clearly spelled out in a single document that is distributed to:

1. Agencies such as education, health, and social services
2. Coordinators of programs such as Head Start, childcare, and perinatal centers
3. Organizations such as parent groups and professional associations

This collaborative process of establishing formal agreements among state leaders and their agencies models the actions that local agencies must take in creating smooth transitions in their communities. The state plan also offers local interagency groups necessary guidance regarding relevant philosophies, practices, and funding mechanisms and options. Despite the benefits of such an approach, recent research shows that, in many states, individual agencies are still devising discrete guidelines for transition planning. These guidelines often conflict with one another, which in turn hinders the process of transition planning as a whole (Shotts, Rosenkoetter, Streufert, & Rosenkoetter, in press).

Provide Collaborative Inservice and Continuing Education Activities Agency leaders across the nation listed personnel training regarding transition as a top priority in a recent needs assessment (Shotts et al., in press). Priorities for training include: legal requirements of the state and federal governments, family participation in the transition process, strategies for child preparation, models for local interagency agreements (and suggestions of ways to devise them), agency roles, timelines, and funding options. When training in this regard is planned or coordinated by a state's technical assistance system(s), parents and professional personnel across the state receive accurate information that is consistent with that state's transition plan and its procedures.

Equip Parents To Participate Actively in Decision-Making Regarding Transition and in Their Child's New Program Preparing parents for their child's transition was also recognized as a top priority in the national needs assessment discussed above (Shotts et al., in press). Each state has a designated information and training center for parents (often referred to by other names) selected to receive and compile federal information relevant for parents. Many of these centers have the potential to facilitate training, often parent-to-parent training. Information regarding transition should be provided to parents in a variety of formats and languages and at numerous times and places in order to accommodate the diversity of families whose children will be making transitions.

Challenges for Local Agency Leaders

Incorporate State and Federal Guidelines into Local Interagency Agreements and Community Transition Policies Cooperative planning, delineation of responsibilities in local (written) interagency agreements, and the development of timelines for accomplishing tasks in a timely manner allow families and individual service providers to anticipate and prepare for transition events.

Provide Resources To Accomplish Transition Tasks Release time from teaching or direct service delivery will be necessary for staff members to visit other programs, receive training on issues regarding transition, and work with families in accomplishing transition objectives.

Provide Guidance Regarding Least Restrictive Placements and Curricular Reform The direct service staff may hesitate to recommend community-based placements if they have never done so before. However, administrative leadership may encourage creativity in this regard and subsequently elicit the most appropriate placement for individual children and their families. Similarly, such leadership can initiate curricular review and promote the adoption of developmentally appropriate curricula that foster success for groups of children functioning at different levels and learning at various rates.

Evaluate Transition Practices in Order To Improve Them Administrative leadership will be necessary for the systematic evaluation of a community's transition practices to occur and for its results to alter existing transition procedures.

Challenges for Interventionists

Help Families To Anticipate Their Children's Transitions Families have often described their grief at the thought of leaving a familiar program and its people in order to move into a new and different setting. Some have said that they coped with the change by denying (to themselves) that the transition was indeed inevitable. Feelings such as these can be eased if personnel from the sending and receiving programs raise issues regarding transition repeatedly, thus helping families to adjust to the idea. Indeed, they can describe the transition as a milestone in growth for the child and his or her family both by focusing on the positive aspects of the change and by promoting trusting relationships with receiving personnel.

Share Information in a Timely Manner with Those People Who Need It To Make Decisions This includes information-sharing with both parents and professionals before, during, and after transition.

View the Transition as a Shared Challenge When successes as well as problems are shared, joint ownership, including cooperative problem-solving, develops. Indeed, transitions should never be the exclusive responsibility of a single person or agency.

Seek the Least Restrictive Environment Possible, and Prepare Children To Function There Mentors from other families and professionals who work with families most closely are the primary advisors regarding placement. Honest exploration of placement options coupled with the careful preparation of relevant professionals may have lasting significance for those young children making a transition.

Examine Curricula To Facilitate Program Changes Senders and receivers can work together to bridge services by developing curricula that promote success for an increasing diversity of children.

Communicate Needs to the Community's Policy-Makers The agency leaders who write and/or revise transition policies for the community may have little if any knowledge of the transition issues that arise daily. Therefore, family service coordinators, teachers, and therapists contribute significantly when they suggest new or improved practices to these individuals.

Challenges for Families

Parents are ultimately responsible for navigating multiple systems in attempts to locate the best available services for their children. Consequently, they are the people who suffer when the community fails to coordinate its efforts in facilitating smooth transitions for children.

Parents contribute most to state and local planning when they focus planners' attention on the overlying purpose of interagency transition planning—helping individual children and their families to get a good start in future learning environments (and on the rest of their lives). However, they may find it challenging to: 1) find the time to locate acceptable channels from which to gather needed information, 2) participate actively in their child's transition, 3) help in formulating local transition policies, and 4) request the development of appropriate services when none are presently available. Additionally, parents may be charged with discerning the generalizable strategies that were effective during previous transitions in order that they may be applied in making future transitions successful as well.

Challenges for Researchers

Several questions continue to confront the research community. These questions are summarized in Table 14.1.

MEASURES OF SUCCESS

How do we judge a transition to be "effective" or "successful?" This question has perplexed scholars for years (Hutinger, 1981). The following criteria are suggested in this regard:

- The child continues to develop in all domains in the new environment, up to the limits imposed by his or her disability. The IFSP/IEP was used in planning activities that help the child to cope successfully with the changes required by transition. In idiosyncratic ways, he or she shows signs of enjoying the new placement and the peers and adults encountered there. Symptoms of stress—crying, tantrumming, and nausea related to school attendance—are absent after 6 weeks in the new program.
- Opportunities for interaction with typically developing peers are frequent.
- Necessary resources—additional equipment or services, adaptations in instructional materials, and/or information for program planning and staff training—are in place by the child's first day of attendance.

Table 14.1. Research questions regarding transition

General Questions

- Which components of transition planning (e.g., timelines, staff inservices, parent program visits) contribute most to successful transitions? Which are less needed?
- What factors drive decisions regarding placement when comprehensive transition planning has occurred? What factors drive these decisions when transition planning is not evident? Are decisions typically driven by professionals, families, or a consultation between the two?
- Which strategies are proving to be effective in helping states and local communities to overcome differences regarding eligibility and service provision across agencies?
- What kinds of leadership foster interagency transition planning? Community-based placements? Curriculum changes to accommodate diverse developmental levels?
- How can policies (e.g., due process), procedures (e.g., interagency enrollment forms), and service options (e.g., family coordination) be universalized across programs to reduce the families' stress during transition?

Family Concerns

- What skills and coping mechanisms do families need (and want) to develop during specific early transitions? Which of these skills can be carried over into new environments under different conditions?
- What evidence indicates that family empowerment during early childhood transitions produces benefits for future transitions as well?
- What supports are essential for families during transitions? Which supports reduce stress, promote adjustment, and result in family satisfaction?
- What accommodations are needed to ensure that transition planning is sensitive to families of diverse cultures? Which maximize their opportunities for participation?
- How does family choice and partnership in transition planning change the educational system (e.g., does it increase placements in community-based programs and decrease segregated special education placements, or does it cause the reverse?)?
- How do specific characteristics (of families and children) influence the timing and activities of transition planning?
- What are the personal and financial consequences of using an IFSP throughout the preschool years?

Professional Concerns

- How does visitation across programs influence professionals' attitudes toward alternative environments?
- To what extent do sending and receiving staff members hold similar expectations for individual children and their families who are in the process of leaving one program and entering another? Do these expectations match respective perceptions of the child's current skills? To what extent can transition planning, staff visits, and inservices influence a match in this regard? To what extent can they foster congruent accommodations in sending and receiving programs to meet individual needs so that expectations do indeed match skills? What strategies help receiving professionals to focus on individual potential rather than on perceived deficits?
- What curricular changes result from joint planning and inservice activities?

(*continued*)

Table 14.1. (*continued*)

- What evidence supports this statement: "The more developmentally appropriate different programs are, the smoother and more successful children's transitions will be between different programs or groups" (Bredekamp, 1987, p. 60)?
- How do timelines and interagency agreements assist professionals in transition planning? Are they seen as entailing extraneous deadlines and paperwork or as guidelines toward meaningful activities?
- To what extent do agencies' job descriptions and expectations reflect individual responsibilities regarding transition activities? Do they consider transition planning with families and other professionals in addition to direct service provision?
- Will closer curricular linkages between sending and receiving programs produce greater learning over the long term?
- How can IFSP outcomes and IEP objectives relevant to transition be truly useful for children and their families?
- Which training procedures are most effective in preparing staff to facilitate effective transitions?

Interagency and Interdisciplinary Concerns

- How do transition practices change over time? One study suggests that system changes first occur through activities that are "easy" to implement (Hains, 1990)—are these results widespread?
- How do disciplines other than education view their roles with regard to transitions? What supports exist for the creation of interdisciplinary teams in transition planning?
- Which conditions are necessary to support local interagency collaboration for developing, implementing, and evaluating effective transitions?
- What do local providers identify as the major barriers to effective transition planning? Have improvements occurred over time? If so, what facilitates change? If not, what is needed for change?
- Which funding options are proving most effective in facilitating early childhood transitions?
- How has evaluation data obtained from professionals and families changed over time regarding their satisfaction with local transition practices?

- Family members have the opportunity to participate actively in making decisions and to communicate freely with the receiving staff before as well as after the transition. Indeed, the family transfers loyalty as it becomes involved with the new program.
- Professionals follow the procedures and timelines agreed upon by the interagency team to accomplish the transition in a timely manner.

An effective transition—a strong bridge—may initially seem simple to construct. It can in fact be straightforward when each participant is prepared to perform his or her duties properly in collaboration with other relevant individuals—their partners in bridge-building. Similarly, transitions are further facilitated when available tools and materials are efficiently used. Given such optimal conditions, everyone can focus on the task at hand—launching a child toward higher levels of education and independence with the support necessary to succeed there.

JUST DO IT!

Efforts to improve early childhood transitions may influence many aspects of service delivery for young children and their families as well as for older students. Indeed, transition planning may lead to local program improvement and interagency collaboration in several areas, even beyond the early childhood years. Building a dependable bridge is likely to preclude many expensive and time-consuming detours for children and their families. It is worth doing, doing well, and doing now.

Appendix A

National Projects Focused on Transition

The following outreach projects of the U.S. Department of Education, Early Education Program for Children with Disabilities, provide information, training, and technical assistance regarding transition.

HOSPITAL TO HOME

Project STEPS (Sequenced Transition to Education in the Public Schools)
Child Development Centers of the Bluegrass, Inc.
465 Springhill Drive
Lexington, KY 40503
(606)278-0549
Beth Rous

Project Continuity Outreach
Meyer Rehabilitation Institute
University of Nebraska Medical Center
600 South 42nd Street
Omaha, NE 68198-5450
(402)559-5765
Barbara Jackson

Magnolia Circle Outreach
Peabody College, Box 328
Vanderbilt University
Nashville, TN 37203
(615)322-8277 or (800)288-7733
Steven F. Warren

NICU Follow-Through Project
Experimental Education Unit, WJ-10
University of Washington
Seattle, WA 98105
(206)543-0925
Forrest C. Bennett and Rodd Hedlund

Bridging Early Services Transition Project—Outreach
Associated Colleges of Central Kansas
105 East Kansas Avenue
McPherson, KS 67460
(316)241-7754
Sharon E. Rosenkoetter

EARLY INTERVENTION TO PRESCHOOL

Preschool Preparation and Transition (PPT) Outreach Project
Department of Special Education/ UAP
University of Hawaii
1776 University Avenue, UA4-7
Honolulu, HI 96822
(808)956-6917
Mary Jo Noonan

Project Vision
Center on Developmental Disabilities
University of Idaho
129 West 3rd Street
Moscow, ID 83843
(208)885-6605
Jennifer Olsen and Helen Ingalls

FACTS/LRE
Department of Special Education
University of Illinois
1310 South Sixth Street
Champaign, IL 61821
(217)333-0260
Susan A. Fowler

Bridging Early Services Transition Project—Outreach
Associated Colleges of Central Kansas
105 East Kansas Avenue
McPherson, KS 67460
(316)241-7754
Sharon E. Rosenkoetter

Project STEPS (Sequenced Transition to Education in the Public Schools)
Child Development Centers of the Bluegrass, Inc.
465 Springhill Drive
Lexington, KY 40503
(606)278-0549
Beth Rous

VIDEOSHARE Outreach Project
Division of Educational Research and Service
School of Education
The University of Montana
Missoula, MT 59812
(406)243-5344
Rick van den Pol

Project Ta-kos Outreach
Alta Mira Specialized Family Services, Inc.
P.O. Box 7040
Albuquerque, NM 87194-7040
(505)842-9948
Betty Yoches and Linda Askew

Ninos Especiales Outreach Project
Family Support/Early Intervention
Westchester Institute for Human Development
New York Medical College
Cedarwood Hall, Room 423
Valhalla, NY 10595-1689
(914)285-7052
Mary Beth Bruder

Magnolia Circle Outreach
Peabody College, Box 328
Vanderbilt University
Nashville, TN 37203
(615)322-8277 or (800)288-7733
Steven F. Warren

The Integrated Outreach Project
Center for Persons with Disabilities
Utah State University
Logan, UT 84322-6845
(801)750-3381
Sarah Rule

Portage Multi-State Outreach Project
CESA 5
626 East Slifer Street
Portage, WI 53901
(608)742-8811
Julia Herwig

PRESCHOOL TO KINDERGARTEN/PRIMARY

The Community Integration Project
Department of Teacher Preparation & Special Education
The George Washington University
2201 G. Street, NW #524
Washington, DC 20052
(703)826-0723
Penelope J. Wald

Project Vision
Center on Developmental Disabilities
University of Idaho
129 West 3rd Street
Moscow, ID 83843
(208)885-6605
Jennifer Olsen and Helen Ingalls

FACETS: Family-Guided Approaches to Collaborative Family Intervention Training and Services
Kansas University Affiliated Program
2601 Gabriel Street
Parsons, KS 67357
(316)421-6550 ext. 1859
Juliann Woods Cripe and David P. Lindeman

FACTS/LRE
Department of Special Education
University of Illinois
1310 South Sixth Street
Champaign, IL 61821
(217)333-0260
Susan A. Fowler

Project SLIDE (Skills for Learning Independence in Diverse Environments)
Juniper Gardens Children's Project
The University of Kansas
1614 Washington Road
Kansas City, KS 66102
(913)321-3143
Judith Carta

Bridging Early Services Transition Project—Outreach
Associated Colleges of Central Kansas
105 East Kansas Avenue
McPherson, KS 67460
(316)241-7754
Sharon E. Rosenkoetter

Comprehensive Model of Appropriate Preschool Practices and Services (CAPPS)
Kansas University Affiliated Program
2601 Gabriel Street
Parsons, KS 67357
(316)421-6550, ext. 1859
Lee K.S. McLean and David P. Lindeman

Project STEPS (Sequenced Transition to Education in the Public Schools)
Child Development Centers of the Bluegrass, Inc.
465 Springhill Drive
Lexington, KY 40503
(606)278-0549
Beth Rous

VIDEOSHARE Outreach Project
Division of Educational Research and Service
School of Education
The University of Montana
Missoula, MT 59812
(406)243-5344
Rick van den Pol

Magnolia Circle Outreach
Peabody College, Box 328
Vanderbilt University
Nashville, TN 37203
(615)322-8277 or (800)288-7733
Steven F. Warren

The Integrated Outreach Project
Center for Persons with Disabilities
Utah State University
Logan, UT 84322-6845
(801)750-3381
Sarah Rule

Portage Multi-State Outreach Project
CESA 5
626 East Slifer Street
Portage, WI 53901
(608)742-8811
Julia Herwig

National TEEM Outreach: Transition Into the Elementary Education Mainstream
Center for Developmental Disabilities
The UAP of Vermont
499C Waterman Building
University of Vermont
Burlington, VT 05405-0160
(802)656-4031
Wayne L. Fox and Jane Ross-Allen

MISCELLANEOUS

Trans/Team Outreach
Williamsburg Area Child Development Resources
P.O. Box 299
Lightfoot, VA 23090-0299
(804)565-0303
Corinne W. Garland

HEAD START TO ELEMENTARY SCHOOL

In September 1991, the Administration on Children, Youth, and Families awarded 32 grants to community-based consortia to demonstrate effective strategies for supporting children and families as they make the transition from the Head Start program through kindergarten and the first three grades of public school. The grants were awarded for up to $650,000 per project for each of 3 years. Of the 32 transition grantees, 23 are Head Start grantees. Six of these 23 are public school systems. The remaining 9 transition grantees are public school systems that do not operate a Head Start program.

These demonstration sites are testing the hypothesis that the provision of continuous comprehensive services to Head Start children will maintain and enhance the early benefits attained by the children and their families. An integral part of this national demonstration is a rigorous evaluation to determine the effectiveness of local programs.

The local projects are:

Albina Ministerial Alliance
Portland, Oregon

Anchorage School District
Anchorage, Alaska

Area Committee To Improve
Opportunities, Inc.
Athens, Georgia

Black River Area Development
Corporation
Pocahontas, Arkansas

Cen-Clear Child Services, Inc.
Philipsburg, Pennsylvania

Chapel Hill-Carrboro Head Start
Chapel Hill, North Carolina

Child Development Council of
Franklin County, Inc.
Columbus, Ohio

Community Services Agency
Reno, Nevada

Dade County Public Schools
Miami, Florida

Dallas Independent School District
Dallas, Texas

Fairfax County Office for Children
Fairfax, Virginia

Hardin County School System
Savannah, Tennessee

Human Services Center, Inc.
Idaho Falls, Idaho

Jefferson County Committee for
Economic Opportunity
Birmingham, Alabama

Kokomo-Center Township
Consolidated School Corporation
Kokomo, Indiana

Lincoln Action Program, Inc.
Lincoln, Nebraska

Mid-Iowa Community Action, Inc.
Marshalltown, Iowa

Montgomery County Government
Division of Community Action
Rockville, Maryland

Muskegon Heights Public Schools
Muskegon Heights, Michigan

Newport Public Schools
Newport, Rhode Island

New York City Schools
Brooklyn, New York

Renewal Unlimited, Inc.
Baraboo, Wisconsin

Santa Clara County Office of
Education
San Jose, California

School District No. 300,
Community Unit
Carpentersville, Illinois

South Central Child Development,
Inc.
Wagner, South Dakota

Southwest Human Development,
Inc.
Phoenix, Arizona

Southwestern Community Action
Council, Inc.
Huntington, West Virginia

School District of Independence
Independence, Missouri

St. Paul Public Schools
St. Paul, Minnesota

Trenton Board of Education
Trenton, New Jersey

The Navajo Nation
Window Rock, Arizona

Worcester Public Schools
Worcester, Massachusetts

Appendix B

Additional Sample Interagency Agreements

INTERAGENCY AGREEMENT between

The Outagamie County Early Intervention Program
Judith L. Gaines, Program Coordinator
(Point of Contact)

3375 West Brewster Street
Appleton, WI 54914
(tel. 749-5870)

and

The School District of Hortonville
Bruce Carew, Elementary Principal
(Point of Contact)

W6822 Greenridge Drive
Greenville, WI 54942
(tel. 757-6971)

The Early Intervention Program and the School District of Hortonville agree to work cooperatively on issues relative to children, birth through age 3, with developmental delays or with conditions having a high probability of affecting development. Some identified issues include childfind, screening, evaluation/assessment, and transition of children/families from the Early Intervention Program to the School District of Hortonville.

Personnel from the School District of Hortonville participate in the Early Intervention Program Informed Referral Network, referring identified children for screening or evaluation. The referring individual is then invited to attend the early intervention team (EI-team) meeting and be a full participant on the designated EI-team.

The Early Intervention Program will keep the School District of Hortonville informed (for planning purposes) regarding those enrolled children from the district. This will include a listing disseminated two times per year, with children identified by the first two letters of their last names (to protect confidentiality), their dates of birth, and some brief descriptions of Exceptional Educational Needs (EEN) eligibility criteria.

Children will be referred to the district 4 months before their third birthdays with consent of the parents/guardians. Referrals will be sent to designated points of contact, along with initial and interim reports to provide background information. The service coordinators' names and telephone numbers are provided (for follow-up contact) as well as the names of other individuals who have been involved with specific children.

The Early Intervention Program's service coordinators will be notified by the school of the multidisciplinary team (M-team) meeting 2 weeks in advance for scheduling purposes. The final report/reports and observations will be provided at M-team meetings.

Families will be supported while becoming acquainted with the district's personnel and facilities aiding in the transition process.

This cooperative agreement will be reviewed annually for possible changes/additions.

Judith L. Gaines, Coordinator Outagamie County Early Intervention Program	Bruce Carew, Elementary Principal School District of Hortonville

January 1993

TRANSITION AGREEMENT

This agreement shall facilitate the timely transition of children with suspected disabilities from the Parent–Child Program of the Development and Training Center (DTC) to the Eau Claire Area School District (ECASD), thus preventing duplication of evaluation efforts.

Parent–Child Program of the Development and Training Center (DTC) When a child with an identified disability or with suspected Exceptional Educational Needs (EEN) attains the age of 2 years, 9 months, and the service providers believe the child will continue to need special education services, staff from the Parent–Child Program of the DTC shall confer with the parent(s) and inform them of the need to refer the child to the school district for a multidisciplinary team (M-team) evaluation. The parent(s) may choose to self-refer, or the staff will facilitate the referral. At this time, the DTC Parent–Child Program shall secure written permission from the parent(s) to release records and send all pertinent information to the ECASD transition coordinator.

Eau Claire Area School District (ECASD) After the transition coordinator receives the information needed to evaluate a child who has been previously identified and served through the DTC Parent–Child Program, the school district shall assemble an M-team.

The first task of the M-team shall be to examine all relevant available data concerning the child, including available records of the child's previous and current educational performance, health, and social behavior (PI 11.04 [3] [a]1.).

If a recent evaluation has been conducted by qualified professionals and the assessment instruments and materials utilized by the DTC Parent–Child Program staff meet the criteria under s. PI 11.04 (3) (d), the school district M-team members may document these results and findings in their individual reports. Additional formal testing may be conducted at the discretion of the M-team members. In the event that an M-team member accepts the findings from a previous report, he or she will cite specific items from it and indicate how they are consistent both with his or her own documented observations of the child and with parental input.

In the event that the M-team documents both the existence of a disabling condition and the need for special education, the following will be adhered to: the parent(s) of an eligible child who is referred at 2 years, 9 months shall receive a placement offer when the child turns 3.

To avoid gaps in service, children who reach the age of 3 after April 1 will be evaluated according to the usual process and may remain at the DTC Parent–Child Program with parental approval until the summer school session (if the child is found to be eligible for the Early Childhood: EEN program, if EC:EEN summer school is offered by the school district, and if summer school is determined to be appropriate for that child by the M-team).

In return for this service the school district may enroll eligible children who attain the age of 3 by November 1 at the beginning of the school year per parental approval.

This agreement shall be reviewed and updated as needed.

______________________________	______________________________
School District Administrator	DTC Parent–Child Program Director

INTERAGENCY AGREEMENT
Coulee Children's Center
School District of LaCrosse
Memorandum of Agreement
Preface

Programs — Coulee Children's Center (CCC) provides early intervention, educational, and therapy services to children with disabilities, ages birth to 3 years in LaCrosse, Wisconsin. The School District of LaCrosse (SDOL) provides public education for children 3–21 years, along with other related services.

Purpose — The CCC and SDOL agree to provide transition services to children and their families through their collaborative efforts. Transition services will be provided so that the movement of the child is as smooth as possible. The SDOL recognizes the responsibility to screen children birth to 21 years. The SDOL will refer children for further evaluation, as needed. In an effort to collaborate on low incidence special services, the SDOL and the CCC will collaborate on joint inservice or share information regarding such services.

Transition Team — These organizations recognize that the transition from early intervention services to public school is a major event in the child's educational history. They recognize that family participation is crucial to a successful transition and will include families in all aspects of transition planning. Each child who makes a transition will receive transition planning services from a transition team. The transition team will include the child's parents or legal guardians, a staff member from the sending program who is familiar with the child and family, and a staff member from the receiving program. Other people also may participate (e.g., family members or others invited by the family, therapists, case managers). The transition coordinators will be responsible for planning.

Transition Dates — The SDOL will make every effort to complete referral and placement procedures to assure that children will transition from CCC on or near their third birthday. In an effort to accommodate this, CCC will refer children at least 90 days prior to their third birthdays. Children with August–September birthdays will be referred to the SDOL in May. Children who turn 3 within 1 month before the end of the school year will be given the option to remain at CCC or enter the public school program.

Goals — The goal of this transition agreement is to specify the commitments and responsibilities of CCC and the SDOL.

Review Dates — The task set forth in this agreement began on August 23, 1989, and is reviewed each year in November. The term of this agreement will be January 1, 1992, to January 1, 1993. Appropriate staff from each agency will reconvene to review the interagency agreement and timeline and revise as needed. Parties to the review will be: Dean Ruppert, Manager of Long Term Support; Polly Neess, SDOL Supervisor of Special Instructional Programs; Diane Nelson, CCC Executive Director; Terry Knothe-Lash, CCC Program Director; SDOL transition coordinator; and CCC transition coordinator. Each program will identify a staff member who will coordinate the transition activities and serve as transition coordinator.

Responsibilities — The transition coordinators will work together to:

(1) Manage the transition process.
(2) Evaluate the success of the child's and family's transition. Plan how transitions can be improved during the coming year.
(3) Revise procedures for transferring records as needed.

The CCC will assume the financial responsibility for providing records to the SDOL. Each program will assume financial responsibility for assessments normally completed by their program.

Individual program responsibilities are specified on the interagency transition plan flowchart, which also serves as a part of this agreement.

Polly Neess *School District of LaCrosse*	Date	Terry Knothe-Lash *Coulee Region Infant Developmental Center*	Date

TRANSITION PORTION OF A COMPREHENSIVE INTERAGENCY AGREEMENT:
TRANSITION PLANNING IN ITS INITIAL STAGES

LOCAL INTERAGENCY COOPERATIVE AGREEMENT

NEK-CAP Doniphan County Head Start
Doniphan County Education Cooperative 616
Special Needs Preschool

November 1991

NEK-CAP Head Start
P.O. Box 380
Hiawatha, KS 66434

Transition

An ongoing process of information sharing will be developed between the staffs of both agencies to ensure smooth transitions for children and families.

Meetings will be held once a month to maximize the benefits to the child through coordinated implementation of each child's specific plan.

For each child, a designated staff member from one program will be assigned as the primary contact and liaison with the family of the child. This person will be responsible for gathering information from all persons involved in providing services to the child.

Sundance/Stevensville Transition Process for Children with Special Needs and Their Families
October 1, 1993

Preamble

This process has been designed to promote smooth transition planning from one program to another for young children with special needs, parents, teachers, and other sending and receiving staff in school districts, agencies, or programs who provide services in the Sundance and Stevensville County areas. Although these procedures are written primarily for the transition into kindergarten, the process can be adjusted for other transitions as well.

We believe practices for young children should be developmentally appropriate—that is, age-appropriate and individually appropriate.

We believe that decisions concerning early childhood transitions should include opportunities for informed participation.

We believe that IEP goals and objectives regarding transition will help to prepare young children and their families for the next environment.

School district and program personnel will understand these procedures and work together to implement them.

Fall Transition Planning

1. Identify the person responsible for coordinating transitions in school district.
2. Inform parents of children enrolled in the Early Childhood Special Education (ECSE) who are potentially eligible for kindergarten the following year about transition. This may happen at the first early childhood parent orientation meeting, a general parent meeting, or during a home visit. Individual school districts are encouraged to provide a videotape of a typical fall kindergarten classroom setting; parents are encouraged to review it.
3. With prearrangement, parents have the option of visiting a kindergarten, preferably during November. The sending teacher may meet with the parent(s) to discuss their observations, questions, and concerns.

4. The person coordinating early childhood transitions will send each building principal a list of all students within their district of residence who will be eligible to enter kindergarten the following year and request that they be placed on the kindergarten enrollment list by September 1.
5. Kindergarten teachers (receivers) meet as a group or separately and complete the classroom checklist for the senders by September 15.
6. Early preschool teachers (senders) visit all possible kindergarten settings during the month of September (as appropriate) to make observations. ECSE and kindergarten teachers may also choose to exchange teaching time (if prearranged with the teachers and principals).
7. Early preschool teachers (senders) and kindergarten teachers (receivers) meet either as a group or individually during September or October to discuss the classroom checklist and make observations.
8. Discuss transition at IEP staffings and reviews. Transition goals and objectives are incorporated into the IEP.

Spring Transition Planning

1. By February 15, the early childhood team revises the list of students transitioning. The person coordinating early childhood transitions sends the revised list to the appropriate elementary principal by March 1 to ensure that students are placed on the kindergarten enrollment list.
2. The person coordinating early childhood transitions ensures that discussions regarding the potential placement of children take place among the principals, special education director, and early childhood and/or special education coordinators to consider the following:
   1) Building boundaries
   2) Degree of disability
   3) Parent rights and requests
   4) Regular education class size including special education ratios
   5) Senders' and receivers' input
   6) Caseloads of the special education teacher
   7) Support service needs (i.e., interpreters, therapists, medical issues)

8) Transportation
9) Other issues and concerns

3. Early childhood staff continue transition communication with parents during spring IEP staffings, reviews, and home visits. Expectations for kindergarten such as classroom interactions and routines continue to be reviewed.
4. All preschool teachers (senders) complete their classroom checklists for the receivers by March 30.
5. The kindergarten teachers and special education teacher(s) (receivers) visit the early childhood classroom between March 30 and April 30.
6. The sending and receiving teachers meet to discuss the classroom checklists and their observations.
7. Any assessments needed will be conducted and completed by April 1.
8. The assessment summary meeting and staffings, per child study procedures, will be conducted in the receiving school and will include the receiving regular and special education staff by May 1 to enable children to participate in kindergarten orientation in their neighborhood school.
9. The transition staffing is held in the receiving school with both the sending and receiving staff. Receiving teachers and support staff receive inservice training as identified.
10. Records for the child are sent to the receiving school by the conclusion of the school year. Parents' permission is obtained first.

Summer

1. The building principal responds to questions or concerns regarding the child's placement and/or service needs expressed by parents during the summer.
2. The special education procedures apply for children moving in during the summer.
3. A letter of confirmation specifying assigned teacher, support staff, and transportation arrangements is sent by the receiving building principal to the family by August 15.

Fall (After Transition)

1. The receiving teacher invites the parents for a brief visit to kindergarten.

2. During the first month of placement, the sending staff provides support and assistance as needed to the receiving staff.
3. The person responsible for coordinating early childhood transitions also coordinates the evaluation of the transition process and its effectiveness with input from senders and receivers. Results are shared with the interagency councils and changes are recommended.

Appendix C

Additional Sample Timelines

POLICIES AND PROCEDURES FOR TRANSITIONING

1. All students receiving Early Childhood Special Education (ECSE) services and related services (vision, occupational, speech, physical therapy) will be transitioned using the approach agreed upon previously.
2. The elementary school system will be informed by the early childhood facilitator of children who will enter through the interagency system.

   January/February—20 months prior to transition

   Person responsible: the transition coordinator
3. Parents will be provided with a copy of the "Parent's Guide to Transition."
4. A transition coordinator will be identified for each student. This person will meet with the parents individually and explain transition processes and forms. The family will be encouraged to be involved with the process. Available services and placement options will also be covered.
5. A team transition meeting will be held in which families will be introduced to the teachers who will take part in the transition process (this meeting can be held in conjunction with a periodic review).
6. The ECSE teacher, special education administrator, and principal will meet to discuss most challenging children and identify potential resources and/or adaptations that will require budget-

ary allocations and/or community support (e.g., bond issues). Identify additional members of individual transition planning teams.

7. The superintendent will be notified in writing regarding those transition plans to which adaptations will require budgetary allocations and/or community support.

   March/April—16 months prior to transition

   The transition coordinator will notify the people listed in items 8 and 9:

8. The elementary school principal, secretary, and kindergarten teacher will be notified in writing as to which children will be transitioned in 6 months and 18 months, respectively.
9. Families will be given opportunities to observe their children in preschool. They will also have opportunities to observe the kindergarten classrooms (during the spring before spring roundup).

TRANSITION PLAN

Algonquin's Early Childhood Special Education to Kindergarten Programs

I. Preliminary transition plans/initiating contacts
   A. IEP planning (ongoing)
      1. Reviewing progress with parents
      2. Identifying goals; include kindergarten survival skills: self-help, social interaction, play skills; and the ability to function independently
   B. Contact case manager and building principal to establish timeline
   C. Invite parents to observe kindergarten program
   D. Invite sending teachers to observe kindergarten program

II. Developing placement options
   A. Early childhood coordinator arranges staffing with principals and kindergarten teachers
   B. Classroom placements are made so receiving teachers can get to know children individually
   C. Receiving teachers observe early childhood classrooms
   D. Any adaptations that need to be made for a particular child are discussed with kindergarten teacher and principal
   E. Kindergarten teachers are invited to be part of IEP planning committee

III. Placement in kindergarten
   A. Children come to new school with parent(s) and early childhood teacher prior to first day of school
   B. Support person is available for the child and teacher during the first week (early childhood coordinator, speech pathologist, counselor, early childhood teacher)
   C. Team meeting occurs within first month of school to reassess needs (including Exceptional Educational Needs personnel and specialists such as art, music, or Instructional Materials Center)
   D. Support is provided as needed by early childhood staff
   E. Receiving school gradually assumes primary responsibility for the child

NORTH SHORE EXCEPTIONAL EDUCATION COOPERATIVE
Transition Checklist

Child's name: ____________ Birthdate: ____________
Parents: ____________ Address: ____________
Phone number: ____________ Home school: ____________
Case manager: ____________ Principal: ____________

Date Com-pleted	**Responsibility**	**Preliminary Transition Plans**
________	____________	Ongoing IEP planning: identifying goals, kindergarten survival skills, play/social skills
________	____________	Contact case manager and building principal to establish timeline for transition
________	____________	Invite parents to observe kindergarten program
________	____________	Invite sending teachers to observe kindergarten program
		Developing Placement Options
________	____________	Early childhood coordinator arranges staffing with kindergarten teachers and principals
________	____________	Classroom placements are made so that receiving teachers can get to know children individually
________	____________	Receiving teachers observe Early Childhood: Exceptional Educational Needs (EC:EEN) classrooms
________	____________	Discuss with the kindergarten teacher and principal any adaptations that need to be made for the child
________	____________	Kindergarten teachers are invited to be part of IEP planning committee

Placement in Kindergarten

________	__________	Children come to new school with parents and the early childhood teacher prior to first day of school
________	__________	Support person available for the child and teacher during the first week of school (dates)
________	__________	Team meeting within first month of school to re-assess needs
________	__________	Support provided as needed by EC:EEN staff
________	__________	Receiving school gradually assumes primary responsibility for child's program

Appendix D

Materials for a Toddler Transition Playgroup

EARLY INTERVENTION PROGRAM
Brown County

April 6, 1993

Dear Parents:

Our toddler transition playgroup is all set and ready to begin. The four sessions will be on Monday and Thursday mornings from 9:00 to 11:00 at the Unified School District's early childhood classroom. The dates are May 3, 6, 10, and 13.

Our planning for staff, equipment, space, activities, and field trips depend on families' commitment to each transition session. Therefore, your child must plan to attend on at least three of the four dates in order to participate. If you need transportation, please call us.

The purpose of the transition playgroup is to provide a transition from home to school. We will help children separate from their parents as we provide them with the opportunity to participate in small group activities while spending time with an early childhood class from Unified School District. The small group activities will focus on the areas of gross motor, fine motor, cognition, self-help, and language. The teachers, therapists, and other staff from both programs will conduct and assist in activities.

We are very excited about this playgroup. We look forward to working together to provide a smooth transition for each child and family.

If you have any questions, please call one of us at the office at 352-0000. We also invite any comments you may have regarding this project.

Sincerely,

Donna Lange, EIP

Jenny Miller, EC

Note: Map follows

TODDLER TRANSITION PLAYGROUP SCHEDULE FOR 1993–1994

Meeting with early intervention and early childhood staff to plan:
September 4, 1993 at 11:30 A.M.

Monday	September 14, 1993	9:00–11:00 A.M.
Thursday	September 17, 1993	9:00–11:00 A.M.
Monday	September 21, 1993	9:00–11:00 A.M.
Thursday	September 24, 1993	9:00–11:00 A.M. (field trip)

* *

Meeting with early intervention and early childhood staff to plan:
January 5, 1994 at 11:30 a.m.

Monday	January 11, 1994	9:00–11:00 A.M.
Thursday	January 14, 1994	9:00–11:00 A.M.
Monday	January 18, 1994	9:00–11:00 A.M.
Thursday	January 21, 1994	9:00–11:00 A.M. (field trip)

* *

Meeting with early intervention and early childhood staff to plan:
April 23, 1994 at 11:30 a.m.

Monday	May 3, 1994	9:00–11:00 A.M.
Thursday	May 6, 1994	9:00–11:00 A.M.
Monday	May 10, 1994	9:00–11:00 A.M.
Thursday	May 13, 1994	9:00–11:00 A.M. (field trip)

EARLY INTERVENTION PROGRAM

TO: EIP staff

FROM: Donna Lange, EIP, Brown County
Jenny Miller, EC, Unified School District

DATE: January 5, 1994

RE: Preparation for children participating in toddler transition class

---

Child's name: ______________________________
Chronological age: ______________________________
Approximation of cognitive level:

Allergies / food intolerances / feeding problems / self-feeders / require assistance

Special precautions: medical, shunts, or otherwise:

Equipment needed:

Level of supervision:
Minimal: ______________________________
Maximum: ______________________________
Precautions (including any food intolerances or special instructions):

Toileting procedures:
Sit/stand: ____ Potty chair: ____ Potty seat: ____
Supported on toilet: ____ Urinal: ____ Diaper: ____

Comments:

Do you anticipate requiring any special aids for managing behavior? We will *ignore* attention seeking behavior that does not harm.

We will provide short *time out* for destructive or hurting behavior.

We will reinforce good effort, compliance, and cooperation with praise, smiles, and hugs.

Comments:

ORIENTATION MEETING FOR PARENTS OF CHILDREN IN HOMEBASE ENTERING CENTERBASE IN FALL

Agenda

I. Welcome and introductions

II. Explanation of toddler group and transition program

III. Scheduling classes
- A. Classroom arrangements
- B. Classroom assignments
- C. A.M./P.M. preferences and hours

IV. Services offered in centerbase
- A. Speech-language therapy
- B. Occupational and physical therapy
- C. Pool therapy
- D. School nurse
- E. Audiologist (hearing screenings)
- F. Teacher for the visually impaired (vision screenings)

V. Daily schedules
- A. Entrance through children's entry
- B. Free choice play
- C. Circle time
- D. Individual work time
- E. Snack time
- F. Recess/outdoor time
- G. Group times (music, motor, science, language, art)
- H. Therapy times
- I. Weekly themes
- J. Goodbye time

VI. Medical issues
- A. Medical/immunization updates
- B. Giving medicines at school
- C. Daily health checks
- D. Medical concerns noted at school
- E. Need to have physician's permission for therapy

VII. Transportation
- A. Transportation to and from school
  - 1) Nickerson (USD 309) 663-7141

    2) Fairfield (USD 310) 596-2152
    3) Pretty Prairie (USD 311) 459-6241
    4) Haven (USD 312) 465-7727
    5) Buhler (USD 313) 543-6829

B. Transportation on field trips/permission for field trips

REMINDER:

Toddler Group starts on Monday, January 11, 1992, at 9:00–10:30 A.M. and 1:00–2:30 P.M. Tuesday, January 12, 1992, 9:00–10:30 A.M.

Your child ______________________________

will attend: Yes __ No __

We're looking forward to seeing you at school.

Homebase Staff
EARLY EDUCATION CENTER

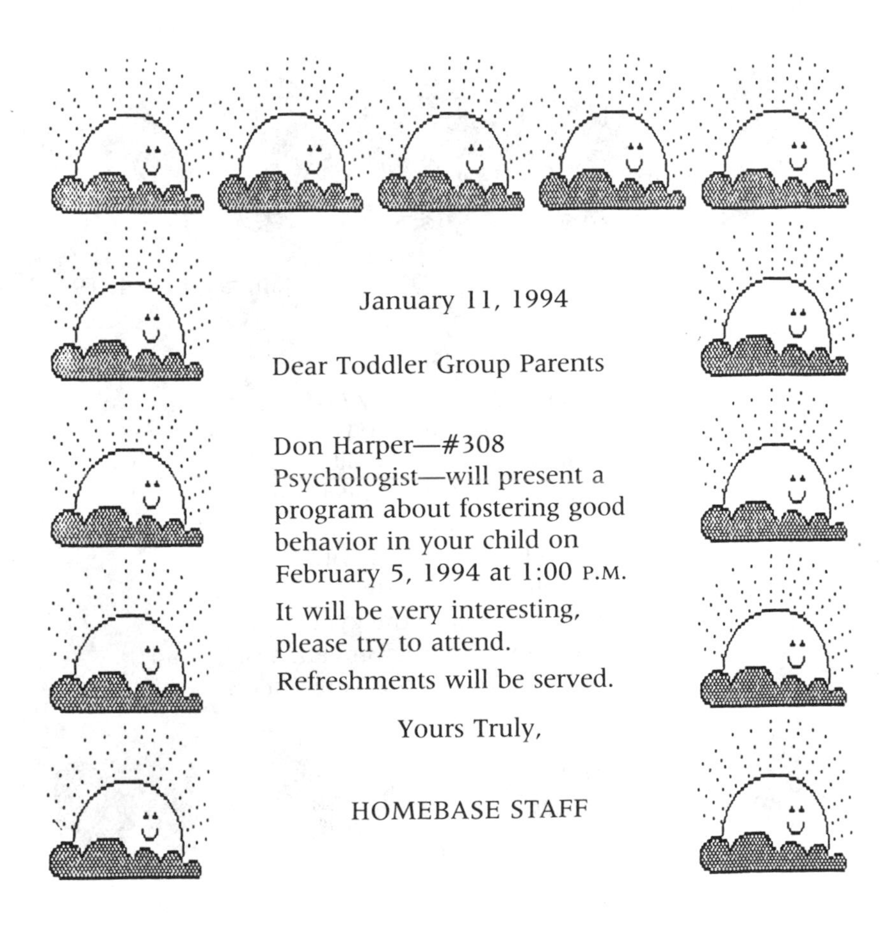

January 11, 1994

Dear Toddler Group Parents

Don Harper—#308
Psychologist—will present a program about fostering good behavior in your child on February 5, 1994 at 1:00 P.M.
It will be very interesting, please try to attend.
Refreshments will be served.

Yours Truly,

HOMEBASE STAFF

January 13–14, 1992

Today at Toddler Group, we...
Played with grocery carts
and pretend foods
Sang songs ("Itsy Bitsy
Spider" and "The Wheels on
the Bus")
We finger painted with
chocolate pudding,
Played ball in the gym
We had peanut butter on bananas,
Read Goldilocks and the Three Bears

Appendix E

A Community Resource Directory

COMMUNITY RESOURCE DIRECTORY

A community resource directory that describes services available in the region can be very useful in exploring placement options, in providing interaction with children without disabilities, and in preparing children for transition. The directory provides general information about

*Available services	*General developmental emphasis
*Contact person	*Facilities
*Location	*Parent involvement
*Hours of service	*Parent/staff communication
*Eligibility	*Cost

A worksheet can be distributed to all programs and individuals in the community that serve children and families. After their responses are collected, the results can be gathered in looseleaf notebooks (for easy updating) and distributed to participating early childhood agencies.

A community resource directory may be a positive choice for an initial interagency effort because it profiles all participants and threatens none. Before undertaking such a directory, however, be sure one is not currently available. Indeed, many Head Start programs have already assembled such a directory that can be used by other community programs.

* * * * * * * *

A number of agencies are cooperating to develop a community resource directory to aid families with young children. The information you provide about your program(s) will be used in assembling a guide to services available for families with young children from birth through age 5. Please be specific in your responses. Use the back of the sheet if you need more space. Feel free to photocopy this sheet if you represent more than one program. If your program has unique characteristics that are not addressed on this form, please describe them in response 11.

1. Services available

____
____
____
____
____
____

2. Program director (Name, address, telephone number, and hours)

____
____
____
____
____
____

3. Location(s)

____
____
____

4. Times when services are provided

____
____
____

5. Description of facilities (Include accessibility for persons with disabilities.)

____
____
____
____
____
____

6. Population served and eligibility for services (Are any children with special needs now receiving services?)

____

____

____

____

7. Developmental skills emphasis (Social, recreation, language, fine and gross motor, self-care, cognitive, math, and reading)

____

____

____

____

____

8. Parent involvement (Describe parents' responsibilities and options for involvement.)

____

____

____

____

____

9. Parent/staff communication (Describe the frequency and type of contact.)

____

____

____

____

____

10. Cost (Is scholarship help available? Criteria for receiving it?)

____

____

11. Other comments

____

____

____

____

____

____

Appendix F

Additional Sample Evaluation Tools

August, 1993

Dear Parent,

As you know, Unified School District's preschool program is starting an exciting new way to provide services to young children with special needs and their families. A number of children will stay in their home community of Springfield and receive their special education services there at the local Children's Center when they graduate from the early intervention program. A teacher and a paraprofessional from the County's Special Education Cooperative will be based at the Children's Center.

Because this is a new way to provide special education services, we wish to evaluate very carefully how the change is going. A team of people from Springfield's local interagency coordinating council will help us with this evaluation. Parents and staff members will be interviewed at different times, and children's progress will be monitored very closely. At this time, we would like your consent regarding the following evaluation activities:

1) An interviewer from the local interagency coordinating council will talk with you in August or September before your child starts at the Children's Center, again 3 weeks after your child starts to attend, and again 6 months later. The purpose of this is to learn how you are viewing your child's experience.

2) A preschool staff member will videotape your child playing both before and after his or her transition in order to evaluate the language and play skills exhibited in the two settings.

Of course, your child's progress in achieving IEP objectives will be followed closely at the Children's Center. None of the information gathered will be shared with your child's name attached with anyone but you. Rather, the information will be put together with information from other children and parents to ensure that this new program is meeting the needs of all involved children. We also hope to learn about any special benefits of this new kind of special education placement. As with all special education services, you may withdraw your consent to participate at any time.

We thank you for your willingness to help in this evaluation. Your participation will help to improve services for your child and for others who follow.

Sincerely,

Virginia Brown John Walker

CONSENT TO PARTICIPATE

I agree to participate in three interviews at a mutually agreeable time and place. The interviews will concern transitions into preschool services in Springfield. I also consent to having my child videotaped for purposes of assessing his or her play and language patterns. I realize that I may withdraw this consent at any time.

_______________________ _______________________

Parent's name Date

PARENT INTERVIEW #1

Thank you for letting me visit you in your home today. As stated in the letter you received, we are looking very closely at the move of children from the early intervention program to the Children's Center to be sure that every child's needs are met. We also want to know any special benefits that may come from this new arrangement and any problems that may arise. We want to know how it seems to you to be going now. There are no right answers, just how it seems to you. Anything that you tell me will be kept confidential from both the Children's Center staff and the early intervention program staff. I will share information only for a group of families, not specifically for your child or your family. The reason we want to record our conversation is so that I can go back later and double check the words that I have jotted down.

1. First, please tell me about your child with special needs and your family.
2. How are you feeling about your child's going to the Children's Center?
3. How do you feel about the way the arrangements are being made for your child to move to the Children's Center?
4. What are some of the benefits anticipated for your child when [he or she] begins going to the Children's Center?
5. What are some of the benefits anticipated for your family when your child goes to the Children's Center?
6. At this point, would you rather have your child at the Children's Center or in the self-contained special education classroom?
7. Do you foresee any problems or disadvantages for your child attending the Children's Center?
8. Do you foresee any problems or disadvantages for your family with your child attending preschool at the Children's Center?
9. What are the most important things that you hope your child will learn at the Children's Center?

10. Is there any information that you would like to receive from either the early intervention program or the Children's Center to make this transition easier for your child or your family?

Thank you very much for visiting with me and answering these questions. Now I'd like to ask you to take one more minute to fill out this sheet of paper. You mark 5 if you agree very much, 1 if you don't agree at all, or anything in the middle that fits your opinion about the question.

PARENT OPINION SURVEY #1

	Don't Agree				Strongly Agree
1. I am eager for my child to attend the Children's Center.	1	2	3	4	5
2. I am pleased with the information I have received thus far.	1	2	3	4	5
3. I would like to receive more information.	1	2	3	4	5
4. The early intervention staff listened carefully to my wishes about the Children's Center.	1	2	3	4	5
5. I feel free to ask any questions I have regarding the move to the Children's Center.	1	2	3	4	5
6. I am worried about how my child will do at the Children's Center.	1	2	3	4	5
7. I believe that it will be helpful for my child to spend lots of time with children without disabilities.	1	2	3	4	5
8. I believe that any therapy my child needs will be provided well at the Children's Center.	1	2	3	4	5
9. I believe that the Children's Center staff will help my child to accomplish IEP objectives.	1	2	3	4	5
10. I hope there will be opportunities for parents to visit the Children's Center.	1	2	3	4	5
11. I hope there will be opportunities for parents/families to be involved at the Children's Center.	1	2	3	4	5

12. I hope that there will be opportunities for parent education at the Children's Center.	1	2	3	4	5
13. I would like to be a parent volunteer at the Children's Center.	1	2	3	4	5

Any other comments are welcome. Thank you for your help.

PARENT INTERVIEW #2

Thank you for letting me visit you in your home today. Your child has been at the Children's Center for about 3 weeks now, and again we really want to know how it's going from your perspective. Again, anything that you tell me will be kept confidential from both the Children's Center staff and the early intervention program staff. I will share information only for a group of families, not specifically for your child or your family. The reason we want to record our conversation is so that I can go back later and double check the words that I have jotted down.

1. First, please tell me how the first 3 weeks have gone for your child and family.
2. How are you feeling about your child's going to the Children's Center?
3. How do you feel about the way the arrangements have been made for your child to move to the Children's Center?
4. Are you seeing any benefits for your child as [he or she] goes to the Children's Center?
5. Are you seeing any benefits for your family as your child goes to the Children's Center?
6. At this point, would you rather have your child at the Children's Center or at the self-contained special education classroom?
7. Are you seeing any problems or disadvantages for your child attending the Children's Center? (If there are several children in the family, you will need to ask this for each child.)
8. Are you seeing any problems or disadvantages for your family with your child attending preschool at the Children's Center?
9. What are some of the things that your child is learning at the Children's Center?
10. Are there other things you would like your child to learn at the Children's Center?
11. Is there any information that you would like to receive from the Children's Center to make this transition easier for your child or your family?
12. Do you have any suggestions for the early intervention program staff or the Children's Center staff to help children with special needs feel comfortable at the Children's Center?

Thank you very much for visiting with me and answering these questions. Now I'd like to ask you to take one more minute to fill out this sheet of paper. You mark 5 if you agree very much, 1 if you don't agree at all, or anything in the middle that fits your opinion about the question.

PARENT OPINION SURVEY #2

		Don't Agree				Strongly Agree
1.	I am pleased my child is attending the Children's Center.	1	2	3	4	5
2.	I am pleased with the information I have received so far about my child's progress.	1	2	3	4	5
3.	I would like to receive more information.	1	2	3	4	5
4.	I feel free to ask any questions I have.	1	2	3	4	5
5.	My child is learning what preschool-age children need to learn.	1	2	3	4	5
6.	The move to the Children's Center has gone well.	1	2	3	4	5
7.	My child is happy at the Children's Center.	1	2	3	4	5
8.	My child is making friends at the Children's Center.	1	2	3	4	5
9.	I believe that it is helpful for my child to spend time with children with disabilities.	1	2	3	4	5
10.	I have concerns about my child attending school with children with disabilities.	1	2	3	4	5
11.	I have been pleased with opportunities for parents to visit the Children's Center.	1	2	3	4	5
12.	I have been pleased with opportunities for parents/families to be involved at the Children's Center.	1	2	3	4	5

13.	I am pleased with the opportunities for parent education at the Children's Center.	1	2	3	4	5
14.	I would recommend that other children with special needs attend preschool in their home community.	1	2	3	4	5

Any other comments are welcome. Thank you for your help.

PARENT INTERVIEW #3

Thank you for letting me visit you in your home today. Your child has been at the Children's Center for about 6 months now, and again we really want to know how it's going from your perspective. Again, anything that you tell me will be kept confidential from both the Children's Center staff and the early intervention program staff. I will share information only for a group of families, not specifically for your child or your family. The reason we want to record our conversation is so that I can go back later and double check the words that I have jotted down.

1. First, please tell me how these 6 months at the Children's Center have gone for your child and family.
2. How are you feeling about your child's going to the Children's Center?
3. How do you feel about the way the arrangements have been made for your child to receive special education services at the Children's Center?
4. What benefits are you seeing for your child as [he or she] continues going to the Children's Center?
5. Are you seeing any benefits for your family as a result of your child's going to the Children's Center?
6. At this point would you rather have your child at the Children's Center or at the self-contained special education classroom?
7. Are you seeing any problems or disadvantages for your child attending the Children's Center?
8. Are you seeing any problems or disadvantages for your family with your child attending preschool at the Children's Center?
9. What are the most important things that your child has learned at the Children's Center?
10. If your child is eligible for services next year, would you prefer to have them delivered at the Children's Center or the self-contained special education classroom?
11. Do you have any suggestions for the early intervention program staff or the Children's Center staff to help other children with special needs and their families feel comfortable at the Children's Center in the future?

Thank you very much for visiting with me and answering these questions. Now I'd like to ask you to take one more minute to fill out this sheet of paper. You mark 5 if you agree very much, 1 if you don't agree at all, or anything in the middle that fits your opinion about the question.

PARENT OPINION SURVEY #3

		Don't Agree				Strongly Agree
1.	I am pleased my child is attending preschool.	1	2	3	4	5
2.	I am pleased my child is attending the Children's Center in Springfield.	1	2	3	4	5
3.	My child is learning what all preschool-age children need to learn.	1	2	3	4	5
4.	My child is receiving excellent help for his or her special needs.	1	2	3	4	5
5.	The move to the Children's Center has gone well.	1	2	3	4	5
6.	My child is happy at the Children's Center.	1	2	3	4	5
7.	My child has made friends at the Children's Center.	1	2	3	4	5
8.	My child sees these friends outside the school day.	1	2	3	4	5
9.	I believe that it is helpful for my child to spend lots of time with children without disabilities.	1	2	3	4	5
10.	I believe that any therapy my child needs is being provided well at the Children's Center.	1	2	3	4	5
11.	I have been pleased with opportunities for parents to visit the Children's Center.	1	2	3	4	5
12.	I have been pleased with opportunities for parents/families to have social evenings at the Children's Center.	1	2	3	4	5

13. I am pleased with opportunities for parent education at the Children's Center.	1	2	3	4	5
14. I would recommend that other children with special needs attend preschool in their home community.	1	2	3	4	5

Any other comments are welcome. Thank you for your help.

STAFF INTERVIEW #1

Thank you for letting me visit with you today. As you know, we are looking very closely at the move of children from the early intervention program to the Children's Center to be sure that every child's needs are met. We also want to know any special benefits that may come from this new arrangement and any problems that may arise. We want to know how it seems to you to be going now. There are no right answers, just how it seems to you. Anything that you tell me will be kept confidential. I will share information only, not names or identifying information. The reason we want to record our conversation is so that I can go back later and double check the words that I have jotted down.

1. First, please tell me how you are feeling about the plan to serve the children with special needs and the children without special needs together at the Children's Center.
2. What are some of the benefits of serving all the children and families together in Springfield?
3. Do you foresee any problems or disadvantages for either the children, families, or staff by serving the children with special needs and those without special needs together at the Children's Center?
4. How are you feeling about the move to the new facility?
5. How do you feel about the way the arrangements are being made for the transition to the new facility?
6. What suggestions do you have for improving the situation? How can we better help the children and families make the transition to the new center?
7. At this point, would you rather have the program at the special education preschool or at the new Children's Center? Why?
8. What are your most important goals for the new Children's Center?
9. Is there any information or training that you would like to receive during the school year?
10. Is there any information or training that other people involved in this transition need to improve their services?
11. Any other comments about the changes that are underway?

Thank you very much for visiting with me and answering these questions. Now I'd like to ask you to take one more minute to fill out this sheet of paper. You mark 5 if you agree very much, 1 if you don't agree at all, or anything in the middle that fits your opinion about the question.

STAFF OPINION SURVEY #1

	Don't Agree				Strongly Agree
1. I am eager for all of the children to be served together at the new center.	1	2	3	4	5
2. I have concerns about what will happen when all of the children are served together at the new center.	1	2	3	4	5
3. I am pleased with the information that I have received so far about the changes.	1	2	3	4	5
4. I would like to receive more information.	1	2	3	4	5
5. I have been able to have the input that I wanted regarding the process.	1	2	3	4	5
6. I feel free to ask any questions I have regarding the move to the Children's Center.	1	2	3	4	5
7. I think the work for each staff member will be manageable at the new center.	1	2	3	4	5
8. I think the staff will be adequately prepared for their responsibilities at the new center.	1	2	3	4	5
9. I believe that it will be helpful for children without special needs to spend lots of time with children who have special needs.	1	2	3	4	5
10. I believe that the needed therapy will be provided well at the Children's Center.	1	2	3	4	5

11.	I believe that children will be able to accomplish their IEP objectives at the Children's Center.	1	2	3	4	5
12.	I look forward to the expanded opportunities for parents at the new Children's Center.	1	2	3	4	5
13.	I hope there will be opportunities for parents/families to have social evenings at the Children's Center.	1	2	3	4	5
14.	I hope that there will be opportunities for parent participation at the Children's Center.	1	2	3	4	5
15.	I would be happy to work with community volunteers at the Children's Center.	1	2	3	4	5

16. I most look forward to this aspect of the Children's Center:

17. I have most concerns about this aspect of the Children's Center:

Any other comments are welcome. Thank you for your help.

STAFF INTERVIEW #2

Thank you for letting me visit with you today. You've been at the Children's Center for several weeks now, and again we really want to know how it's going. Again, anything that you tell me will be kept confidential. I will share comments only, not names or identifying information. The reason we want to record our conversation is so that I can go back later and double check the words that I have jotted down.

1. First, please tell me how the first weeks have gone for children with special needs and their families being served together with other children and families in the community.
2. How are you feeling about the move to the new facility?
3. What are some of the benefits you are seeing from serving all the children in Springfield together? Benefits for children without disabilities? Benefits for children with disabilities? Benefits for families? Benefits for staff?
4. What are some of the problems you are seeing from serving the children with special needs and the children without special needs together? Problems for children? For families? For staff?
5. What suggestions do you have for overcoming these problems?
6. How do you feel about the way the arrangements were made for the transition to the new facility?
7. How can we better help the children and families make the transition to the new facility?
8. At this point, would you rather have the program at the special education preschool or at the Children's Center? Why?
9. What are your most important goals for the Children's Center?
10. Is there any information or training that you would like to receive during the school year?
11. Is there any information or training that other people involved in this transition need to improve the services?
12. Any other comments about the changes that are underway?

Thank you very much for visiting with me and answering these questions. Now I'd like to ask you to take one more minute to fill out this sheet of paper. You mark 5 if you agree very much, 1 if you don't agree at all, or anything in the middle that fits your opinion about the question at hand.

STAFF OPINION SURVEY #2

		Don't Agree				Strongly Agree
1.	I am pleased that all of the children are being served together at the center.	1	2	3	4	5
2.	I have some concerns about some things that are happening when all of the children are served together at the center.	1	2	3	4	5
3.	I am pleased with the information that I have received about the changes.	1	2	3	4	5
4.	I would like to receive more information.	1	2	3	4	5
5.	I have been able to have the input that I wanted regarding the process.	1	2	3	4	5
6.	I feel free to ask any questions I have regarding the upcoming plans at the Children's Center.	1	2	3	4	5
7.	I think the work for each staff member will be manageable at the new center.	1	2	3	4	5
8.	I think the staff are adequately prepared for their responsibilities at the new center.	1	2	3	4	5
9.	I believe that it will be helpful for children without special needs to spend lots of time with children who have special needs.	1	2	3	4	5
10.	I believe that the needed therapy is provided well at the Children's Center.	1	2	3	4	5
11.	I believe that children will be able to accomplish their IEP objectives at the Children's Center.	1	2	3	4	5

(continued)

12.	I look forward to the expanded opportunities for parents at the new Children's Center.	1	2	3	4	5
13.	I hope there will be opportunities for parents/families to have social evenings at the Children's Center.	1	2	3	4	5
14.	I hope that there will be opportunities for parent education at the Children's Center.	1	2	3	4	5
15.	I would be happy to work with community volunteers at the Children's Center.	1	2	3	4	5

16. My primary concern regarding my experience with the Children's Center is:

17. The best thing so far about my experience with the Children's Center is:

Any other comments are welcome. Thank you for your help.

STAFF INTERVIEW #3

Thank you for letting me visit with you today. You've been at the Children's Center for about 6 months now, and again we really want to know how it's going. Again, anything that you tell me will be kept confidential. I will share comments only, not names or identifying information. The reason we want to record our conversation is so that I can go back later and double check the words that I have jotted down.

1. First, please tell me how the first 6 months have gone for children with special needs and their families being served together with other children and families in the community.
2. How are you feeling by now about the move to the new facility?
3. What are some of the benefits you are seeing from serving all the children in Springfield together? Benefits for children without disabilities? Benefits for children with disabilities? Benefits for family? Benefits for staff?
4. What are some of the problems you are seeing from serving the children with special needs and the children without special needs together? Problems for children? For families? For staff?
5. What suggestions do you have for overcoming these problems?
6. How do you feel about the way the arrangements were made for the transition to the new facility?
7. At this point, would you rather have the program at the special education preschool or at the new Children's Center? Why?
8. What are your most important goals for the new Children's Center?
9. Is there any information or training that you would like to receive during the next school year?
10. Is there any information or training that other people involved in the Children's Center need to improve the services?
11. Any other comments about the changes that are underway?

Thank you very much for visiting with me and answering these questions. Now I'd like to ask you to take one more minute to fill out this sheet of paper. You mark 5 if you agree very much, 1 if you don't agree at all, or anything in the middle that fits your opinion about the question at hand.

STAFF OPINION SURVEY #3

		Don't Agree				Strongly Agree
1.	I am pleased that all of the children are being served together at the Children's Center.	1	2	3	4	5
2.	The integrated program at the Children's Center is good for children without special needs.	1	2	3	4	5
3.	The integrated program at the Children's Center is good for the children with special needs.	1	2	3	4	5
4.	I have some concerns about some things that are happening when all of the children are served together at the Children's Center.	1	2	3	4	5
5.	I believe that major changes need to be made before we sponsor an integrated program again next year.	1	2	3	4	5
6.	I have been able to have the input that I wanted regarding the Children's Center development.	1	2	3	4	5
7.	I think the work for each staff member has been manageable at the Children's Center.	1	2	3	4	5
8.	I think major changes need to be made in staff assignments before next year.	1	2	3	4	5
9.	It has been fun for staff to work together.	1	2	3	4	5
10.	It has been helpful for my professional development to work with staff from the other programs at the Children's Center.	1	2	3	4	5

11.	I believe that it is helpful for children without special needs to spend lots of time with children who have special needs.	1	2	3	4	5
12.	I believe that the needed therapy has been provided well at the Children's Center.	1	2	3	4	5
13.	I believe that children have accomplished their IEP objectives.	1	2	3	4	5
14.	The children with special needs have become good friends with the typically developing children.	1	2	3	4	5
15.	There are expanded opportunities for parents at the Children's Center.	1	2	3	4	5
16.	I feel that our staff at the Children's Center have learned a lot about problem-solving this year.	1	2	3	4	5
17.	I believe that we are now an effective team at the Children's Center.	1	2	3	4	5

18. My primary concern regarding my experience with the Children's Center is:

19. The best thing about my experience with the Children's Center is:

Any other specific comments or suggestions regarding your experience will be appreciated. Thank you for your help.

References

Administration for Children and Families. (1993). *Head Start program performance standards: Performance standards for services to children with disabilities in the Head Start Program* (*CFR, 45,* Part 1308). Washington, DC: U.S. Department of Health and Human Services, Administration of Children, Youth, and Families.

Allen, K.E. (1992). *The exceptional child: Mainstreaming in early childhood education.* Albany, NY: Delmar.

American Academy of Pediatrics. (1990). Children with health impairments in schools. *Pediatrics, 86,* 636–638.

American Occupational Therapy Association. (1988). *Occupational therapy services in early intervention and preschool services.* Rockville, MD: Author.

American Speech-Language-Hearing Association. (1990). The role of the speech-language pathologist in service delivery to infants, toddlers, and their families. *Asha, 32*(2), 4.

Americans with Disabilities Act of 1990 (ADA), PL 101-336. (July 26, 1990). Title 42, U.S.C. 12101 et seq: *U.S. Statutes at Large, 104,* 327–378.

Bailey, D.B., Jr. (1989). Case management in early intervention. *Journal of Early Intervention, 13,* 120–134.

Bailey, D.B., McWilliam, P.J., & Winton, P.J. (1992). Building family-centered practices in early intervention: A team-based model for change. *Infants and Young Children, 5*(1), 78–82.

Baker, B.L., & Brightman, A.J. (1989). *Steps to independence: A skills training guide for parents and teachers of children with special needs.* Baltimore: Paul H. Brookes Publishing Co.

Balaban, N. (1985). *Starting school: From separation to independence.* New York: Teachers College Press.

Barber, P.A., Turnbull, A.P., Behr, S.K., & Kerns, G.M. (1988). A family systems perspective on early childhood special education. In S.L. Odom & M.B. Karnes (Eds.), *Early intervention for infants and children with handicaps: An empirical base* (pp. 179–198). Baltimore: Paul H. Brookes Publishing Co.

Barbour, N.H., & Seefeldt, C.A. (1993). *Developmental continuity across preschool and primary grades: Implications for teachers.* Wheaton, MD: Association for Childhood Education International.

Barbour, N.H., & Seefeldt, C.A. (1992). Developmental continuity from preschool through primary grades. *Childhood Education, 68*(5), 302–304.

Baumgart, D., Brown, L., Pumpian, I., Nisbet, J., Ford, A., Sweet, M., Messina, R., & Schroeder, J. (1982). Principle of partial participation and individualized adaptations in educational programs for severely handicapped students. *Journal of The Association for the Severely Handicapped, 7*(2), 17–27.

Beckoff, A.G., & Bender, W.N. (1989). Programming for mainstream kindergarten success in preschool: Teachers' perceptions of necessary prerequisite skills. *Journal of Early Intervention, 13*(3), 269–280.

Benner, S.M. (1992). *Assessing young children with special needs: An ecological perspective.* White Plains, NY: Longman Publishing Group.

Bennett, T., Raab, M., & Nelson, D. (1991). The transition process for toddlers with special needs and their families. *Zero to Three, 11*(3), 17–21.

Bernard, B. (1989). Working together: Principles of effective collaboration. *Prevention Forum, 10*(1), 4–9.

Bickman, L., & Weatherford, D.L. (1986). *Evaluating early intervention programs for severely handicapped children and their families.* Austin, TX: PRO-ED.

Blair-Thomas, L., Wilson, T.F., Guida, J.C., & Manning, S. (1986). *Project ENTRANS: A model for transition of preschool children with handicaps into public school.* Monmouth, OR: Teaching Research Division.

Blaska, J.K. (1989). *An exploratory study of current transition practices: Implications for program administration.* Unpublished doctoral dissertation, University of Minnesota, Minneapolis.

Boyer, E.L. (1991). *Ready to learn: A mandate for the nation.* Princeton, NJ: Carnegie Foundation for the Advancement of Teaching.

Bredekamp, S. (1987). *Developmentally appropriate practice in early childhood programs serving children from birth through age 8.* Washington DC: National Association for the Education of Young Children.

Bredekamp, S., & Rosegrant, T. (Eds.). (1992). *Reaching potentials: Appropriate curriculum and assessment for young children* (Vol. 1). Washington DC: National Association for the Education of Young Children.

Bricker, D.D. (1989). *Early intervention for at-risk and handicapped infants, toddlers, and preschool children* (2nd ed.). Palo Alto, CA: VORT Corp.

Bricker, D., & Cripe, J.J.W. (1992). *An activity-based approach to early intervention.* Baltimore: Paul H. Brookes Publishing Co.

Bricker, D.D., Peck, C.A., & Odom, S.L. (1993). Integration: Campaign for the new century. In C.A. Peck, S.L. Odom, & D.D. Bricker (Eds.), *Integrating young children with disabilities into community programs* (pp. 271–276). Baltimore: Paul H. Brookes Publishing Co.

Brinkerhoff, J. (1987). *The Portage Classroom Curriculum.* Portage, WI: Cooperative Educational Service Agency 5, Portage Project.

Brinkerhoff, J., & Vincent, L. (1986). Increasing parental decision making at the individualized educational program meeting. *Journal of the Division for Early Childhood, 11,* 46–58.

Brotherson, M.J., Backus, L.H., Summers, J.A., & Turnbull, A.P. (1986). Transition to adulthood. In J.A. Summers (Ed.), *The right to grow up: An introduction to adults with developmental disabilities* (pp. 17–44). Baltimore: Paul H. Brookes Publishing Co.

Brown, F., & Lehr, D. (Eds.). (1989). *Persons with profound disabilities: Issues and practices.* Baltimore: Paul H. Brookes Publishing Co.

Brown, L., Branston, M.B., Hamre-Nietupski, S., Pumpian, I., Certo, N., & Gruenewald, L. (1979). A strategy for developing chronological age-appropriate and functional curricular content for severely handicapped adolescents and young adults. *Journal of Special Education, 13,* 81–90.

Brown, L., & Irwin, L. (1992). *Parent to parent: Encouraging connections be-*

tween parents of children with disabilities. Madison: University of Wisconsin, Waisman Center, Wisconsin Personnel Development Project.

Brown, L., Nietupski, J., & Hamre-Nietupski, S. (1976). Criterion of ultimate functioning. In M.S. Thomas (Ed.), *Hey, don't forget about me.* Reston, VA: Council for Exceptional Children.

Bruder, M.B. (1990, October). *Children with complex health care needs: Issues in policy and personnel preparation.* Paper presented at the International Early Childhood Conference on Children with Special Needs, Albuquerque, New Mexico.

Caldwell, B.M. (1990). Continuity in the early years: Transitions between grades and systems. In S.L. Kagan (Ed.), *The care and education of America's young children: Obstacles and opportunities: Nineteenth Yearbook of the National Society for the Study of Education* (pp. 69–89). Chicago: University of Chicago Press.

Caldwell, B.M. (1991). Continuity in the early years: Transition between grades and systems. In S.L. Kagan (Ed.), *The care and education of America's young children: Obstacles and opportunities* (pp. 69–90). Chicago: University of Chicago Press.

Caldwell, T.H., & Kirkhart, K.A. (1991). Accessing the education system for students who require health technology and treatment. In N.J. Hochstadt & D.M. Yost, *The medically complex child: The transition to home care.* New York: Harwood Academic Publishers.

Caldwell, T.H., Todaro, A.W., & Gates, A.J. (Eds.). (1989). *Community providers guide: An information outline for working with children with special health needs.* New Orleans: Children's Hospital, National MCH Resource Center.

California Infant Preschool/Special Education Resource Network. (n.d.). Community collaboration. Excerpted from *The file drawer: A resource for consultants to community collaborative groups.* Sacramento: Author.

Campbell, P.H., Garner, J.B., Cooper, M., & Wetherbee, R. (1986). *Strategies for identifying and selecting instructional priorities.* Akron, OH: Family Child Learning Center and Akron City Schools.

Cantor, L. (1976). *Assertive discipline: A take charge approach for today's education.* Los Angeles: Lee Cantor and Associates.

Carden-Smith, L., & Fowler, S.A. (1983). An assessment of student and teacher behavior in treatment and mainstreamed classes for preschool and kindergarten. *Analysis and Intervention in Developmental Disabilities, 3,* 35–57.

Carta, J., Atwater, J.B., Schwartz, I.S., & Miller, P.A. (1990). Applications of ecobehavioral analysis to the study of transitions across early educational settings. *Education and Treatment of Children, 13*(4), 298–315.

Carta, J.J., Elliott, M., Orth-Lopes, L., Scherer, H., Schwartz, I.S., & Atwater, J.B. (1992). *Project SLIDE: Skills for learning independence in diverse environments (teacher's manual).* Kansas City: University of Kansas, Juniper Gardens Children's Project.

Carta, J.J., Sainato, D.M., & Greenwood, C.R. (1988). Advances in the ecological assessment of classroom instruction for young children with handicaps. In S.L. Odom & M.B. Karnes (Eds.), *Early intervention for infants and children with handicaps: An empirical base* (pp. 217–240). Baltimore: Paul H. Brookes Publishing Co.

Carta, J.J., Schwartz, I.S., Atwater, J.B., & McConnell, S.R. (1991). Developmentally appropriate practice: Appraising its usefulness for young children with disabilities. *Topics in Early Childhood Special Education, 11*(1), 1–20.

Chandler, L.K. (1992). Promoting children's social/survival skills as a strategy for transition to mainstreamed kindergarten programs. In S.L. Odom, S.R. McConnell, & M.A. McEvoy (Eds.), *Social competence of young children with disabilities: Issues and strategies for intervention* (pp. 135–164). Baltimore: Paul H. Brookes Publishing Co.

Children's Defense Fund. (1992). *The state of America's children: 1992.* Washington, DC: Author.

Church, G., & Glennen, S. (1992). *The handbook of assistive technology.* San Diego: Singular Publishing Group.

Committee for Economic Development. (1987). *Children in need: Investment in strategies for the educationally disadvantaged.* New York: Author.

Commonwealth of Virginia Early Intervention. (1988). *Collaborative early intervention planning guide.* Richmond: Author.

Conn-Powers, M., & Ross-Allen, J. (1991). *TEEM: A manual to support the transition of young children with special needs and their families from preschool into kindergarten and other regular education environments.* Burlington: University of Vermont, University Affiliated Program, Center for Developmental Disabilities.

Conn-Powers, M.C., Ross-Allen, J., & Holburn, S. (1990). Transition of young children into the elementary education mainstream. *Topics in Early Childhood Special Education, 9,* 91–105.

Cook, R.E., Tessier, A., & Klein, M.D. (1992). *Adapting early childhood curricula for children with special needs.* New York: Macmillan.

Cooper, A.Y., & Holt, W.J. (1982). Development of social skills and the management of common problems. In K.E. Allen & E.M. Goetz (Eds.), *Early childhood education: Special problems, special solutions* (pp. 105–127). Rockville, MD: Aspen.

Cooper, J.O., Heron, T.E., & Heward, W.L. (1987). *Applied behavior analysis.* Columbus, OH: Charles F. Merrill.

Council for Exceptional Children. (1988). *Final report: CEC ad hoc committee on medically fragile.* Reston, VA: Author.

Council of Chief State School Officers. (1989). *Success for all in a new century.* Washington, DC: Author.

Cuomo, M.M. (1988, January). *Governor's state of the state address to the legislature of New York,* Albany.

Curl, R.M., Rowbury, T.G., & Baer, D.M. (1985). The facilitation of children's social interaction by a picture-cue training program. *Child and Family Behavior Therapy, 7*(2), 11–39.

Diamond, K.E., Spiegel-McGill, P., & Hanrahan, P. (1988). Planning for school transition: An ecological-developmental approach. *Journal of the Division for Early Childhood, 12*(3), 245–252.

Division for Early Childhood. (1993). *Recommended practices of quality in programs for infants and young children with special needs and their families.* Reston, VA: Council for Exceptional Children, Division for Early Childhood.

Dodge, D.T. (1991). *The creative curricula for early childhood.* Mt. Rainier, MD: Gryphon House.

Drew, M., & Law, C. (1990). Making early childhood education work. *Principal, 69*(5), 10–12.

Dunst, C.J., Johanson, C., Trivette, C.M., & Hamby, D. (1991). Family-oriented early intervention policies and practices: Family-centered or not? *Exceptional Children, 58*(2), 115–126.

Dunst, C., Trivette, C., & Deal, A. (1988). *Enabling and empowering families: Principles and guidelines for practice.* Cambridge, MA: Brookline Books.

Early Education Center. (1992). *Transition program and curriculum: Home base to center base.* Hutchinson, KS: Author.

East Los Angeles Interagency Coordinating Council. (1992). *Transition Checklist.* California State University at Los Angeles, Los Angeles: SHARE Center for Educational Excellence in Early Intervention.

Edmunds, P., Martinson, S.A., & Goldberg, P.F. (1990). *Demographics and cultural diversity in the 1990s: Implications for services to young children with special needs.* Chapel Hill, NC: National Early Childhood Technical Assistance System.

Education of the Handicapped Act Amendments of 1986, PL 99-457. (October 8, 1986). Title 20, U.S.C. 1400 et seq: *U.S. Statutes at Large, 100,* 1145–1177.

Elder, J.O., & Magrab, P.R. (Eds.). (1980). *Coordinating services to handicapped children: A handbook for interagency collaboration.* Baltimore: Paul H. Brookes Publishing Co.

Elkind, D. (1981). *The hurried child: Growing up too fast too soon.* Reading, MA: Addison-Wesley.

Epps, W.J. (1992). Program coordination and other real-world issues in strengthening linkages. In *Sticking together: Strengthening linkages and the transition between early childhood education and early elementary school—Summary of a national policy forum.* Washington, DC: U.S. Department of Education, Office of Educational Research and Improvement.

Epstein, S.G., Taylor, A.B., Halberg, A.S., Gardner, J.D., Walker, D.K., & Crocker, A.C. (1989). *Enhancing quality: Standards and indicators of quality care for children with special health care needs.* Boston: New England SERVE.

Essa, E.L. (1990). *Practical guide to solving preschool behavior problems.* Albany, NY: Delmar.

Fauvre, M. (1988). Including young children with "new" chronic illnesses in an early childhood education setting. *Young Children,43*(6), 71–77.

Federal Register. (1989, June 22). Rules and regulations, Department of Education, (*CFR 34,* Part 303), Early intervention programs for infants and toddlers with handicaps, *54,* 26322.

Federal Register. (1989, June 22). Rules and regulations, Department of Education, (*CFR 34,* Part 303), Early intervention programs for infants and toddlers with handicaps, *54,* 26322.

Federal Register. (1990, August 24). Rules and Regulations, Department of Education, (*CFR 34,* Part 301), Preschool Grants for Handicapped Children, *55,* 34845.

Fillmore, L.W. (1992). Policy issues of developmentally appropriate curricula, parental involvement, and multiculturalism. In *Sticking together:*

Strengthening linkages and the transition between early childhood education and early elementary school—Summary of a national policy forum. Washington, DC: U.S. Department of Education, Office of Educational Research and Improvement.

Finger, W. (1992). Can I use a constructivist approach with children with special needs? In D.G. Murphy & S.G. Goffin (Eds.), *Project Construct: A curriculum guide* (170–187). Jefferson City: Missouri Department of Elementary and Secondary Education.

Fitz-Gibbon, C.T., & Morris, L.L. (1987). *How to design a program evaluation.* Newbury Park, CA: Sage Publications.

Forest, M., & Lusthaus, E. (1990). Everyone belongs with the MAPS action planning system. *Teaching Exceptional Children, 22,* 32–35.

Fowler, S.A. (1978). *Ecological considerations in the education and integration of young handicapped children.* Paper presented at the Council for Exceptional Children, Kansas City, MO.

Fowler, S.A. (1982). Transition from preschool to kindergarten for children with special needs. In K.E. Allen & E.M. Goetz (Eds.), *Early childhood education: Special problems, special solutions* (pp. 229–242). Rockville, MD: Aspen.

Fowler, S.A. (1988). Promising programs: Transition planning. *Teaching Exceptional Children, 20,* 62–63.

Fowler, S.A., Chandler, L.K., & Johnson, T.E. (1988). *It's a big step: A manual for planning transitions from preschool to kindergarten.* Lawrence: University of Kansas, Bureau of Child Research.

Fowler, S.A., Chandler, L.K., Johnson, T.E., & Stella, E. (1988). Individualizing family involvement in school transitions: Gathering information and choosing the next program. *Journal of the Division for Early Childhood, 12,* 208–216.

Fowler, S.A., Hains, A.H., & Rosenkoetter, S.E. (1990). The transition between early intervention services and preschool services: Administrative and policy issues. *Topics in Early Childhood Special Education, 9*(4), 55–65.

Fowler, S.A., & Ostrosky, M.M. (in press). *Transitions to and from early childhood special education programs.* In P.L. Safford, D. Spodek, & B. Saracho (Eds.), *5th yearbook for early childhood education.* New York: Teachers College Press.

Fowler, S.A., Schwartz, I.S., & Atwater, J. (1991). Perspectives on the transition from preschool to kindergarten for children with disabilities and their families. *Exceptional Children, 58,* 136–145.

Foyle, H.C., Lyman, L., & Thies, S.A. (1991). *Cooperative learning in the early childhood classroom.* Washington, DC: National Education Association.

Freeman, E.B., & Hatch, J.A. (1989). What schools expect young children to know and do: An analysis of kindergarten report cards. *Elementary School Journal, 89*(5), 595–605.

Futrell, M.H. (1987). Public schools and four year olds. *American Psychologist, 2*(3), 251–253.

Gallagher, J., Maddox, M., & Edgar, E. (1984). *Early childhood interagency transition model.* Seattle: University of Washington, Experimental Education Unit.

Giangreco, M.F., Cloninger, C.J., & Iverson, V. (1992). *Choosing options and accommodations for children (COACH): A guide to planning inclusive education.* Baltimore: Paul H. Brookes Publishing Co.

Gibbs, E.D., & Teti, D.M. (Eds.). (1990). *Interdisciplinary assessment of infants: A guide for early intervention professionals.* Baltimore: Paul H. Brookes Publishing Co.

Gilkerson, L. (1990). Understanding institutional functioning style: A resource for hospital and early intervention collaboration. *Infants and Young Children, 2*(3), 22–30.

Goffin, S.G., & Stegelin, D.A. (1992). *Changing kindergartens: Four success stories.* Washington, DC: National Association for the Education of Young Children.

Golant, S., & Golant, M. (1990). *Kindergarten: It isn't what it used to be.* Los Angeles: Lowell House.

Goldstein, H., & Kacsmarek, L. (1992). Promoting communicative interactions among children in integrated intervention settings. In S.F. Warren & J. Reichle (Eds.), *Causes and effects in communication and language intervention* (pp. 81–111). Baltimore: Paul H. Brookes Publishing Co.

Goldstein, H., Wickstrom, S., Hoyson, M., & Jamieson, B. (1988). Effects of sociodramatic script training on social and communicative interaction. *Education and Treatment of Children, 11,* 97–117.

Graue, M.E. (1993). *Ready for what? Constructing meanings of readiness for kindergarten.* Albany: State University of New York Press.

Grusec, J.E, Kuczynski, L., Rashton, J.P., & Simutis, Z. M. (1979). Learning resistance to temptation through observation. *Developmental Psychology, 15,* 233–240.

Guralnick, M.J. (1981). Programmatic factors affecting child–child social interaction in mainstreamed preschool programs. *Exceptional Education Quarterly, 1,* 71–91.

Guralnick, M.J. (1990). Major accomplishments and future directions in early childhood mainstreaming. *Topics in Early Childhood Special Education, 10*(2), 1–17.

Gwost, J. (1992, December). A parent's perspective. In *Strategies for transition planning, a critical component of comprehensive state and local intervention systems.* Workshop presented at The International Division for Early Childhood Conference. Washington, DC.

Hains, A.H. (1990, April). *Teachers' evaluations of transition practices in birth-to-three programs.* Paper presented at the Council for Exceptional Children, Toronto.

Hains, A.H. (1992). Strategies for preparing preschool children with special needs for the kindergarten mainstream. *Journal of Early Intervention, 16*(4), 1–12.

Hains, A.H., Fowler, S.A., & Chandler, L.K. (1988). Planning school transitions: Family and professional collaboration. *Journal of the Division for Early Childhood, 12,* 108–115.

Hains, A.H., & Rosenkoetter, S. (1991). *Planning transitions for young children with special needs and their families: Wisconsin manual.* McPherson: Associated Colleges of Central Kansas, Bridging Early Services Transition Project.

Hains, A.H., Rosenkoetter, S.F., & Fowler, S.A. (1991). Transition planning with families in early intervention programs. *Infants and Young Children, 3,* 38–47.

Hains, A.H., Fowler, S.E., Schwartz, I., Kottwitz, E., & Rosenkoetter, S. (1989). A comparison of preschool and kindergarten teacher expectations for school readiness. *Early Childhood Research Quarterly, 4,* 75–88.

Halpern, A.S. (1985). Transition: A look at the foundations. *Exceptional Children, 51*(6), 479–486.

Hanline, M.F. (1988). Making the transition to preschool: Identification of parent needs. *Journal of the Division for Early Childhood, 12,* 98–107.

Hanline, M.F. (1993). Facilitating integrated preschool service delivery transitions for children, families, and professionals. In C.A. Peck, S.L. Odom, & D.D. Bricker (Eds.), *Integrating young children with disabilities into community programs: Ecological perspectives on research and implementation* (pp. 133–146). Baltimore: Paul H. Brookes Publishing Co.

Hanline, M.F., & Knowlton, A. (1988). A collaborative model for providing support to parents during their child's transition from infant intervention to preschool special education public school programs. *Journal of the Division for Early Childhood, 12,* 116–125.

Hanline, M.F., Suchman, S., & Demmerle, C. (1989). Beginning public school. *Teaching Exceptional Children, 22,* 61–62.

Harbin, G.L. (1988). Implementation of PL 99-457: State technical assistance needs. *Topics in Early Childhood Special Education, 8,* 24–36.

Hart, B., & Risley, T. (1975). Incidental teaching of language in the preschool. *Journal of Applied Behavior Analysis, 8,* 411–420.

Hart, B., & Risley, T. (1980). In vivo language intervention: Unanticipated general effects. *Journal of Applied Behavior Analysis, 13,* 407–432.

Hazel, R., Barber, P.A., Roberts, S., Behr, S.K., Helmstetter, E., & Guess, D. (1988). *A community approach to an integrated service system for children with special needs.* Baltimore: Paul H. Brookes Publishing Co.

Head Start. (1989). *Transition.* Washington, DC: Administration for Children, Youth, and Families.

Heath, S.B. (1983). *Ways with words: Language, life, and work in communities and classrooms.* Cambridge, England: Cambridge University Press.

Heron, T.E., & Harris, K.C. (1993). *The educational consultant: Helping professionals, parents, and mainstreamed students.* Austin, TX: PRO-ED.

High Scope. (1992). *Setting up the learning environment* [Videotape]. Ypsilanti, MI: Author.

High Scope Resource. (1993). Ypsilanti, MI: High Scope Educational Research Foundation.

Hohmann, M., Banet, B., & Weikart, D.P. (1979). *Young children in action.* Ypsilanti, MI: High Scope Educational Research Foundation.

Hohmann, C., & Buckleitner, W. (1992). *K-3 learning environment.* Ypsilanti, MI: High Scope Educational Research Foundation.

Holvoet, J., Mulligan, M., Schussler, N., Lacey, L., & Guess, D. (1984). *The Kansas individualized curriculum sequencing model (KICS): Sequencing learning experiences for severely handicapped children and youth.* Portland, OR: A.S.I.E.P. Education Co.

Hunter, M. (1992). *How to change to a nongraded school.* Alexandria, VA: Association for Supervision and Curriculum Development.

Hupp, S.C., & Kaiser, A.P. (1986). Evaluating educational programs for severely handicapped preschoolers. In L. Bickman & D.L. Weatherford (Eds.), *Evaluating early intervention programs for severely handicapped children and their families* (pp. 233–261). Austin, TX: PRO-ED.

Hutinger, P. (1981). Transition practices for handicapped young children: What the experts say. *Journal of the Division for Early Childhood, 2,* 8–14.

Indiana First Steps. (1991). *Community partners through the individualized family service plan.* Bloomington: Indiana University, Institute for the Study of Developmental Disabilities.

Individuals with Disabilities Education Act of 1990, PL 101-476 (The 1990 Education of the Handicapped Act Amendments, October 30, 1990) 20 U.S.C. 55, 1400–1485.

Individuals with Disabilities Education Act Amendments of 1991, PL 102–119. (October 7, 1991). Title 20, U.S.C. 1400 et seq: *U.S. Statutes at Large, 105,* 587–608.

Jervis, K. (1984). *Separation.* Washington, DC: National Association for the Education of Young Children.

Jesien, G., & Tuchman, L. (1992). *Early intervention self-assessment and planning guide on family-centered services and interagency collaboration.* Madison: Wisconsin Department of Health and Social Services, Birth to Three Program.

Johnson, D.R., Bruininks, R.H., & Thurlow, M.L. (1987). Meeting the challenge of transition service planning through improved interagency cooperation. *Exceptional Children, 53*(6), 522–530.

Johnson, D.W., Johnson, R.T., Holubee, E.J., & Roy, P. (1984). *Circles of learning: Cooperation in the classroom.* Washington, DC: Association for Supervision and Curriculum Development.

Johnson, J.L., Kilgo, J., Cook, M.J., Hammitte, D.J., Beauchamp, K., & Finn, D. (1992). The skills needed by early intervention administrators/supervisors: A study across six states. *Journal of Early Intervention, 16*(2), 136–145.

Johnson, T.E., Chandler, L.K., Kerns, G.M., & Fowler, S.A. (1986). What are parents saying about family involvement in school transitions? A retrospective transition interview. *Journal of the Division for Early Childhood, 11,* 10–17.

Kaczmarek, L.A. (1985). Integrating language/communication objectives into the total preschool curriculum. *Teaching Exceptional Children, 17*(3), 183–189.

Kagan, S.L. (1991a). The strategic importance of linkages and the transition between early childhood programs and early elementary school. In U.S. Department of Education *Sticking together: Strengthening linkages and the transition between early childhood education and early elementary school—Summary of a national policy forum.* Washington, DC: Office of Educational Research and Improvement.

Kagan, S.L. (1991b). *United we stand: Collaboration for child care and early education services.* New York: Teachers College Press.

Kagan, S.L. (1992). Forward. In South Eastern Regional Vision for Education (SERVE), *Sharing success in the Southeast: Promising programs in preschool-to-school transition.* Tallahassee, FL.

Kagan, S.L., Rivera, A.M., & Parker, F.L. (1990). *Collaborations in action: Reshaping services for young children and their families.* New Haven, CT: Yale

University, Bush Center in Child Development and Social Policy. (ERIC Document Reproduction Service No. ED 328 363)

Kansas State Board of Education. (1992). *Kansas guidelines for implementation of early childhood special education services: A technical assistance guide.* Topeka: Author.

Karweit, N. (1988). Quality and quantity of learning time in preprimary programs. *Elementary School Journal, 89,* 119–133.

Katz, K.S. (1992). *Headed home: Developmental intervention for hospitalized infants and their families.* Palo Alto, CA: VORT Corp.

Katz, L.G., Evangelou, D., & Hartman, J.S. (1989). *The case for mixed-age grouping in early education.* Washington, DC: National Association for the Education of Young Children.

Kilgo, J.L., Richard, N., & Noonan, M.J. (1989). Teaming for the future: Integrating transition planning with early intervention services for young children with special needs and their families. *Infants and Young Children, 2,* 37–48.

Killoran, J., Rule, S., Stowitschek, J.J., Innocenti, M., & Levine, L.M. (1982). *Let's be social: Language-based social skills for preschool at-risk children.* Tucson, AZ: Communication Skill Builders.

King, J.A., Morris, L.L., & Fitz-Gibbon, C.T. (1987). *How to assess program implementation.* Newbury Park, CA: Sage Publications.

Kohler, F.W., & Strain, P.S. (1990). Peer-assisted interventions: Early promises, notable achievements, and future aspirations. *Clinical Psychology Review, 10,* 441–452.

Kohler, F.W., & Strain, P.S. (1993). The early childhood social skills program: Making friends during the early childhood years. *Teaching Exceptional Children, 25*(2), 41–42.

Koop, C.E. (1987). *Surgeon general's report: Children with special health care needs—Campaign '87.* Washington, DC: U.S. Government Printing Office.

Kostelnik, M.J., Stein, L.C., Whiren, A.P., & Soderman, A.K. (1993). *Guiding children's social development.* Albany, NY: Delmar.

Ladd, G.W. (1990). Having friends, keeping friends, and being liked by peers in the classroom: Predictors of children's early school adjustment? *Child Development, 61,* 1081–1100.

Lazzari, A.M. (1991). *The transition sourcebook: A practical guide for early intervention programs.* Tucson, AZ: Communication Skill Builders.

Lazzari, A.M., & Kilgo, J.L. (1989). Practical methods for supporting parents in early transitions. *Teaching Exceptional Children, 22,* 40–43.

Leach, L. (1992). *Interchange.* Champaign: University of Illinois at Urbana-Champaign, College of Education, Transition Research Institute.

LeBlanc, J.M. (1982). Instructing difficult-to-teach children. In K.E. Allen & E.M. Goetz (Eds.), *Early childhood education: Special problems, special solutions* (pp. 229–251). Rockville, MD: Aspen.

Lehr, D.H. (1990). Preparation of personnel to work with students with complex health care needs. In A.P. Kaiser & C.M. McWhorter (Eds.), *Preparing personnel to work with persons with severe disabilities* (pp. 135–151). Baltimore: Paul H. Brookes Publishing Co.

Lobato, P.J. (1990). *Brothers, sisters, and special needs: Information and activities for helping young siblings of children with chronic illnesses and developmental disabilities.* Baltimore: Paul H. Brookes Publishing Co.

Logue, M.E., & Love, J.M. (1992). Making the transition to kindergarten. *Principal, 71*(5), 10–12.

Lovaas, O.I. (1977). *The autistic child: Language development through behavior modification.* New York: Irvington.

Love, J.M., Logue, M.E., Trudeau, J.V., & Thayer, K. (1992). *Transitions to kindergarten in American schools* (Final Report of the National Transition Study). Washington, DC: U.S. Department of Education, Office of Policy and Planning.

Lowman, D.K. (1992). *Planning for preschoolers with complex health care needs.* Presentation at the International Early Childhood Conference on Children with Special Needs, Washington, DC.

Lynch, E.W., & Hanson, M.J. (Eds.). (1992). *Developing cross-cultural competence: A guide for working with young children and their families.* Baltimore: Paul H. Brookes Publishing Co.

Magrab, P., Elder, J.O., Kazuk, E., Pelosi, J., & Wiegerink, R. (1981). *Developing a community team.* Washington, DC: U.S. Department of Health and Human Services, Head Start Bureau.

Mahoney, G., Robinson, C., & Powell, A. (1992). Focusing on parent–child interactions: The bridge to developmentally appropriate practices. *Topics in Early Childhood Special Education, 12*(1), 105–120.

Mallory, B.L., & Kerns, G.M. (1988). Consequences of categorical labeling of preschool children. *Topics in Early Childhood Special Education, 8,* 39–50.

McCollum, J.A., & Bailey, D.B. (1991). Developing comprehensive personnel systems: Issues and alternatives. *Journal of Early Intervention, 15*(19), 57–65.

McCollum, J.A., & Hughes, M. (1988). Staffing patterns and team models in infancy programs. In J.B. Jordan, J.J. Gallagher, P.L. Hutinger, & M.B. Karnes (Eds.), *Early childhood special education: Birth to three* (pp. 129–146). Reston, VA: Council for Exceptional Children.

McCormick, L.P. (1985). Keeping up with language intervention trends. *Teaching Exceptional Children, 18*(2), 123–129.

McCracken, J.B. (Ed.). (1986). *Reducing stress in young children's lives.* Washington, DC: National Association for the Education of Young Children.

McDonald, L., Kysela, G.M., Siebert, P., McDonald, S., & Chambers, J. (1989). Parent perspectives: Transition to preschool. *Teaching Exceptional Children, 22,* 4–8.

McDonnell, A., & Hardman, M. (1988). A synthesis of "best practice" guidelines for early childhood services. *Journal of the Division for Early Childhood, 12*(4), 328–341.

McEvoy, M.A., Twardosz, S., & Bishop, N. (1990). Affection activities: Procedures for encouraging young children with handicaps to interact with their peers. *Education and Treatment of Children, 13,* 159–167.

McGonigel, M.J., Kaufmann, R.K., & Johnson, B.H. (Eds.). (1991). *Guidelines and recommended practices for the individualized family service plan* (2nd ed.). Bethesda, MD: Association for the Care of Children's Health.

McLaughlin, J.A., & Covert, R.C. (1984). *Evaluating interagency collaborators.* Chapel Hill: University of North Carolina, Technical Assistance Development System.

McNulty, B.A. (1989). Leadership and policy strategies for interagency planning: Meeting the early childhood mandate. In J.J. Gallager, P.L. Trohanis, & R.M. Clifford (Eds.), *Policy implementation & PL 99-457: Planning for young children with special needs* (pp. 147–167). Baltimore: Paul H. Brookes Publishing Co.

Meichenbaum, D. (1977). *Cognitive behavior modification: An integrative approach.* New York: Plenum.

Meisels, S.J. (1992). Early intervention: A matter of context. *Zero to Three, 12*(3), 1–12.

Meisels, S.J., & Provence, S. (1989). *Screening and assessment: Guidelines for identifying young disabled and developmentally vulnerable children and their families.* Washington, DC: National Center for Clinical Infant Programs.

Meisels, S.J., & Shonkoff, J.P. (1990). *Handbook of early childhood intervention.* New York: Cambridge University Press.

Mental Health Law Project, NEC*TAS, & DEC/CEC. (1990). *Strengthening the role of families in states' early intervention systems: Policy guide to procedural safeguards for infants and toddlers and their families under Part H of the Education of the Handicapped Act.* Washington, DC: Mental Health Law Project, and Reston, VA: Division for Early Childhood of the Council for Exceptional Children.

Michigan inclusive education position statement. (1992). Lansing: Michigan Department of Education, State Board of Education.

Mitchell, A., & David, J. (Eds.). (1992). *Explorations with young children: A curriculum guide from the Bank Street College of Education.* Mt. Rainier, MD: Gryphon House.

Mitchell, A., Seligson, M., & Marx, F. (1989). *Early childhood programs and the public schools: Between promise and practice.* Cited in Caldwell, B.M., (1991). Continuity in the early years: Transition between grades and systems. In S.L. Kagan (Ed.), *The care and education of America's young children: Obstacles and opportunities* (pp. 69–90). Chicago: University of Chicago Press.

Moore, W., & Toews, J. (1985). *Early intervention advisory group workbook: A guide for writing local comprehensive plans for early intervention.* Monmouth, OR: Teaching Research.

Morgan, J.L., Guetzloe, E.C., & Swan, W.W. (1991). Leadership for local interagency coordinating councils. *Journal of Early Intervention, 15*(3), 255–268.

Morgan, J., & Swan, W.W. (1988). *Local interagency councils for preschool handicapped programs.* Bloomington: Indiana University, Department of School Administration/Council of Administrators of Special Education.

Morris, L.L., Fitz-Gibbon, C.T., & Freeman, M.E. (1987). *How to communicate with evaluation findings.* Newbury Park, CA: Sage Publications.

Morse, M.T. (1990). PL 94-142 and PL 99-457: Considerations for coordination between the health and the education systems. *Children's Health Care, 19*(4), 213–218.

Mulligan, S.A., Green, K.M., Morris, S.L., Maloney, T.J., McMurray, D., & Kittleson-Aldred, T. (1992) *Integrated child care.* Meeting the challenge. Tucson, AZ: Communication Skill Builders.

Mulligan-Ault, M., Guess, D., Struth, L., & Thompson, B. (1988). The implementation of health related procedures in classrooms for students with severe multiple impairments. *Journal of The Association for Persons with Severe Handicaps, 13,* 100–116.

Murphy, D.G., & Goffin, S.G. (1992). *Project Construct: A curriculum guide.* Jefferson City: Missouri Department of Elementary and Secondary Education.

Murphy, L., & Corte, S.D. (1985). Getting your child ready for school. *Special Parent—Special Child, 1*(5), 1–6.

Murphy, M., & Vincent, L.J. (1989). Identification of critical skills for success in day care. *Journal of Early Intervention, 13,* 221–229.

National Academy of Early Childhood Programs. (1985). *Guide to accreditation.* Washington, DC: National Association for the Education of Young Children.

National Association for the Education of Young Children. (1984). *Accreditation criteria and procedures of the national academy of early childhood programs.* Washington, DC: Author.

National Association for the Education of Young Children. (1988a). NAEYC position statement on developmentally appropriate practice in the primary grades, serving 5 through 8 year olds. *Young Children, 43*(2), 64–84.

National Association for the Education of Young Children. (1988b). Position statement on standardized testing of young children 3 through 8 years of age. *Young Children, 43*(3), 42–47.

National Association for the Education of Young Children. (1990). NAEYC position statement on school readiness. *Young Children, 46*(1), 21–23.

National Association for the Education of Young Children. (1991). Guidelines for appropriate curriculum content and assessment in programs serving children ages 3 through 8. *Young Children, 46*(3), 21–38.

National Association of Early Childhood Specialists in State Departments of Education. (1987). *Unacceptable trends in kindergarten entry and placement.* Unpublished paper.

National Association of Elementary School Principals. (1990). *Early childhood education and the elementary school principal: Standards for quality programs for young children.* Alexandria, VA: Author.

National Association of State Boards of Education. (1988). *Right from the start: The report of the NASBE task force on early childhood education.* Alexandria, VA: Author.

National Association of State Boards of Education. (1991). *Caring communities: Supporting young children and families.* Alexandria, VA: Author.

National Association of State Boards of Education. (1992). *Winners all: A call for inclusive schools.* Alexandria, VA: Author.

National Commission on Children. (1991). *Beyond rhetoric: A new American agenda for children and families.* Washington, DC: Author.

National Conference of State Legislatures. (1989). *Child care and early childhood education policy: A legislator's guide.* Denver: Author.

National Conference of State Legislatures. (1991). *Americans with developmental disabilities: Policy directions for the states.* Washington, DC: Author.

National Education Association. (1983). *How to prepare your child for school.* New York: Avon.

National Governors' Association. (1990). *Education America: State strategies for achieving the national education goals.* Washington, DC: Author.

National Head Start Association. (1990). Family-centered Head Start. *Young Children, 45*(6), 30–35.

National Policy Forum. (1991). *Sticking together: Strengthening linkages and the transition between early childhood education and early elementary school—Summary of a national policy forum.* Washington, DC: U.S. Department of Education, Office of Educational Research and Improvement.

National Policy Forum. (1992). Sticking together, *Strengthening linkages and the transition between early childhood education and early elementary school—Summary of a national policy forum.* Washington, DC: U.S. Department of Education, Office of Educational Research and Improvement.

Nebraska Department of Education, & Iowa Department of Education. (1993). *The primary program: Growing and learning in the heartland.* Lincoln: Nebraska Department of Education.

NEC*TAS. (1992a). *Section 619 profile: A profile of Part B—Section 619 services.* Chapel Hill, NC: Author.

NEC*TAS. (1992b, March). *Procedural safeguards based on review of fourth and fifth year applications.* Unpublished manuscript.

Noonan, M.J. (1989, October). *Hawaii preparing for integrated preschool (PIP): An eco-behavioral approach to curriculum development for infants with special needs.* Paper presented at the Division for Early Childhood Conference, Minneapolis.

Noonan, M.J., & Ratokolau, N.B. (1991). Project profile—PPT: The Preschool Preparation and Transition Project. *Journal of Early Intervention, 15*(4), 390–398.

O'Brien, M. (1991). *Promoting successful transition into school: A review of current intervention practices.* Lawrence: University of Kansas, Kansas Early Childhood Research Institute.

Odom, S.L., McConnell, S.R., & McEvoy, M.A. (Eds.). (1992). *Social competence of young children with disabilities: Issues and strategies for intervention.* Baltimore: Paul H. Brookes Publishing Co.

Odom, S.L., & McEvoy, M.A. (1988). Integration of young children with handicaps and normally developing children. In S.L. Odom & M.B. Karnes (Eds.). *Early intervention for infants and children with handicaps: An empirical base* (pp. 241–267). Baltimore: Paul H. Brookes Publishing Co.

Odom, S.L., & Warren, S.F. (1988). Early childhood special education in the year 2000. *Journal of the Division for Early Childhood, 12*(3), 263–273.

Office of Special Education Programs (OSEP). (1992). *To assure the free appropriate public education of all children with disabilities: Fourteenth annual report to Congress on the implementation of the Individuals with Disabilities Education Act.* Washington, DC: U.S. Department of Education.

Ohio Department of Health. (1989a). *Collaboration for early intervention services in Ohio, 1982–1988.* Columbus: Author.

Ohio Department of Health. (1989b). *Early intervention: Everyone's investment for the future.* Columbus: Author.

Orelove, F.P., & Sobsey, D. (1991). *Educating children with multiple disabilities: A transdisciplinary approach* (2nd ed.). Baltimore: Paul H. Brookes Publishing Co.

Paulu, N. (1992). *Helping your child get ready for school with activities for birth through age 5.* Washington, DC: U.S. Department of Education, Office of Educational Research and Improvement.

Peck, C.A., Appolloni, T., Cooke, T., & Raver, S.A. (1978). Teaching retarded preschoolers to imitate the free-play behavior of nonretarded classmates: Trained and generalized effects. *Journal of Special Education, 12,* 195–207.

Peck, C.A., Carlson, P., & Helmstetter, E. (1992). Parent and teacher perceptions of outcomes for typically developing children enrolled in integrated early childhood programs: A statewide survey. *Journal of Early Intervention, 16*(1), 53–63.

Peck, C.A., Odom, S.A., & Bricker, D.D. (Eds.). (1993). *Integrating young children with disabilities into community programs: Ecological perspectives on research and implementation.* Baltimore: Paul H. Brookes Publishing Co.

Peck, J.T., McCaig, G., & Sapp, M.E. (1988). *Kindergarten policies: What is best for children.* Washington, DC: National Association for the Advancement of Young Children.

Pennsylvania Office of Mental Retardation. (1991). *Pennsylvania local interagency coordinating councils.* Harrisburg: Author.

Pensacola ARC. (1992). *Building bridges: A family's guide to transition.* Pensacola, FL: Pearl Nelson Child Development Center.

Peterson, N.L. (1987). *Early intervention for handicapped and at-risk children: An introduction to early childhood special education.* Denver: Love Publishing Co.

Peterson, N.L. (1991). Interagency collaboration under Part H: The key to comprehensive multidisciplinary, coordinated infant/toddler intervention services. *Journal of Early Intervention, 15,* 89–105.

Quinn, J., & Jackson, B. (n.d.). *Case coordination: The project continuity model.* Omaha: University of Nebraska Medical Center, Meyer Rehabilitation Institute.

Ratajczak, L. (1992). *Reflections of 1991–1992. Our assignment: Student success: Twin Willows Early Childhood Center.* Appleton, WI: Twin Willows School Newsletter.

Rice, M.L., & O'Brien, M. (1990). Transitions: Times of change and accommodation. *Topics in Early Childhood Special Education, 9*(4), 1–14.

Robbins, P. (1991). *How to plan and implement a peer coaching program.* Alexandria, VA: Association for Supervision and Curriculum Development.

Rosenkoetter, S.E. (1990a). Age three transition tip. *Rural Links Social Education, 3,* 1.

Rosenkoetter, S.E. (1990b, April). *First day of kindergarten: What teachers expect from children.* Paper presented at the Council for Exceptional Children, Toronto, Canada.

Rosenkoetter, S.E. (1992, November). *Bridging early services for* all *children.* Paper presented at the National Transition Forum, Washington, DC.

Rosenkoetter, S.E., & Fowler, S.A. (1986). Teaching mainstreamed children to manage daily transitions. *Exceptional Children, 19,* 20–23.

Rosenkoetter, S., & Shotts, C. (1992). *Bridging early services: Interagency transition planning.* McPherson: Associated Colleges of Central Kansas, Bridging Early Services Transition Project.

Rosenkoetter, S.E., & Rosenkoetter, L.I. (1993, March). *Starting school: Perceptions of parents of children with and without disabilities.* Presented at the Society for Research in Child Development, New Orleans.

Ross-Allen, J., & Conn-Powers, M. (1991). *TEEM: A manual to support the transition of young children with special needs and their families from preschool into kindergarten and other regular education environments.* Burlington: University of Vermont, Center for Developmental Disabilities.

Rowbury, T. (1982). Preacademic skills for the reluctant learner. In K.E. Allen & E.M. Goetz (Eds.), *Early childhood education: Special problems, special solutions* (pp. 201–228). Rockville, MD: Aspen.

Rule, S., Fiechtl, B.J., & Innocenti, M.S. (1990). Preparation for transition to mainstreamed post-preschool environments: Development of a survival skills curriculum. *Topics in Early Childhood Special Education, 9,* 78–90.

Rusch, F.R., & Phelps, L.A. (1987). Secondary special education and transition from school to work: A national priority. *Exceptional Children, 53*(6), 487–492.

Safford, P.L. (1989). *Integrated teaching in early childhood: Starting in the mainstream.* White Plains, NY: Longman.

Sainato, D.M., & Strain, P.S. (1993). Integration success for preschoolers with disabilities. *Teaching Exceptional Children, 25*(2), 36–37.

Sainato, D.M., Strain, P.S., Lefebre, D., & Rapp, N. (1987). Facilitating transition times with handicapped preschool children: A comparison between peer mediated and antecedent prompt procedures. *Journal of Applied Behavior Analysis, 20*(3), 285–291.

Sainato, D.M., Strain, P.S., Lefebre, D., & Rapp, N. (1990). Effects of self-evaluation on the independent work skills of preschool children with disabilities. *Exceptional Children, 56,* 540–549.

Sainato, D.M., Strain, P.S., & Lyon, S.R. (1987). Increasing academic responding of handicapped preschool children during group instruction. *Journal of the Division for Early Childhood, 12,* 23–30.

Salisbury, C.L., & Vincent, L.J. (1990). Criterion of the next environment and best practices: Mainstreaming and integration 10 years later. *Topics in Early Childhood Special Education, 10*(2), 78–89.

Sapon-Shevin, M. (1990). Schools as communities of love and care. *Holistic Education Review, 3,* 22–24.

Schaps, E., & Solomon, D. (1990). Schools and classrooms as caring communities. *Educational Leadership, 48*(3), 39–42.

Schauls, L. (1991). Integrated family-centered birth to 3 services: MAPS (rewritten) to get you there. In R. Paisley, *Interagency transition guide.* Cumberland, WI: Northern Pines Area Early Intervention Project.

Schorr, L. (1988). *Within our reach: Breaking the cycle of disadvantage.* New York: Anchor.

Schuster, J.W., & Griffen, A.K. (1990). Translating research into classroom practice: Using time delay with task analyses. *Teaching Exceptional Children, 22*(4), 49–53.

Shelton, T.L., Jeppson, E.S., & Johnson, B.H. (1989). *Family-centered care for children with special health care needs.* Bethesda, MD: Association for the Care of Children's Health.

Shepard, L., & Smith, M. (1988). Escalating academic demands in kindergarten: Some nonsolutions. *Elementary School Journal, 89*(2), 135–146.

Shotts, C.K., & Rosenkoetter, S.E. (1992). *Bridging early services: Interagency planning for transitions* [Videotape]. Jefferson City: Missouri Department of Education.

Shotts, C.K., Rosenkoetter, S.E., Streufert, C.A., & Rosenkoetter, L.I. (in press). Transition policies and issues: A view from the states. *Topics in Early Childhood Special Education.*

Sirvis, M. (1988). Students with special health care needs. *Teaching Exceptional Children, 20*(4), 40–44.

Skrtic, T. (1986). The crisis in special education knowledge: A perspective on perspective. *Focus on Exceptional Children, 18,* 1–16.

Smith, B.J., Rose, D.F., Ballard, J.B., & Walsh, S. (1991). The preschool (Part B) and infant/toddler (Part H) programs of the Individuals with Disabilities Education Act (IDEA) and the 1991 Amendments (PL 102-119): Selected comparison. *DEC Communicator, 19*(1), insert.

Smith, B.J., & Strain, P.S. (1988). Implementing and expanding PL 99-457. *Topics in Early Childhood Special Education, 8,* 37–47.

Smith, D.D., Smith, J.O., & Edgar, E. (1976). Research and application of instructional materials development. In N.G. Haring & L. Brown (Ed.), *Teaching the severely handicapped* (Vol. 1). New York: Grune & Stratton.

Smith, B.J., & Schakel, J.A. (1986) Noncategorical identification of preschool handicapped children: Policy issues and options. *Journal of the Divison for Early Childhood, 11,* 78–86.

Snell, M.E., & Zirpoli, T.J. (1987). Intervention strategies. In M.E. Snell (Ed.), *Systematic instruction of persons with severe handicaps.* Columbus, OH: Charles E. Merrill.

Snow, J.A. (1991). Dreaming, speaking, and creating: What I know about community. *Developmental Disabilities Bulletin, 19*(12), 12–27.

Snyder-McLean, L.K., Solomonson, B., & McLean, J.E. (1984). Structuring joint action routines: A strategy for facilitating communication and language development in the classroom. *Seminars in Speech and Language, 5*(3), 213–227.

South Eastern Regional Vision for Education (SERVE). (1992). *Sharing success in the Southeast: Promising programs in preschool-to-school transitions.* Tallahassee, FL, Author.

Southwest Educational Development Laboratory. (1992). *Follow through: A bridge to the future.* Austin, TX: Author.

Spiegel-McGill, P., Reed, D.J., Konig, C.S., & McGowan, P.A. (1990). Parent education: Easing the transition to preschool. *Topics in Early Childhood Special Education, 9,* 66–77.

Spodek, B., Saracho, O.N., & Lee, R.C. (1984). *Mainstreaming young children.* Belmont, CA: Wadsworth.

Stainback, S., & Stainback, W. (Eds.). (1992). *Curriculum considerations in inclusive classrooms: Facilitating learning for all students.* Baltimore: Paul H. Brookes Publishing Co.

Stecher, B.M., & Davis, W.A. (1987). *How to focus an evaluation.* Newbury Park, CA: Sage Publications.

Stephens, P., & Rous, B. (1992). *Facilitation packet for the development of a system for the transition of young children and families.* Lexington, KY: Child Development Centers of the Blue Grass.

Stokes, T.F., & Baer, D.M. (1977). An implicit technology of generalization. *Journal of Applied Behavior Analysis, 10,* 349–367.

Strain, P.S. (1990). LRE for preschool children with handicaps: What we know, what we should be doing. *Journal of Early Intervention, 14*(4), 291–296.

Strain, P.S., & Odom, S.L. (1986). Peer social initiations: Effective intervention for social skills development of exceptional children. *Exceptional Children, 52*(6), 543–551.

Strickland, B., & Turnbull, A.P. (1990). *Developing and implementing individualized educational programs.* Columbus, OH: Merrill/Macmillan.

Striefel, S., Killoran, J., & Quintero, M. (1991). *Functional integration for success.* Austin, TX: PRO-ED.

Summers, J.A., Dell'Oliver, C., Turnbull, A.P., Benson, H.A., Santelli, E., Campbell, M., & Siegel-Causey, E. (1990). Examining the individualized family service plan process: What are family and practitioner preferences? *Topics in Early Childhood Special Education, 10,* 78–99.

Swann, W.W., & Morgan, J.L. (1993). *Collaborating for comprehensive services for young children and their families: The local interagency coordinating council.* Baltimore: Paul H. Brookes Publishing Co.

Trostle, S., & Yawkey, T. (1990). *Integrated learning activities for young children.* Boston: Allyn & Bacon.

Turnbull, A.P., & Turnbull, H.R. (1990). *Families, professionals, & exceptionality: A special partnership.* Columbus, OH: Charles E. Merrill.

Urbano, M.T. (1992). *Preschool children with special health care needs.* San Diego: Singular Publishing Group.

U.S. Congress, Office of Technology Assessment. (1987). *Technology-dependent children: Hospital v. home care—A technical memorandum* (OTS-TM-H-38). Washington, DC: U.S. Government Printing Office.

U.S. Department of Education. (1992). *To assure the free appropriate public education of all children with disabilities: Fourteenth annual report to Congress on the implementation of the Individuals with Disabilities Education Act.* Washington, DC: Author.

U.S. Department of Education. (1991). *Preparing young children for success: Guideposts for achieving our first national goal.* Washington, DC: Author.

Vandercook, T., York, J., & Forest, M. (1989). The McGill action planning system (MAPS): A strategy for building the vision. *Journal of The Association for Persons with Severe Handicaps, 14*(3), 205–215.

Vaughn, S., Bos, C.S., & Lund, K.A. (1986). . . . But they can do it in my room. *Teaching Exceptional Children, 25*(1), 176–180.

Vincent, L.J., Madrid, J., & Martinez, I. (1992, December). *Family driven transition planning with Latino families.* Session presented at the International Early Childhood Conference on Children with Special Needs, Washington, DC.

Vincent, L.J., Salisbury, C., Walter, G., Brown, P., Gruenewald, L., & Powers, M. (1980). Program evaluation and curricular development in early childhood/special education: Criteria of the next environment. In W. Sailor, B. Wilcox, & L. Brown (Eds.), *Methods of instruction for severely handicapped students* (pp. 303–328). Baltimore: Paul H. Brookes Publishing Co.

Vincent, L.J., Salisbury, C.L., Strain, P., McCormick, C., & Tessier, A. (1990). A behavioral-ecological approach to early intervention: Focus on cultural diversity. In S.J. Meisels & J.P. Shonkoff (Eds.), *Handbook of early childhood intervention* (pp. 173–195) Cambridge, England: Cambridge University Press.

Vygotsky, L.S. (1962). *Thought and language.* Cambridge, MA: MIT Press.

Vygotsky, L.S. (1978). *Mind in society: The development of higher psychological processes.* Cambridge, MA: Harvard University Press.

Walker, H.M., & Rankin, R. (1983). Assessing the behavioral expectations and demands of less restrictive settings. *School Psychology Review, 12,* 274–284.

Wallace, E. (1992). Transitions for learning. *First Teacher, 13*(2), 14–15.

Wasserman, S. (1990). *Serious players in the primary grades: Empowering children through active learning experiences.* New York: Teachers College Press.

Will, M. (1984). *Bridges from school to working life: OSERS programming for the transition of youth with disabilities.* Washington, DC: U.S. Department of Education, Office of Special Education and Rehabilitative Services.

Winton, P., & Bailey, D. (1993). Communicating with families: Examining practices and facilitating change. In J. Paul & R. Simeonsson (Eds.), *Understanding and working with parents of children with special needs* (2nd ed.). New York: Holt, Rinehart & Winston.

Wolery, M. (1989). Transitions in early childhood special education: Issues and procedures. *Focus on Exceptional Children, 22,* 1–16.

Wolery, M., Ault, M.J., & Doyle, P.M. (1992). *Teaching students with moderate to severe disabilities: Use of response prompting strategies.* New York: Longman.

Wolery, M., Strain, P.S., & Bailey, D.B. (1992). Reaching potentials for children with special needs. In S. Bredekamp & T. Rosegrant (Eds.), *Reaching potentials: Appropriate curriculum and assessment for young children* (Vol. 1, pp. 92–113). Washington, DC: National Association for the Education of Young Children.

York, J., Doyle, M.B., & Kronberg, R. (1992). A curriculum development process for inclusive classrooms. *Focus on Exceptional Children, 25,* 1–16.

Ziegler, P. (1985). Saying good-bye to preschool. *Young Children, 41,* 11–15.

Index

Page numbers followed by "t" or "f" indicate Tables or Figures, respectively.